Christ — The Hope of Glory

Christological Eschatology

by WM. CHILDS ROBINSON, D.D.

"We look to the Holy Spirit to convince men that the Christian Revelation is God's provision for the deepest needs of the heart, the head, the hand, His answer to the most searching questions of the soul."

"Our hope is in—Jesus Christ the Messiah, God's mighty amen to His precious promises. His majestic message turns our eyes from the angry inferno of a warring world to the golden spires of the City of God." This, in a few words, is the theme of this profound and scholarly book on Eschatology.

Christ—The Hope of Glory is a survey of the findings of Biblical research and Christian scholarship upon this subject. The Union Theological Seminary of Virginia, sponsoring the Sprunt lectureship, chose Dr. William Childs Robinson to deliver these lectures on this vital theme.

Dr. Robinson maintains that only those whose spiritual eyes have been opened in the new birth are in a position to understand these things truly. It is out of the entire body of revealed truth in the Word of God that our "hope of glory" springs. "Christian thinking must find its canon in Christian revelation."

The entire structure of the Old Testament and the New involves the eschatological expectation, as does the history of the primitive Church which lived daily in the hope of the Second Coming. Christ spoke of Himself as the Coming One. If the Kingdom of God were not going to be manifested in a real kingdom on this

(*Continued on back flap*)

Christ — The Hope of Glory

Christ — The Hope of Glory

CHRISTOLOGICAL ESCHATOLOGY

By

WM. CHILDS ROBINSON, M.A., Th.D (Harv.) D.D.
Professor of Historical Theology
Columbia Theological Seminary
Decatur, Ga., U.S.A.

WM. B. EERDMANS PUBLISHING CO.

Grand Rapids   1945   Michigan

CHRIST — THE HOPE OF GLORY
by
Wm. Childs Robinson

PRINTED AND BOUND IN THE UNITED STATES OF AMERICA

TO MY BROTHER,
DAVID W. ROBINSON, Jr.

TABLE OF CONTENTS

THE JAMES SPRUNT LECTURES

In 1911, Mr. James Sprunt, of Wilmington, North Carolina, established a perpetual lectureship at Union Theological Seminary in Virginia, which would enable the institution to secure from time to time the services of distinguished ministers and authoritative scholars as special lecturers on subjects connected with various departments of Christian thought and Christian work. The lecturers are chosen by the Faculty of the Seminary and a Committee of the Board of Trustees, and the lectures are published after their delivery in accordance with a contract between the lecturer and these representatives of the institution. The series of lectures on this foundation for the year 1941 is presented in this volume.

B. R. Lacy, Jr.
President.

Union Theological Seminary
in Virginia.

INTRODUCTION

Every writer has a point of view. We believe, therefore we speak and write. And we invite a sympathetic liaison with the reader when we have taken him into our confidence and state this point of view at once.

THE POINT OF APPROACH. The frame with which one approaches a subject often determines the findings of the investigation. *Finis origine pendet.* We propose to begin intellectually where God has graciously placed us, that is, in the Christian Revelation. We start neither with an axiom of reason, nor with a datum of experience, but with what God has told us in His Word concerning Himself, His gracious intervention for our salvation, and the hope He has laid up for those who trust in Him. Accordingly, we invite Christian brethren who differ with details of our eschatology to recognize that we stand together at the beginning, and to seek with us the ever more complete subordination of religious experience, philosophy, pedagogy, and eschatological programs to the authority of the Word. For, "the Bible stands above our theology."

This is the approach of both the conservatives and "the Barthians," the former because they accept the Holy Scriptures as the Word of God written and the latter because they hold that the Word is bound to Scripture, its authentic witness. According to Thurneysen, a preacher can only expect the living Word to speak through his pulpit when that pulpit presents Christ from the written Word. "God's revelation is always objectively present in Christ, the Bible and faithful preaching."* By the illumination of the Holy Spirit, it becomes the life-giving Word which makes one wise unto salvation. Since faith comes by hear-

---

* Bromiley, G. W., *The Evangelical Quarterly,* 12, 4, 323.

ing and hearing by the Word of Christ, one properly begins with the Scripture and preaches unto men Jesus.

THE ANALOGY OF FAITH. We not only begin with the Christian Revelation, we also seek our measure of truth in this Revelation rather than in the canons of general history, natural science, psychology, sociology, economics, education, philosophy, or religion. Since man has fallen as a totality, any general set of principles which he may excogitate for himself and use as a norm by which to judge the Christian faith can only curtail and pervert the Divine Revelation. Christianity is a definite datum which is entitled to give its own account of itself and may not be transmutted into something different in a historical crucible.* To approach the interpretation of Christ with the assumption that He must be conformed to other historical analogies is inevitably to confuse the issue. No man has ascended into heaven, but on the other hand the Son of Man has descended out of heaven. Hence there is no parallel, and we are not to judge Him by our ready-made standards. Rather we are to recognize that He sovereignly creates the faith by which He is approached. He brings with Him His own norm and standard for estimating truth.

In the early Church the baptismal confession or the Apostles' Creed was the canon of truth, the rule of faith. Calvin accepted this good form of sound words as the outline and analogy for Institutes. Barth finds in the careful Christological formulation of the first several ecumenical councils the best guide in interpreting Christian truth. Consequently, he is re-reading even such matters as election and ethics in the Name of the Lord Jesus Christ, true God and true man. P. T. Forsyth found the focus of the action of the holy God in saving sinners in the work of Christ, in the cruciality of the Cross. Professor H. Shelton Smith suggests that the covenant of grace, which furnished the architectonic principle of much Reformed Presbyterian and Con-

---

* Paterson, W. P., *The Rule of Faith*. cf. Mackintosh, H. R., *Types of Modern Theology*. pp. 155, 157, 187, 247.

gregational theology, be revived as an antidote for the humanism of current religious education.* Luther rediscovered justification by faith as the message of Romans and Galatians and the heart of the Church. Jonathan Edwards' series of sermons on justification by faith alone initiated the Great Awakening. For J. H. Thornwell, "the central principle of all theology is *justification.*" Near the close of the last century Edouard Boehl called for a new recognition of the regulative place of justification as a verdict of God, based on a gracious imputation of Christ's active and passive obedience to the sinner.

This volume is not designed to say which of these evangelical themes is the most logical point about which to organize Christian thinking. Complete logical coherence is in God, rather than in His interpreters. And the sovereignty of God means first submission to His authority, trembling at His Word. What we do seek is that Christian thinking find its canon in the Christian Revelation.

This method of procedure does not forbid true inquiry, it does not mean the sacrifice of the intellect, it does not call for blind obedience to dogma. It does mean that the Christian faith is studied and presented according to its own intrinsic logic. Then the Christian world and life view is set in comparison and contrast with other world and life views, and the reader is invited to choose. Our Lord Himself challenges the inquirer to *come and see.* We look to the Holy Spirit to convince men that the Christian Revelation is God's provision for the deepest needs of the heart, the head, and the hand, His answer to the most searching questions of the soul.

APPRECIATION

The Lecturer records his deep appreciation to the President, to the Faculty, and to the Board of Union Theological Seminary for the honor and privilege of delivering the Sprunt Lectures. And scarcely less is his appreciation due to the Faculty for

---

* Smith, H. S., *Faith and Nurture.*

suggesting as a theme for investigation and presentation in lectures the subject of eschatology. Without this suggestion, it is doubtful whether he would have had the temerity to select this theme, and so would have missed the information and blessing that this study has been to him. The reader may regard the same suggestion as an invitation to study here as well as elsewhere the riches of the Christian hope.

The sympathetic attention of the students of Union Theological Seminary and of the Assembly's Training School, as well as of citizens of Richmond, facilitated the delivery of the lectures. The thoughtful and gracious hospitality of President and Mrs. Ben R. Lacy, Jr., made the week in their home a memorable occasion. Professor James E. Bear read the lectures and offered valuable suggestions.

WM. CHILDS ROBINSON

Columbia Theological Seminary.

Christ — The Hope of Glory

CHAPTER I.

CHRIST JESUS — OUR HOPE
I Tim. i.1.

● *"In Christ all our hope may rest and be satisfied."*

Institutes, III.xx.2.

I. THE PLACE OF HOPE IN THE CHRISTIAN PICTURE.
   A. Windows of Hope.
   B. An Anchor of the Soul.
   C. The Pillars that Support the Christian Edifice.
   D. The Rising Tide of Christian Hope.

II. THE FOUNDATION OF OUR HOPE - CHRIST JESUS.
   Christ is the hope of glory and other foundation can no man lay.

   A. Is Natural Theology an Additional Foundation? What God has written of Himself into Nature can only be truly read by those whose eyes have been opened by the great revelation in Christ.

   B. Fellowship in Everlasting Life.
      The Eternal Life was with the Father and was given us in His Son.
      The Incarnation and Eschatology.
      Spes Mea, Crux Christi.
      The Power of His Resurrection.
      The Lord of History.
      The Blessed Hope.

15

CHRIST JESUS, OUR HOPE

These four words present two tremendous truths: In Christ there is hope, and our hope is Christ. In Jesus Christ we not only have faith and love, but also the hope of glory. And the Christian hope is not a series of vague premonitions, poetic phantasies or philosophical speculations; rather it is Jesus the Messiah, God's mighty Amen to His precious promises. His majestic message turns our eyes from the angry inferno of a warring world to the golden spires of the City of God.

I. THE PLACE OF HOPE IN THE CHRISTIAN PICTURE.

A. *Windows of Hope.* In the First Presbyterian Church of Charlotte there are two windows depicting Christian hope. One represents a woman whose feet are in chains, whose head and shoulders are shrouded in mists, but who is reaching through the clouds into the light of Heaven. The other shows the Holy City, New Jerusalem, coming down out of Heaven from God. God has let down His gracious promises of a new heaven and a new earth which our Lord will bring with Him when He comes in His glory. Though our feet be chained by the sordidness of earth and our heads lost in the smoke of battle and the turmoil of trivialities, we can still grasp the promises of God that are Yea in Christ. For, "everywhere hope looks out of the windows of the Christian Scriptures." [1]

The black-outs of earth do not dim the lights of heaven. It is when the night becomes dark that the stars appear. In the hour of darkness the Lord of hosts becomes a crown of glory and a diadem of beauty unto the residue of His people, and a spirit of justice to him that sitteth in judgment and strength to them that turn back the battle at the gate (Isa. xxviii.6). We have lost our hope in man, but God is still the strength of our hearts. We have failed, but Christ has overcome the world. Western civilization is collapsing, but His truth is marching on. Above the travail of nations shines the star of Christian hope.

1. Webb, R. A., *The Christian's Hope*, p. 12.

As this is written, the white horseman of Conquest is over-throwing nations and conquering millions. The red horseman of War has taken peace from nine-tenths of the population of the earth, turning industry into the business of killing. The black horseman of Famine is stalking the length and breadth of Eurasia from the valleys of China to the coasts of Belgium, from the Acropolis of Athens to the ghettos of Poland. With sword, with hunger, with pestilence and with beasts the "pale" horse-man of Death is destroying a fourth part of the earth.

Tragedy, however, is no new thing to the people of God. They have made brick without straw, trodden the furnace heated sevenfold, wept by the waters of Babylon, been accounted as sheep for the slaughter. They have accepted tribulation as a step on the path of hope (Rom. v.3-5), the reproach of Christ as an assurance of the Spirit of glory (I Pet. iv.14), persecution for His sake as the testimony of His beatitude and the promise of His reward (Mt. v.11-12). Even when they are prisoners, still are they prisoners of hope. Weeping may endure for a night, but joy comes in the morning. If we suffer with Him, we shall also reign with Him. If we are conformed to the Head of the elect first in the Cross, we shall also be conformed in the Crown. Even a Roman dungeon cannot stifle the bugle notes of victory, Rejoice in the Lord always. Through the tears of suffering and the shame of oppression shines the Crown of Life.

When the dreams of men vanish in the battle smoke, when oppression blasts the vision of humanism, when idealism reels before the realism of mechanized might, His people are neither without God nor without hope in the world. Only that hope is not pinned on the world, on that world whose princes crucified the Lord of glory. It is based on the Lord of glory who over-came the world, whose unsullied life of love is the harbinger of the new heavens and the new earth, whose Cross is our redemp-tion, whose Resurrection is the revelation of the day that shall know no end. The resurrection reveille that sounded from the emptied tomb of Joseph of Arimathea sheathed the flaming sword of exclusion from God's presence and announced the City of God in which there is no more death, nor separation, nor mourning, nor crying, nor pain. The darkness of secular despair passes with the dawn of Christian faith.

God, who has revealed Himself as our Lord Jesus Christ and God our Father, has loved us and given us eternal comfort and good hope through grace (II Thess. ii.16). According to the doctrine of God our Saviour the saving grace of God has appeared to all men, teaching us to the intent that denying ungodliness and wordly lusts we should live soberly and righteously and godly in this present age, expectantly awaiting the blessed hope, even the epiphany of the glory of our great God and Saviour, Jesus Christ (Tit.ii.10-13). "Christ also having been once offered to bear the sins of many, shall appear a second time, apart from sin, to them that wait for Him unto salvation" (Hebr. ix.28). The Book of Revelation is stretched from two poles, the first and the second comings of Christ.

The Apocalypse does not stand alone, but its vision of the New Jersusalem only visualizes the hope of the primitive disciples and of Paul. Galatians, Romans, Hebrews, First Peter and First John are all eschatological.[2] The same vibrant note sounds in the primitive Gospel which Paul cites (I Cor. xv.3f.; xvi.22; I Thess. i.10), in "the oral gospel" as preserved in Acts (iii.13), in the primitive narrative, in the primitive sayings, in the passion and resurrection preaching (Mk. xiv.61-62) which is recognized as the earliest element in the church praxis. Indeed, the footsteps of Christ are heard all along the Old Testament way, while the New Testament is occupied with that which the Old Testament saw in prospect, namely, the appearance of the Messiah and the inauguration of His work at His first coming, the continuance of that work in His appearing in the presence of God for us, and the consummation thereof by His appearing again on earth (Hebrews ix.24-28).

2. Schmidt, K. L., *New Testament Eschatology*, lectures 1937-38.

B. *An Anchor of the Soul.* Our hope is born of the Resurrection of Christ, and feeds on the unchanging promises of God. Hence, the darker the day and the more dismal the dawn, the brighter does this hope appear. When Jesus entered within the veil as our Forerunner, He gave the *Yea* and *Amen* to the promises of God and set before us the hope of glory as a sure and steadfast anchor for our souls (Hebrews vi.13-20). While fear hath torments that point to the pit, Christian hope hath promises that reach unto glory. Those who are separated from Christ and alienated from the covenants of promise are without God and without hope (Eph. ii.12) ; but the Christian has hope in Christ both in this life and in that which is to come (Cf. I Cor. xv.19). Even as he walks through the Valley of the Shadow, he sorrows not as those who have no hope (1 Thess. iv.13). By the Resurrection of Jesus Christ he has been begotten again unto a living hope (I Peter i.3), and cherishes the blessed hope of the appearing of the glory of our great God and Saviour, Jesus Christ (Tit. ii.13). By faith in Christ Jesus and love toward all the saints he nourishes the hope which is laid up for him in the heavens, according to the true Word of the Gospel (Col. i.4-5).

The primitive Christian life is characterized as worshipping God and waiting for His Son from heaven (I Thess. i.9). The whole creation, having been subjected in hope of its deliverance, is in eager expectancy, awaiting its redemption at the revelation of the sons of God (Rom. viii.19-20). For, according to His promise, we look for a new heaven and a new earth wherein dwelleth righteousness (II Peter iii.13). Hence, as sons of light and as daughters of the dawn, we wear the breastplate of faith and love ; and for a helmet, the hope of salvation. (I Thess. v. 8).

In the Apostle Paul's matchless hymn of Christian love, these three parts of the soldier's armor become the Christian graces of faith, hope and love, the gifts of God that abide. Given by the same Spirit, these graces all grasp the unseen Christ and so fuse in Christian character that he who has one will not be destitute of the others. *Faith* embraces the exceeding great and precious promises; clings to the Maker of these promises; and, acting upon them, commits the believer to his Lord and Saviour. Through the Spirit by *faith* we wait for the *hope* of righteousness (Gal. v. 5). Hope is the confident expectation of the fulfillment of the promises, the anticipation that *spes erit res. Faith* is an assurance of things *hoped* for, a certainty of things not seen (Hebr. xi.1). *"Love* is based upon *faith,* especially, that element in it we call confidence."[3] Faith is the receptive principle, by which God's spontaneous "uncaused" love, shed abroad in our hearts by the Holy Spirit, is apprehended, and the living hope of salvation in the heavenly inheritance fills us with joy unspeakable and full of glory (Rom. v. 5; I Peter i.3-9). *Faith* worketh by *love* and glorieth in *hope* (Gal. v. 6; Rom. v. 2). *Faith* and *hope* are the two stimuli for the life of love. By the grace of God we are saved through faith (Eph. ii.8), and through *hope* (Rom. viii.24); while our *love,* in so far as it reflects God's great *agape,* "seeketh not her own," but poureth itself out on others.[4] Hence we pray, "Lord, work in our hearts a true *faith,* a purifying *hope,* and an unfeigned *love* to thee."[5] "By God's inspired arrangement, in the triad of Christian grace, *Hope* stands betwixt *Faith* and *Love,* and lifts the eyes of the soul up to the throne of God. Then let not thy soul be disquieted within thee! *Hope* thou in God! For Hope can find grandeur in graves and glory in gloom when its foundation rests on God-Incarnate . . . 'which is Christ in you the *Hope* of glory'."[6]

Now the Christian revelation is proved true by the fact that it shines in its own light and illumines everything with which it comes in contact. "In Thy light, we shall see light" (Psa. xxvi.9). The testimony of the Holy Spirit lays a compulsion on the mind to believe the Word.

> "It gives a light to every age;
> It gives, but borrows none."

3. Dr. Frazier Hood.
4. Nygren, A., *Agape and Eros,* translated by Hebert, 1937, p. 105.
5. *The Imitation of Christ.*
6. Hutton, J. B., *Christmas Message,* 1939.

The wealth of God's Revelation is beyond human reason and may not be scaled down to conform to the canons of fallen and fallible natural man. Hence, we do not begin with a general concept of hope and force Christian hope to conform to this preconceived mould. But having begun with the Christian revelation, we may notice that, in recognizing hope as an anchor of the soul, Christianity has laid hold on one of the potent forces in the life of man. Often "hopes deceive and fears annoy;" nevertheless, hope hath her achievements in every field of human endeavor. "Hope is undoubtedly an elementary principle in our rational nature." [7] Her hope triumphant o'er her fears, the mother brings a child into the world. In the midst of crushing disappointments and continuous sufferings, hope keeps the lamp of life alight and refuses the suicide's grave. Nerved by hope, the sailor struggles through the storms that buffet his boat. Sustained by hope, the scientist continues his ceaseless experimentation until discovery crowns his tireless search. The patient, battling for life against the white plague, conquers by hope. The patriot fights on for freedom, hope strengthening the hand that wields the sword. Undismayed by countless rebuffs, Columbus was led by hope to the New World. Often, "Hope points beyond this to a life to come."[8] "Religion without a great hope would be like an altar without a living fire."[9] Hope is the vision without which the people perish. By hope, captive Israel was lifted as on eagle wings, enabled to run and not be weary, to walk and not to faint, until Jerusalem was rebuilt.

By the hope of a brighter tomorrow, Henry W. Grady encouraged the prostrate South to rise from the ashes of war and reconstruction. One of his most telling figures is a comparison of the South to a soldier left sorely wounded on the battlefield, with only a faint gleam of hope in a doctor's assurance that if he lives until tomorrow's sundown he will get well. And, as life ebbs 'neath the fierce rays of the sun, the hopes of his heart

7. Palmer, B. M., *The Threefold Fellowship and the Threefold Assurance*, p. 134.
8. Luthardt, C. E., *The Saving ruths of Christianity*, 1886, p. 291.
9. Van Dyke, Henry, *The Other Wise Man*.

whisper their messages of courage. He thinks of the home among the hills with roses climbing to its doors, and trees whispering about its windows; of the aged parents who need his supporting arm; of the girl who has come from a neighboring farmhouse and put her hand shyly into his, and brought love into his life and light into his home; of the bairns who climb upon his lap and tangle their hands in his heart strings, making to him a music that earth shall not equal, nor heaven surpass. And, as hope steadies the heroic soldier, the Son of God puts the hand that was nailed to the Cross on ebbing life and holds on the staunch until the sun goes down and the stars come out and shine down in the brave man's heart and blurr in his glistening eye, and he is taken from death to life. But the saving of that soldier is also a parable of the saving of the South, by *hope*. Therefore, neither as children of humanity's tragedies and triumphs, nor as children whom God has begotten again unto a living hope, can we forget the place that hope has in life and in our faith.

Today, as the lights go out, as the dreams of Humanism turn into the nightmare of Nazism, and the triumphs of peace dissolve in the ashes of war, there is but one refuge from blank pessimism and cynical despair. Man's inability to achieve his ideals of justice and progress will lead to this one sure hope, if from his defeat and failure, he learns to hope in God. Whether or not "Heideyger is the symbol of modern man's confession of defeat, with his hopes in the dust,"[10] Christ is God's declaration of victory and our hope of glory.

C. *The Pillars that Support the Christian Edifice.* The Church of the New Testament has been compared to an audacious trestle, stretched on a single lofty arch over a raging torrent, and supported by only two pillars, one standing on this and the other on that shore of world history. If either of these pillars is shattered the whole bridge collapses and everything is lost. The one pillar is the event of Golgotha, and the other pillar is the still outstanding event, namely, the Son of God's visible,

10. Davies, D. R., *The Two Humanities*, p. 49, cf. p. 60.

mighty laying-hold of His own Authority. As the trestle stands only by the tension between both these pillars, so the Church exists only by the inseparable unity between this which has occurred, and that which is to come.[11] She lives in the faith that the same One who has come will come. "Having tasted the powers of the world to come" (Hebr. vi.5), she looks to that coming act of God and the glory of the new age.

Professor Karl Barth describes the Old Testament as the witness of expectation of the coming Messiah, and the New Testament as the witness of remembrance of this same Messiah. The two Testaments are related as the rightly given answer to the rightly put question. But having said this, Barth immediately adds that the New Testament remembrance of the Word made flesh straightway turns itself in an hundred and eighty degree angle, and becomes the witness of expectation of the same Christ whom she knows as true God and true man. The testimony of hope irradiates both Testaments; but the New Testament saint knows the Messiah upon whom he waits in a way that the Old Testament did not. "His coming is really only His coming again." "The New Testament is, as the Old Testament, the witness of the revelation in which God is present to men as the coming God."[12]

This means that the current continental theology is rediscovering the great foundations on which the life of God's people has ever rested. We look *back* by *faith* to the First Coming of Christ; and we look *forward* by *hope* to the Second Coming. "In the enjoyment of the fruit of the first, we anticipate the fulness of the second. Between these two the apostle has beautifully placed the Christian's present holy walk. These are the two *pivots* on which turns the Christian life—the two *wings* on which the believers mount up as eagles. If either is clipped, the soul's flight heavenward is low, feeble and fitful." "To the *grace* brought by the one we look backward by faith, and forward by

11. Heim, Karl, *Jesus der Weltvollender*, p. 172.
12. Barth, K., *Kirchliche Dogmatik*, I.2 pp. 131, 104.

hope to the glory which is to be brought by the other."[13] "The remembrance of the first advent, culminating in the sacrifice of love on Golgotha, and the hope of the Lord's return, bringing glory and joy to His ransomed Bride; this past and this future form the element in which the Christian lives; they are, so to speak, blended in his consciousness, and form his true present, his real, blessed, eternal life." "The grace of God, bringing salvation, hath appeared—this is our sunrise—teaching us to wait for the appearing of our great God and Saviour—this is our perfect, and never-ending day." "The Lord's Supper . . . is the most vivid remembrance and realization of the death of Christ and the most vivid anticipation of the return of the Bride-groom."[14] That return is the

> "Hope of the sacramental host,
> Their only glory, joy and boast."[15]

"We need two motives, memory and hope, to keep the soul in equilibrium. Memory must constantly draw us back to the cross, and hope must constantly attract us to the crown, if our hearts are to be kept in even and balanced communion with God. As the waters of the sea are held between two mighty gravitations, the moon now drawing the waters to itself, and the earth now drawing them back again, thus giving us the ebbing and flowing tide by which our earth is kept clean and healthful, so must the tides of the soul's affection move per-petually between the Cross of Christ and the Coming of Christ, influenced now by the power of memory, and now by the power of hope."[16]

Since "the Christian expectation of the end is an inseparable part of the Christian faith in God," [17] the Church ought not allow any other interest to obscure this hope. In his moderatorial

13. Brown, David, *Christ's Second Advent*, pp. 29, 77.
14. Saphir, A., *The Hidden Life*, pp. 266-268.
15. Girardeau, J. L. quoted by Webb, R. A., *The Christian's Hope*, p. 110. The eschatol-ogical school finds the past suffering and the eschatological expectation bound together in the Lord's Supper, and, in the latter aspect, describes it as a foretaste of the Messianic meal of triumph.—Schweitzer, A., *Das Abendmahl*, I. 1.
16. Gordon, E. B., *Life of A. J. Gordon*, Revell, 1898, pp. 267-9.
17. Lilje, H., *Das Letzte Buch der Bibel*.

sermon, Professor Edward Mack exhorted the Synod of Virginia not to permit temporal services and social concerns to dim her concentration upon the supreme goal of the Church: the return of the Lord in glory. Professor Paul Althaus opposes a mysticism which, professing a present eternal life in a super-world of "True Being," forgets life and history and erases the tension of waiting to see God in the eschatological age.[18] There is a modernism which has abandoned belief in the Second Coming of Christ and has transformed the Kingdom of God into the conception of a righteous society to be evolved out of the existing social order.[19] "According to the idealistic philosophy of history, the Kingdom comes through the immanent Logos of history itself as a result of progressive evolution." When one identifies the Kingdom of God with any form of messianism— be it democracy, the League of Nations, socialism, nationalism, or anti-alcoholism—which does not have Jesus Christ as its center and its realization in the eschatological state, he turns *the Kingdom of God* into *the Kingdom of man,* into a humanism in which man wants to redeem and perfect the world by his sovereignty. "The preaching of the Coming of God, who as Lord and King of the world will be and is its sole consummator and redeemer, is the most drastic criticism of these utopias."[20]

Modern tragedy has destroyed nineteenth century belief in a progressive evolution of mankind to moral and spiritual perfection and has revived the long suppressed question of what lies on the other side of death. The hearts of men are famishing for that blessed note that runs through all Scripture: the assured return of the Lord and the glory that shall follow.

D. *The Rising Tide of Christian Hope.* Tracing a close parallelism between the historical sequence in the formulation of Christian dogmas and the logical unfolding of the theological

---

18. Althaus, P., *Die letzten Dinge,* vierete auflage, pp. 4-11, 23.
19. Cadoux, C. J., *The Case for Evangelical Modernism;* Smith, B. G. B., *Principles of Christian Living,* p. 26; Fosdick, H. E., *The New Knowledge and the Christian Faith;* Wilder, A. N., *Eschatology and Ethics in the Teaching of Jesus,* pp. xi. 4, 7, 21, 197, 235.
20. Wendland, H. D., *The Kingdom of God and History,* Oxford Conference Books, III: 170, 172. Cf. Smith, H. S., *Faith and Nurture.*

system, James Orr predicted that our age would give itself with special earnestness to eschatological questions, moved thereto, perhaps, by the solemn impression that on it the ends of the world have come, and that some great crisis in the history of human affairs is approaching.[21] Orr's forecast is fast becoming true.

In 1910, Archbishop Soderblom declared, "To our generation the knowledge of the fundamentally eschatological character of the Gospel comes as a needed call to awake." Deissmann told the delegates at Lausanne, "For the last thirty years or so the discernment of the eschatological character of the Gospel of Jesus has come more and more to the front in international Christian theology . . . We must lay the greatest possible stress upon the eschatological character of the Gospel." To this Zwemer added at the Jerusalem Council, "This is indeed our missionary message, the everlasting Gospel of One who came, who died, who rose, who ascended and who is coming again."[22]

In the New Testament field this change of viewpoint, traceable by such signposts as Wilhelm Wrede, Albert Schweitzer, Franz Overbeck, Karl Barth, Paul Althaus, Walter Kunneth, has progressed so far that Nygren can say, "Probably the weightiest contribution of modern exegesis to the study of the Gospels has been its clear delineation of the eschatological outlook."[23]

From the latest school, the theologians of the Word, come such testimonies as the following: "All the fantastic ideas which have brought the Christian hope into discredit must not lead us into any mistake about the thing itself, about the truth that the End is coming." "Grace cometh and the world passeth away." "Without this burning expectation of the end the true thought of God cannot live." "Without eschatology genuine faith in God is impossible." [24] "For Christianity—as for Israel, Islam and Parseeism—the belief of the End becomes the ruling

21. Orr, J., *The Progress of Dogma,* pp. 17-30.
22. Zwemer, S. M., Jerusalem Meeting *I. M. C.,* I.300-301.
23. Holmstrom, F., *Das eschatologische Denken der Gegenwart,* Germany, 1936, pp. I, 19, 23 citing Soderblom, Aulen and Nygren.
24. Heim, K., *The New Divine Order,* p. 88; *Jesus der Herr,* p. 39.

thought of the whole religion." [25] "The whole Jesus Christ of
the New Testament can really only be understood as this coming
Redeemer. If He is not the Coming One, then He is not the
One who did come. If the reconciliation accomplished in Him
is not futuristically understood, then it is not perfect, then it
is not understood. Our rebirth, our justification, our sanctification, the Church and the sacraments, the whole existence and
the whole work of Jesus Christ in the present are realized
eschatologically, that is, only in the coming Redeemer. What
have we here that we have not in hope?" [26] "The eschatological
construction of Christianity has become the battle standard
erected in the struggle for the freedom of the Christian message
from the speculative interpretations with which many centuries
of thoroughly idealistic delusions within the Christian theology
have hidden the genuine Gospel." "The strife concerning the
role and significance of eschatology for the present understanding
of Christianity is in reality a more tense as well as a more sublime
and a more tragic battle, just because thereby the Biblical Gospel
will be freed from the alien fetters of a timeless metaphysics."[27]

The writings of Barth, Brunner, W. D. Wendland, K. L.
Schmidt, G. T. Thomson, H. M. Relton, A. Keller and N.
Ehrenström show that eschatology has come into the consideration of the doctrine of the state. Is the state God's representative
and priest according to Romans thirteen, or is it the beast rising
out of the sea according to Revelation thirteen? If the former,
does it not become demonized when it gives up the idea of a just
government and persecutes the Church of God? "The National
Gospel comes under the same condemnation as the social gospel
in so far as in it interest is concentrated upon the efforts and
problems which concern this world alone and upon the contribution which Christianity can make toward their solution, not upon
the Divine Word and its message of judgment and grace to fallen

25. Althaus, *op. cit.*, p. 7.
26. Barth, K., *Kirchliche Dogmatik*, I.2:979.
27. Holstrom, F., *op. cit.* pp. 1, 19, 23.

man. When the emphasis is laid upon the evanescent historically relative factors, men have forgotten that this earth with all that belongs to it must be regarded 'from the eschatological point of view. The emphasis must be removed from man and his world to God as judge and redeemer and His coming Kingdom."[28] The announcement of the coming Kingdom defines the states as provisional and relative.

The eschatological destiny of the Church was proclaimed by B. M. Palmer to our first General Assembly and was emphasized by Abraham Kuyper in the Stone Lectures. It has received renewed recognition in W. D. Wendland's *Die Eschatologie des Reiches Gottes bei Jesus,* in K. L. Schmidt's article on *Ekklesia* in Kittel's *Theologisches Wörterbuch,* in H. Kraemer's, *The Jesus and His Church.* The eschatological consummation of the Church was kept to the forefront in the 1939 meeting of the continuation committee of the World Conference of Faith and Order at Clerens. Much of the discussion was based upon the following definition of the Church offered by Professor J. de Zwaan of the Reformed Church of the Netherlands:

> "The one Church of God is not an institutional but a super-natural entity which is in process of growth towards an eschatological end, as being the sphere of action of the heavenly Christ; all its members being in Christ and being knit together by a supernatural kinship; all their gifts and activities continuing the work of Christ, originating from Christ and being co-ordinated by Christ to the one final result, which will appear in the eschatological future as the one People of God united in one *qehala* before the Throne, or as the one celestial City."[29]

28. Ehrenstrom, N., *Christian Faith and the Modern State,* p. 81.
29. *World Conference on Faith and Order,* pamphlet 92, p. 46.

The Oxford Conference volume on *The Kingdom of God and History* contains Professor Wendland's insistence that the Kingdom is realized at the *Parousia* of the Lord toward which the history of the world is moving. In his volume written for the Madras Conference, Professor Kraemer "looks forward to a consummation which transcends our human strivings and achievements, the realization of the Kingdom of God by God Himself." "The integral realization of this new order of the Kingdom of God is the object of expectation." "The community, the *Koinonia* of those who live in Christ, is waiting with long expectation for the coming of the Kingdom." When the Tambaram meeting of the International Missionary Council seemed to give inadequate recognition to this aspect of the Church's message, the chairman of the German delegation added: "In the Apostles' Creed, we all confess together that Christ will come again to judge the living and the dead. In spite of changes which have taken place in the aspect of the world and history since the days of the Apostles, we believe according to the Scriptures that through a creative act of God His Kingdom will be consummated in the final establishment of a New Heaven and a New Earth."

II. The Foundation of Our Hope - Christ Jesus.

The opening verse of First Timothy describes Christ Jesus as our hope. In an epistle written from prison, the Apostle asserted that Christ in you is the hope of glory (Col. i.27). In one of his major epistles, Paul declared that other foundation can no man lay than that which is laid, which is Jesus Christ (I Cor. iii.11). Calvin apprises us that the hope of the pious has never been placed anywhere but in Christ, and that when we face the tribunal of God we must turn our eyes from ourselves and fix them *solely* on Christ, for the believer has no other justifying righteousness than that obtained from the Mediator *(Institutes* II.vi.3; II.xvi.19; III.xix.2; III.xiv.11). For Wm. S. Plumer, "All we have and all we hope for is through

His grace." To Thomas Scott, "Christ is my all, He is my hope." [30] In one of the great evangelical hymns, we sing:

> "My hope is built on nothing less
> Than Jesus' blood and righteousness.
> I dare not trust the sweetest frame,
> But wholly lean on Jesus' Name.
>
> His oath, His covenant, His blood,
> Support me in the whelming flood;
> When all around my soul gives way,
> He then is all my hope and stay.
>
> On Christ, the solid Rock, I stand
> All other ground is sinking sand."

At the present time, the loss of confidence in man and his natural ability to evolve a kingdom of peace, prosperity, culture, plenty, truth, and justice is driving the hopes of men back to the promises of God which are Yea and Amen in Christ. "God has revealed in history, in Jesus Christ, the ultimate meaning and destiny of human existence."[31] "The eschatology of the early Church was founded on the life of Christ. Because of what He had done for them during His earthly life they could entertain a firm hope for the future. His life was the model to which by the Holy Spirit they hope to be conformed."[32] Or more briefly, Jesus Christ *alone* is the hope of the Church, just as Jesus Christ *alone* is her comfort.[33] The Christmas Message in *the Atlanta Constitution,* 1940, carried this title: *Christ is our Hope.*[34]

A. *Is Natural Theology a Prior Foundation?* However, someone is already asking: Have we not many reasons for hope in the intimations of immortality which nature gives us? May we not use the arguments of natural religion to reach the reason of men, and then by appealing to faith let the grace of Christ

30. Plumer, W. S., *The Grace of Christ,* pp. 345, 365.
31. Smith, H. S., *Faith and Nurture,* 1941, pp. 105-107.
32. Piper, O. A., *USR,* August, 1942, p. 284.
33. Barth, K., *The Knowledge of God and the Service of God.* p. 241.
34. By Bishop Arthur J. Moore.

supplement what nature has begun? Before one hastily answers
these questions in the affirmative, he ought to recognize that
Karl Barth's celebrated NEIN! calls for careful rather than
superficial thinking on this subject.

Finis origine pendet. The Roman Catholic thesis that grace
does not destroy nature but perfects it overlooks the fact that
the foundation of a building determines its superstructure, and
flies in the face of the Saviour's warning against pouring new
wide into old wineskins. Both Luther and Tyndale protested
against a system of education that filled a student's mind with
Aristotle before it allowed him to study the Word. In the
Dedication of the Institutes Calvin quoted the Romanist com-
plaint against "our pleading the Word of God" as "the way to
overturn, I know not what blind light of nature." The organizing principle in the first chapters of both the first and the
second books of the Institutes is the inability of fallen man to
attain an adequate knowledge of God and the consequent necessity of beginning with the Word of God. Rome says begin
with nature and complete the building on this natural foundation with grace; Calvin says begin with the Word and use the
Word as spectacles through which alone will you be able to
read God's revelation in nature. "The Reformation took its
position not in natural reason, in order gradually to lead this on
to faith, but in the Christian faith. And it declared as positively
as possible . . . that that faith rests on the authority of God
and is wrought only by the Holy Spirit."[35]

Man is fallen as a totality and as a concrete unit he needs
the saving light of Christ and the renewing grace of the Holy
Spirit. There is "an extreme and brutish blindness in things
of religion which naturally possesses the hearts of mankind."[36]
Due to the depravity of man and the malignity of Satan, "no
just and consistent notions of God's nature, His character and
His attributes are compassed by natural light."[37] "If Christian

---

35. Bavinck, H., *Gereformeerde Dogmatiek,* I. 427-442.
36. Edwards, J., *Works,* IV.7.
37. Thornwell, J. H., *Writings,* I.76-77.

revelation which assumes the darkness and error of the natural man should surrender herself beforehand to the judgment of reason, she would contradict herself."

One never gets a true view of the Christian revelation when he approaches it by setting up certain principles as to what constitutes nature, history, philosophy, education, religion or criticism and then modifies or rejects whatever in the Christian faith refuses to be confined in these rationalistic preconceptions. God does not stand at our judgment bar. We do not take knowledge of Him and fit Him into our schemes, He takes knowledge of us and fits us into His whole, else were the puny fragments of human knowledge wiser than God's unsearchable omniscience. "The very first condition to be fulfilled by the Church is clear, Christian thinking. Not merely clear thinking, but clear Christian thinking—a distinction with the profoundest of differences."[38] This necessity of beginning with the Christian revelation may be illustrated by a study of the problem of evil,[39] by the doctrine of the Holy Trinity, or by a consideration of whether the heavens declare the glory of God to a sun-worshipper, to an experimentalist who admits no mind but the human, or to the Psalmist to whom the LORD has already revealed Himself as Rock and Redeemer (Psalm xix.1,14).

The Gestalt psychology is calling men to begin logically with the whole and then study the parts, to start with the final and then take up the preparatory stages. If God was not content to stop even with the revelation He had made of Himself through diverse portions and in diverse manners unto the prophets but finally spoke unto us in His Son, why should we assume that our sin-darkened eyes can begin aright with the diffused gleams in nature, or possible sparks of truth in human philosophy or whatever dim reflections of general revelation may lie buried in the mass of heathen superstition and pagan worship? God shines in the believer's heart to give the light of the knowledge of His glory in the face of Jesus Christ (II

38. Davies, D. R., *On To Orthodoxy*, p. 227.
39. "Evil remains the great problem for religion." H. F. Rall, *Christianity*, p. 343.

Cor. iv.6). The Christian ought to begin where the Dayspring from on High has visited him, rather than ignore His shining and begin with the darkness and the shadow of death (Lk. i.78-79). Experiments show that a rodent in a covered box will come to any point at which light is introduced into the box. Is the Christian, then, to begin with the twilight of nature, or the darkness of words without wisdom when he might begin intellectually where God has graciously placed him? Since the revelation of God in nature is not understood by fallen man, "God is and must be His own revealer." [40] God does not confront man for his salvation either "in His world" or in "the empirical idealism" out of which the Laymen's Inquiry offers to build "a world faith."** Christian faith cometh by hearing and hearing by the Word of Christ (Rom. x.17). When the Father in heaven has revealed Himself to us in His only Son, why should we refuse the foundation that He has laid, which is Jesus Christ? (Matt. xvi.17; I Cor. iii.11).[40] "Even what God has written of Himself into Nature can only be truly read by those whose eyes have been opened by the great revelation in Jesus."[41] It is from this vantage point that we can study the vestiges of the Creator in nature and in the life of the spirit.[42]

While the vestiges of immortality impressed upon man by God's primitive revelation are indelible *(Institutes* I.iv.5), between man's original destination and its fulfillment sin has entered darkening man's understanding, and death has come testifying to man's changed status before God. All of Plato's argument only proved the possibility not the certainty of immortality, only this possibility for Socrates, not for every man, only for Socrates' thinking soul, not for his complete personality. Reason may argue that as a dependent existence the soul may cease, if God please, and that He will probably quench the sinful soul to purify the universe. Even "the certainty of continued existence can be a deep certainty of being lost, and in any case an uncertainty

** *Re-thinking Missions.*
40. Smyth, T., *Works,* IX.62-63.
41. Mackintosh, J. R., *Types of Modern Theology,* p. 147.
42. Cf. Dodd, C. H., *History and the Gospel,* pp. 19-36, 58.

of salvation."§ When man comes face to face with the Word, *our God is a consuming fire,* and *the soul that sinneth it shall die,* he finds himself under the curse of God.

B. *Fellowship in Life Everlasting.* However, just here where the curse hangs heaviest, where God speaks judgment, He also speaks grace. "The deepest root of the belief in an eternal life is, according to the Bible, singly and alone our terrified conscience that says to us unmistakably: There is an eternal judgment."[43] The Word of the Cross speaks our condemnation at the same moment that it speaks our justification. We deserved all that He received, and He received all that we deserved. He was delivered for our offenses and raised for our justification (Rom. iv.25). Luther begins with the Word of the eternal God: "Where or with whom God speaks, whether it be in wrath or in grace, is certainly immortal. The Person of God speaks it and the Word declares it, that we are such creatures as those with whom God would speak even unto Eternity and in an immortal way."

It is certainly more reasonable to begin our consideration of everlasting life with God, the self-existent, eternal Being than with the souls of transient, dependent creatures. "Why should it be thought a thing incredible with you, that *God* should raise the dead?" Both the Old and New Testament teachings of the hereafter are centered not in the Hellenic conception of the inherent ability of the soul to attain immortal life, but in the Hebraic idea of an immortal or indissoluable relationship which God establishes with the believer. Since Jehovah has said, *I am the LORD, thy God,* therefore, *the eternal God is thy stay, and underneath are the arms that will last for aye* (Ex. xx.2; Deut. xxxiii.27). God will be true to His gracious covenant. "Thus has Jesus grounded the certainty of eternal life. In that God named Himself the God of Abraham, and the God of Isaac, and the God of Jacob He attested the eternal life of these men before Himself."[44]

§ Althaus, *DvD.*v.a.110.
43. Heim, K., *Glaube und Denken,* p. 344f.
44. Althaus, P., D.L.D.v.v.S. 106, 109.

The Incarnation and Eschatology. According to the Bible, the eternal life was with the Father and was manifested to us in the Word of Life (I John i.1-2). This is eternal life: to know the only true God and Jesus, the Messiah whom He sent (John vii.3). "God hath given unto us eternal life, and this life is in His Son. He that hath the Son hath the life; he that hath not the Son hath not the life." (I John v.11-12). Or if one wishes to begin with the primitive "oral gospel" the Apostles preached in Jesus the Resurrection of the dead (Acts iv.2), the judgment (xvii.31), the times of the restoration of all things (iii.20) and deliverance from the wrath to come (I Thess. i.9). It is our Saviour Jesus Christ who has abolished death and brought immortality to life through the Gospel (II Tim. i.10). God hath begotten us again unto a living hope by the Resurrection of Christ (I Peter i.3). He that hath the words of eternal life is our hope, not only in His words, but also in His Person, in His work, "in His mission as a whole." [45] Christ has been made unto us wisdom, righteousness, sanctification and complete redemption (I Cor. i.30). As the Saviour of the world Jesus is *der Weltvollender*,[46] for "in Jesus Christ God disclosed the ultimate meaning of existence."[47] "Incarnation gave men the assurance that their eschatological expectations were substantially true." [48]

"To us a Child of hope is born,
To us a Son is giv'n,
The Wonderful, the Counsellor,
The mighty Lord of heaven."

Yea, "the intuition of the Church as revealed in the Chalcedonian doctrine of the two natures was absolutely sound; for it did justice to the fact that Jesus was both God and Man at the same time. On the truth of that fact depends the realization by mankind of its hopes of a perfect social order."[49]

45. Wendland, H. D., *op. cit.* p. 147.
46. Heim, K., *Jesus der Weltvollender.*
47. Smith, H. S., *op. cit.* p. 106.
48. Piper, Otto, *God in History*, p. 38.
49. Davies, D. R., *On to Orthodoxy*, pp. 136-137.

In a representative spokesman, even philosophy, which has so often arrayed her Platonic doctrines against our Christian hopes, has turned her face toward *The Christian Hope of Immortality* and bases her hopes upon the maintenance of the central doctrine of Christianity. Thus, Professor A. E. Taylor reasons, you are not to withhold from Christ any jot of the worship due to the supreme Creator; equally you are not to exempt Him from anything incidental to full human normality—hunger, thirst, weariness, pain, temptation. He is to be thought of neither as a deity of second rank, or as a "superman." For "obviously if the life of Christ is to be evidence that our highest human values are also eternal and absolute values, it is precisely this union in one historical person of Deity and complete humanity which must be maintained. To whittle away either the divinity or the humanity—to be either 'Liberal Protestant' or Docetist— is to surrender the very 'ground of all our hopes'." (p. 73).

For the same thinker "eternal life is always represented in the New Testament as a *gift* from God" and "a gift which Christ is empowered to confer on His followers, and only on them." "The gift is not represented in the New Testament as bestowed upon men by the fact of their creation. Men are not thought of as already sons of God and heirs of eternal life in virtue of their birth into the world as men; that is a modern 'humanitarian' remodelling of the thought; according to the New Testament, men acquire sonship to God and the inheritance of eternal life by being 'adopted' into the Christian fellowship; they are adopted, not natural sons of the Father in Heaven." "Those who are still outside the Christian fellowship are said, on the contrary, to be without hope in the world, and are spoken of not as sons of God, but as 'Children of wrath'." (p. 59).[50]

Spes Mea Crux Christi. It is Christ and Christ alone who delivers us from this wrath to come. "Our only hope is in the Cross." [51] The Christian hope is no utopian illusion. It sees the

50. Cf. Smith, S. M., in *Memorial of Westminster Assembly*, 1897, pp. 236-241.
51. Thornwell, I.629.

tragedy of life under the curse of God, but believing that Christ
was made a curse for us it lays hold of a hope and an assurance
that is beyond tragedy. "The only hope of all the pious who
groan under the burden of a corruptible flesh and amidst the
infirmities of this life is that we have a Mediator, Jesus Christ;
and He is the propitiation for our sins."[52] Therefore, "preach
Christ and Him crucified, as the world's last and only hope."[53]

In the third of Romans Paul wrestles with the passing over
of sins done aforetime; in the twelfth of Revelation, Satan
appears as the accuser of his brethren; and in the third of Zechariah, Joshua first appears clothed with filthy garments. How can
God be just and the justifier of the ungodly? Satan never ceased
to accuse God of unrighteousness in making Himself the God
of sinners until God set forth Christ, in His own blood, as the
propitiation for sin, as the vindication of His justice (Rev.
xii.10-11; Rom. iii.25; viii.33-34). "In Him the verdict on us
has been not only given, but put into effect."[54]

Calvin, as well as Luther, recognized that the preaching of
the Cross was not agreeable to human reason. But, according
to His Divine Wisdom, God showed Himself just in justifying
the believer, by making Him who knew no sin to be sin for
us that we might be made the righteousness of God in Him.[55]
Justice was satisfied when Love endured the punishment we
deserved. Since Christ is the end of the law for justifying
righteousness, no one can lay anything to the charge of God's
elect. It is God who justifieth. Clothed in the white and spotless
robes of Christ, Jehovah-our-Righteousness, we may our fierce
Accuser meet and tell him Christ hath died. By the blood of
the Lamb and the word of their testimony, Christian confessors have overcome the Devil. Michael has answered Satan's
accusations against his brethren, and God has manifested His
righeousness and shown Himself to be at once a just God and a

---

52. Augustine.
53. Baker, Daniel, cited Wells, J. M. *Southern Presbyterian Worthies*, p. 99.
54. Barth, K., *The Knowledge of God and the Service of God*, p. 242.
55. I Cor. i.23-25; II Cor. v.21, cf. Luther, *Weimar Ausgabe, XXV*, p. 329. Sermon
on Is. liii, and Calvin, *Institutes*, II.vi.1.

Saviour. The power of sin has been broken, the sting has been drawn from death, and victory has been snatched from the grave of His people. "Through the death of Christ they are filled with the future of God." [56] The expiation, accomplished by the Incarnate Lord, is the pledge that He will appear a second time, apart from sin, unto salvation (Hebrews ix.28). Since Jesus is the Lamb of God that taketh away the sin of the world, He is the Saviour of the world. He is the propitiation for the sins of the world; therefore, He is the Redeemer, the Deliverer, the Consummator of the world. And, according to His promise, we look for a new heaven and a new earth in which dwelleth righteousness. If, when we were enemies, we were reconciled unto God by the death of His Son; much more, being justified by His blood, we shall be saved from the coming wrath of God by His life (Rom. v.9-10).

> "The Saviour's blood and righteousness
> My beauty is and glorious dress;
> Thus well arrayed, I need not fear
> When in His presence I appear."

The Power of His Resurrection. Christ *was delivered up for our trespasses and was raised for our justification,* so that God in His great mercy *begat us again unto a living hope by the resurrection of Jesus Christ from the dead.* His Resurrection declares His justification as the Head of the elect. His entrance into glory after His sufferings is our assurance of an inheritance, incorruptible, undefiled, unfading, reserved in heaven for us who are kept by the power of God through faith unto that salvation which is ready to be revealed in the eschatological era. "If His righteousness means resurrection from the dead and eternal life and if His righteousness is our righteousness, then what we have to await and what is revealed to us as our hope can only be resurrection and eternal life. Such is the hope in which we live."[57]

Christ's resurrection is the first fruits of the harvest of life.

56. Barth, K., *The Epistle to the Romans,* translated by Hoskyns, p. 164.
57. Barth, K., *The Knowledge of God and the Service of God,* p. 242.

The first blessed notes, declaring that the spring time of a new
heaven and a new earth shall come, have already reached our
anxious hearts. Stand beside the bed of a loved one as life
ebbs away and your confidnce in the logic of Plato's *Phaedus*
or Kant's practical reason, your testimonies of a hope of a hereafter from the burial customs of all races, your poetic intimations of immortality drawn from natural analogies will vanish
'neath the staggering realism of the chariot of death. Like a
torrent of the merciless lava of Vesuvius, death sweeps all
before it. The dizzy dance of death has apparently gathered
everything into its sweep for these milleniums. As you look into
its awful face it seems to have gripped even the innermost essence
of that dear one. But the reign of terror is broken; for *now is
Christ risen from the dead.* Here the avalanche of death has
been stayed; the reign of life has begun. And He must reign
until He hath placed even that last enemy—Death—under His
feet. As a boulder once started down the mountain cannot be
stopped, so shall the march of life, that began in the Resurrection of Christ and that continues in His ever-victorious Name,
never be stopped. If death were final, then all the pains by
which life enters this world, or is prolonged here, were in vain.
But Christ has the last word and that word is not death but
Life. As in Adam all die, even so in Christ shall all be made alive
(I Cor. xv.22). His resurrection is the sign and assurance of
our resurrection, of a glorious, mighty, incorruptible Spiritual
body. His risen Presence is the channel through which moves this
regenerating power for our souls, our bodies, our world and
our society. His resurrection from the dead points to a new
consummation.

The Lord of History. "He who has risen again is Lord of
history, Lord of all times and dimensions of historical reality
in the past, the present and the future."[58] Christ has ascended
the throne of the universe. He sits at the right hand of Jehovah

58. Wendland, W. D., *op. cit.* p. 147.
59. *Calvin's Catechism,* 80.

until His enemies are made the footstool of His feet. "He hath received into His hands the governance of heaven and earth, whereby He is King and Ruler over all (Matt. xxviii.18)."[59] In overflowing grace He sits as priest upon His throne, ever living to make intercession for His people. The foundation of the Church is this session of Christ at God's right hand, in the glory of the Father's throne interceding as the Lamb that hath been slain. God hath made Him reign at His own right hand in the heavenlies as Head over all things for the Church which is His body (Eph. i.20-23). God hath given all authority in heaven and earth into His hands. We go into life believing that the time which lies before us, even as that which lies behind us, is in the nail-pierced hands of our Redeemer. He is leading things to their destined end. "History points to Christ and is derived from Him; the ages lead to Him as their goal or take their origin from him."[60] Natural theology is powerless to confront man with the God which it describes;[61] but through the Church which He has instituted, by the Word He has spoken, and the Spirit He imparts, Christ is confronting men, institutions and systems with His claims and declaring Himself the true Lord of History.[62]

The Blessed Hope. Christ directs our eyes ever toward His Second Appearing as "the very pole star of the Church,"[63] the focus of hope for the Kingdom of Glory, the manifestation of His victory, the resurrection of the dead and the new heavens and the new earth. That He did come in grace is the assurance that He shall come in glory. In the blessed hope of His glorious Appearing are included or involved the several events of the eschatological drama. Christ will return with the plan of the ages in His own hand. The wonderful Counsellor, the mighty God will need no human eschatologist to direct Him, no human chart to instruct Him (Isa. ix.6; xl.14); but as He doeth all

60. Wendland, *op. cit.* p. 150.
61. William Temple, Archbishop of York in the Gifford Lectures.
62. Piper, O., *op. cit.*, pp. 134, 141.
63. Brown, D., *op. cit.* p. 22.

things well all creation shall wonder at *the depth of the riches both of the wisdom and the knowledge of God. How unsearchable are His judgments and His ways past tracing out! For who hath known the mind of the Lord? or who hath been His counsellor?*

God in Christ hath made full provision for sinners. Let us take care that He is robbed of none of the glory of His gracious work for us and that we are deprived of none of the comfort and hope that is in Him. As we abide in Him now, we shall have confidence and not be ashamed before Him at His coming in glory (I John ii.28). By the love that hath been bestowed on us in Him, now are we the sons of God; and when He shall appear, we shall be like Him, for we shall see Him as He is. Now by faith in Him we have fellowship in life everlasting; then, as we gaze upon Him who is the life indeed, we shall be like Him. And everyone that hath this hope in Him purifieth himself even as He is pure (I John iii.2-3).

> "When He shall come with trumpet sound,
> O, may I then in Him be found,
> Clothed in His righteousness alone,
> Faultless to stand before the Throne."

CHAPTER II

THE FAITHFUL WITNESS
Rev. i.5

● *"Fulfilled is now what David told*
In true prophetic song of old;
How God the heathen's King should be,
For God is reigning from the Tree."

Jesus Christ is represented as the Faithful Witness prior to His Resurrection, thereafter as the Prince of the kings of the earth.

    I. The Reign to which He witnessed.

        Reign or Realm?

        The coming nigh of a Reign already known.

        The providential Reign and the redemptive Reign.

    II. The Messanic Hope which He fulfilled.

        The Redemptive Reign in Israel.

        The Messiah King.

        Jesus' Greater Confession.

    III. The Heavenly Kingdom which He embodied.

        The King as servant of the Lord and citizen of the Kingdom.

        The Kingdom of Christ is the Kingdom of God.

IV. THE KINGDOM GOSPEL WHICH HE PREACHED.
The Kingdom preached.
The preaching of the Kingdom a Gospel.
The Gospel of the Kingdom is Christ.

V. THE COMINGS OF THE KINGDOM WHICH HE ATTESTED
The Reign of Glory
The Reign of Grace

THE FAITHFUL WITNESS

In the interesting summary of the Christian faith given in Revelation i.4-8, Jesus Christ is described as the faithful witness, the first-born of the dead, and the Prince of the kings of earth. This chapter, which deals primarily with His testimony prior to the Resurrection, may then be entitled *The Faithful Witness;* while the following one, dealing largely with His work after the Resurrection, may be described as the Prince of the kings of the earth, or *The King upon His Invisible Throne.*

During His ministry our Lord insisted on the propriety of His own witness to Himself (Jn. viii.14). He was born a King to witness to the Kingdom of truth (Jn. xviii.37). When His interpreters looked back upon His earthly life they remembered that He had witnessed the good confession before Pontius Pilate (I Tim. vi.13), and so presented Him as still the Amen, the Witness, faithful and true, the beginning of the new creation of God (Rev. iii.14). Our Saviour refused the ways of attaining the Kingdom which Satan offered Him and accepted instead the role of the Servant of the Lord which the voice of the Father ascribed to Him at His baptism (Mk. i.11; Isa. xlii.1). As one who serveth, He both portrayed the life of the perfect citizen in the Sermon on the Mount and lived it in His ministry. Thus His life is the witness to and the prophecy of the New Jerusalem; and, as the basis on which God deals with sinners, justifying them and creating them anew for this Holy City, it is the beginning of the Gospel (Mk. i.1). Moreover, as the Yea and

Amen to the promises of God, He is the answer to the messianic hope of Israel (II Cor. i.20).

I. THE REIGN TO WHICH HE WITNESSED.

Ere discussing this testimony in detail, it is desirable to look at certain aspects of the Kingdom to which He bore witness. In particular, it is necessary to point out here that the Kingdom to which He witnessed is God's redemptive Reign.

In its most general sense *basileia* means the things of a king, either his kingship, power, dignity, dominion, reign, or his realm, sphere of authority, territory. Speaking of earthly authorities, the New Testament uses the term in both senses: as the kingly dignity, the royal crown (Lk. xix.12,15), the authority as king, the reign (Rev. xvii.12,18), and as the realm, nation, kingdom (Mt. xii.25; iv.8;xxiv.7). However recent studies show that in the oriental mind, basileia is less a state than a lordship. It designates less a geographical concept than the fact of the sovereignty of a king, less a realm than a reign. When the Bible speaks of the Kingdom of God the emphasis falls more on His reign than on His realm, on His Kingship more than on His Kingdom, on His power more than on His people. The Kingdom of God is the Reign of God, His kingly rule, His sovereign power, His Divine Lordship.[1] Its immediate reference is Divine glory, sovereign grace, heavenly Lordship. Its primary direction is vertical rather than horizontal. It comes not through the natural evolution of earthly relationships or human strivings, but as the mystery of the Kingdom is revealed by the Word (Lk. viii.10-11; ix.60) and effectuated by the Spirit in regeneration (Jn. iii.3; Mt. xix.28; Lk. xxii.30). It comes by the direct action of God from Heaven revealing His own Lordship.

The pious Jewish circles from which the Christian movement sprang were waiting for the Reign of God and the consolation of Israel (Lk. xxiii.51; ii.25,38). Accordingly, neither John nor

---

1. Bruce, F. F., *I.V.F. News Letter* No. 5; *Rawlinson, Mark,* p. 111; Deissman, *The Religion of Jesus and the Faith of Paul,* p. 108; Warschauer, *The Historical Life of Christ;* Schmidt, K. L., *Basilea* in Kittel's *Theologisches Worterbuch,* z. N.T., I.580; Kuhn, *ibid,* I.570, citing also Dalman.

Jesus speak of the Kingdom as a new or unknown term, but as one familiar to their hearers from the Jewish background. The proclamation is not, There is a Reign of God of such and such a kind, but rather, the Reign of God is near.

Moreover, while there is a providential Reign of God proclaimed in the Old Testament and carried over into the New (Gen. xviii.25; Ps. cii.19; cxxxiv.13-16; Isa. xiv.24; Eph. i.11), a Reign based on creation and so exercised through every aspect of Providence that God's holy hand is over even the wicked acts of wicked men (Ps. ii; Acts ii.23; iv.27-28), nevertheless the Reign which is nigh is the redemptive Reign. For "the direct, immediate control of the universe and of every event in it by God Himself with His unlimited power, love and mercy." [2] is not a Kingdom that can be given or taken away or entered, for all men are in it already. The Kingdom of grace came nigh when God came into the world to save and establish a redeemed people, and to be deprived of this Kingdom is the final judgment (Mt. xxv.34; xxi.43). [3]

"The whole of history is a fallen creation and at every moment it is falling afresh." [4] Since God is this world's King and Lord, He is not content that demonical and human power dispute His sway upon the earth, His footstool. Hence, His redemptive Reign comes to earth to meet and vanquish opposing forces and to establish His sovereignty so that the will of God shall be done on earth as it is done in heaven. Indeed, it is the Word of this redemptive Reign that lifts the veil and discloses the significance and issue of history in the covenant of grace in Christ which lies behind the dawn of history. [5] Before the foundation of the world this Kingdom is prepared for a people chosen in Christ, the slain Lamb of God (Mt. xxv.34; Eph. i.4; II Tim. i.9; Rev. xiii.8; I Peter i.19-20; Jn. vi.37; xvii.2). Since the redemptive purpose of God is the centre of this world's history, common grace governs in the interest of saving grace, the provi-

---

2. Grant, F. C., *The Gospel of the Kingdom*, pp. 126-127.
3. Wahlstrom, E. H., in *World Conference on Faith and Order*, 90:60.
4. Wendland, H. D., *op. cit.* pp. 146, 149, 158.
5. Barth, K., *Kirchliche Dogmatik*, II.2.p.6.

dential Reign serves the purpose of the redemptive Reign. A great host that no man can number shall come out of every nation and kindred and tribe and wash their robes and make them white in the blood of the Lamb. And in the new heaven and the new earth, the Holy City shall resound to the praise of the grace of Him that sitteth upon the Throne and of the Lamb.

II. THE MESSIANIC HOPE WHICH HE FULFILLED.

God called the Patriarchs into this redemptive Kingdom (Mt. viii.11) and chose Israel to be unto Him a Kingdom of priests and a holy nation (Ex. xix.6; Deut. xxxii.9). At Sinai Israel accepted God's covenant and God became in a special sense the King of Israel (Deut. xxxiii.5) with the Ark as His throne. Accordingly, one who separates himself from heathenism takes on "the yoke of the Kingdom" (cf. Mt. xi.29); and the Hebrew acknowledges God as King every time he repeats the *Shema*. Prayer for the speedy coming of the time when God's saving rule over Israel shall be a universal and a visible reality is so constant a part of the liturgy that R. Johanan says: A prayer in which there is no mention of (God's) Kingship is no prayer.[6]

The whole structure of the Old Testament prophetic thinking is strongly oriented in the eschatological expectation.[7] "The time will come when all mankind will bow to His rule, and do homage to Him alone, and obey His law."[8] For "the Lord shall be King over all the earth; in that day shall the Lord be one and His Name one" (Zech. xiv.9) and "the kingdom shall be Jehovah's" (Obad. 21). Yea, when the Lord of hosts reigneth in Mount Zion and maketh His glory manifest before his elders the moon shall be confounded and the sun ashamed (Isa. xxiv.23). Sellin has summed up the Old Israelitish eschatology of weal and woe thus, "Jahweh is to come and simply be manifest as Lord—that is the kernel of the whole eschatology."[9] The Kingdom of

---

6. Moore, G.F., *op. cit.*, II.372, 373.
7. Eichrodt, W., *Theol. des Alten Testament*, I.255, 256.
8. Moore, *op cit.*, II.372.
9. Sellin, *Prophetismus*, pp. 172, 274 cited Warfield, *Christology and Criticism*, p. 19.

Heaven proclaims the final consummation in which God shall be "all in all" (I Cor. xv.24-28) ; not "that the All will be dissolved in God and lost in Him, but that every thing will be filled and permeated with God's sovereignty, will and salvation."[10] With the thought of God's Kingship Micah mingles the figure of the Shepherd (v. 4), and Isaiah parallels the concepts of Creator, Redeemer and King (xliii.14f).[11] In the Riches of His grace, God promises to come and be the Saviour of His people (Isa. xxxv|4; xliii.11,3; Hos. xiii.4).

As the promises of the redemptive Reign become fuller, the figure of the Messiah King becomes clearer. The hearts of the pious yearn for the Kingdom His coming will bring. The prophets of Israel tune their ears for the jubilee trumpet of Gospel gladness when He will preach the gracious Reign of God.

Many of the rich messianic promises stem from God's covenant with David (II Sam. vii). It is not that David will build a house for the Lord, but that the Lord will build David a house. In prophecying that David's throne shall stand forever, the foundation is laid for the expectation of a King from the loins of David, whose Reign will last evermore.[12] Solomon sits upon the throne of Jehovah's Kingdom over Israel, yea in the LORD'S Kingdom the "Davidites" shall sit forever upon the throne of Jehovah (I Chr. xxviii.5; xvii.12-14; xxix.23; II Chr. ix.8).[11] David and his successors, insofar as they were theocratic kings, were representatives and types of the Messiah King. As the LORD'S anointed they derive their sovereignty from the heavenly King whose vicegerents they were. When evils come the psalmist pleads the covenant promise of Jehovah to his servant David (Ps. lxxxix), and the prophet predicts the rebuilding of the tabernacle of David in the day when the Gentiles are called by Jehovah's name (Amos. ix.11-12).

Micah expects a Bethlehemite who shall stand and feed his flock in the strength of the LORD and in the majesty of the

---

10. Moore, *op. cit.* II.371; Kuhn in *Theologisches Worterbuch*, I.573; Wendland, H. D., *op. cit.*, p. 166.
11. von Rad, in *Th. W-b.z.N.T.*, I.565, 569.
12. Ridderbos, J., *The Messiah-King*, *The Evangelical Quarterly*, 11.4.289, 292.

name of Jehovah His God (Mic. v.1ff). According to Ezekiel, the Lord Jehovah will shepherd His sheep by setting up his servant David to be their King and Shepherd (Eze. xxxiv.15, 23f; xxvii.24f; cf.xvii.22ff). Jeremiah sees Jehovah raising up unto David a righeous Branch who shall reign as King in righteousness and justice. "And this is his name whereby he shall be called: Jehovah our Righteousness" (xxiii.5-6).

In the Immanuel section of Isaiah (chs. vii-xi) the Branch out of the stock of Jesse is connected on the one hand with the promise of Immanuel and the Governor upon the Throne of David whose name is Wonderful, Counsellor, Mighty God, Everlasting Father, Prince of Peace and on the other with the aeon of the righteousness and the peace of Paradise.[13] "A Messiah who reigns 'without end' (Isa. ix.6), who is called the God-Hero and the Eternal One, who is the personal concentration of the Spirit (Isa. xi.2ff), and destroys the wicked with the breath of his mouth (Isa. xi.4), is not purely human but superhuman wholly apart from this—that the Kingdom over which he reigns is the miraculous kingdom of peace and righteousness, the splendour of which is the light of the benighted peoples" (Isa. ix.1ff; xi.2ff).[14] "Out of the despised house of David (xi.1) rises the great King, who in all respects forms a contrast with the despot upon the throne of Assur." In the course of their history, in the character of their domination and in the fruits of their reigns, "you see the great antithesis of the Kingdom of God and the Kingdom of the world; and the Kingdom of God is concentrated in the Messiah-King. You see also that the expectation which the prophecy will raise has nothing to do with the humanitarian hope that by human efforts a realm of goodwill and of peace may be established; it is the miraculous power of the Lord that does here everything; and it is the Spirit of the Lord that rests upon the Messiah and that makes righteousness the girdle of His loins and faithfulness the girdle of His reins." Immanuel, *"God with us,* and, God with us in a

13. von Rad, *op. cit.,* p. 565, citing R. Kittel, *Hell. Mysterienrel,.* 73ff.
14. Bruckner, Martin, cited Warfield, *Christology and Crrticism,* p. 33.

Man whom He will send, form the real contents of the prophecies of the Messiah-King."[15]

The Suffering Servant of Isaiah is conceived as an eschatological redeemer, since chapters liv-lvi, which prophesy the glorious new age that Yahweh will soon inaugurate, are directly joined to Is. lii.13-liii.12, and especially to the closing verse, which portrays the final victory of the Suffering Servant:

> Therefore will I give Him his portion with the great and
> he shall divide spoil with a numerous host.

Earlier in the fifty-third chapter it is written,

> He shall prolong His days and the pleasure of the Lord
> shall prosper in His hand.

And the fifty-sixth opens,

> Keep ye justice, and do righteousness; for my salvation
> *is near to come,* and my righteousness to be revealed.

Accordingly, the Preacher who graciously and humbly brought the consolation of God to His people, who bare the sin of many and made intercession for the transgressors (liii.12), shall be exalted, and lifted up and be very high (liii.13) as "the future king, the king in the glorious kingdom which ch. livff forthwith portray."[16]

The sharp apocalyptic division between the present and the future aeons, occuring in Daniel, brings with it a much clearer delineation of the kingdom of God. The God of heaven, who ruleth in the kingdom of men and giveth the kingdom to whom He will, shall take away the dominion from the beasts and give the Kingdom to the saints of the Most High (Dan. vii.28,27). Accordingly, the people of the saints of the Most High possess the kingdom for ever (vii.18, 27; ii.44). Hence the phraseology is not God's Kingdom, and Jehovah is not spoken of as King, but the prophecy treats of a succession of human kingdoms until

---

15. Ridderbos, *op. cit.,* 295, 218.
16. Otto, R., *op cit., pp.* 217, 218.

the kingdom of the saints breaks in.[18] And the statement that the everlasting kingdom is given to the Son of Man (vii.14) indicates that "his kingdom," spoken of in verse 27, is to be understood as the Son of Man's Kingdom.

"Daniel has seen the giant forms of empire appear and pass, the kingdoms of the beasts. Those kingdoms were founded in crude ambition and were cemented with blood. Wars and rumors of wars, pillage, rapine, famine, pestilence, marked their progress. They were military monarchies, of the earth earthy. But as Daniel meditated on the vision, another Kingdom came into view, represented not by a bestial form, but by a Son of Man standing in the splendour of the Ancient of Days and receiving from the Eternal Love, a Kingdom of righteousness and peace, a Kingdom human and divine."[19] Thus the Old Testament looks forward to the coming of a Person in whose Kingdom everything good will come into its own. And Daniel presents as the Head of the Kingdom of God one "whose home is the glory of the Divine presence, a Man standing close the 'light-girdled Throne of the Ancient of Days'" and "belonging to the realm of the heavenly and the eternal." [20]

This line of thought is taken up in the subsequent apocalyptical literature. In the Book of Enoch that Son of man is described as God's chosen (xl,viii.3) ; "who was hidden. For the Son of Man was previously hidden, and the Most High kept him before his power" (lxii.6). God promises, "The Elect One shall in those days sit on my Throne" (li.3). Again Enoch says, "The Lord of Spirits seated him on the throne of his glory" (lxii.1). More fully, he sets forth that the name of that Son of Man had been revealed unto the elect ones,

"And he sat on the throne of his glory
And the sum of judgment was given to that Son of Man . . .
For that Son of Man has appeared

---

18. von Rad, *op. cit.,* p. 569.
19. McIntyre, D. M., *Christ the Lord,* p. 47, cited by Ross, *infra.*
20. Ross, Prof. Alexanler, *The Title "Son of Man,"* T.Ev.Q.6.1.38-39.

And has seated himself on the throne of his glory" (lxix.26ff).
Chapter lxii.14-16 gives words which throw light upon several
New Testament eschatological references:

> "The Lord of Spirits will dwell above them, and they will
> eat with that Son of Man, and lie down and rise up unto
> all eternity." "They will be clothed with the garment of
> (imperishable) glory."

In the concluding section, the Lord of Spirits promises His
people, that they shall walk in the paths of uprightness and have
peace in their lives, since "I and my Son will be united with
them forever" (cv).

In the *Assumption of Moses,* the writer portrays the eschatological age thus,

> "And then His kingdom shall appear in all His creation;
> And then Satan shall have an end,
> And sorrow shall depart with him."

The fundamental thought in the Jewish expectation was that
God would intervene and save His people "in the latter days,"
that is, in the Messianic times. In the light of the New Testament we can see that this intervention is in stages, and can
even find intimations of the steps in Enoch and perhaps in
Isaiah.[21] But "to Daniel the Messianic Parousia is as yet an
undivided whole," with distinction between the first and second
comings of Christ not formulated.[22] Erich Winkel has shown
that the concept Son-of-Man together with the expression Kingdom of Heaven arose from Daniel (ii-vii), with which every
hearer of Jesus was familiar.[23] To these Jesus specifically
appealed in His answer to the High Priest, where, "the echo of
the passage in Daniel is unmistakable."[24] Before the Sanhedrin
Jesus confessed His Messianic rank in the form of the Son

---

21. So Otto, R., *op. cit.*
22. Vos, C., *The Self-Disclosure of Jesus,* p. 242.
23. Heim, K., *Jesus der Weltvollender,* p. 149 (citing Winkel) and p. 206.
24. Ross, Alexander, *T.Ev.Q.,* 6.1.37.

of Man which, as Daniel and Enoch show, was a familiar concept in that day.[25] In Enoch the Messiah is the Son of Man, God's Elect, the Son of the Lord of Spirits, who after being hidden comes in Power, to sit on the throne of His glory and execute judgment. The High Priest asked,

"Art thou the Messiah, the Son of the Blessed?"
Jesus answered,

"I am: and ye shall see the Son of Man sitting at the right hand of Power and coming with the clouds of heaven" (Mk. xiv.61-62).

If Peter's answer for the disciples is the Great Confession, then Jesus' answer to the High Priest is the Greater Confession. In this significant affirmation Jesus weaves together the great lines of messianic prophecy. He affirms that He is the Messiah, the Son of the Blessed God, the Lord who sits at the right hand of Jehovah (Psalm cx), the Son of Man who comes with the clouds of a Theophany, the Coming One. And the most primitive Christian testimony confirms this Greater Confession of Jesus representing Him as the Lord of Psalm cx in the triple Gospel tradition, in the oral gospel and in the epistles; representing Him as the Son of Man standing or coming in the clouds of glory in the oldest strata of gospel testimony, in Stephen's dying vision, "the oral gospel" (Acts vii.56), and in the interesting reply of James preserved by Hegesippus: "Why do you ask me concerning the Son of Man, He sits in heaven at the right hand of great power and will return on the clouds of heaven." From His Resurrection and Ascension He is ever the celestial Christ in Acts, Epistles and Revelation. The effect of the earliest preaching of Paul is to leave his converts awaiting God's Son from heaven, whom He raised from the dead, Jesus who delivereth us from the wrath to come (I Thess. i.9).

---

25. Otto, R., *op. cit.*, pp. 225-227.

"There is a real unity between the Old Testament image of the Messiah-King and the figure of Jesus Christ as He is shown to us in the New Testament, and as we see His work in His Church . . . All that was essential in the figure of the Messiah-King is evident in Him, as He has come as the anointed with the Holy Ghost who has brought a Kingdom not of this world but from God, a Kingdom of which the deepest essence is glory to God, and salvation to mankind." In His birth at Bethlehem, in His Divinity (the mighty God), in His atoning death, His Resurrection and Ascension and the outpouring of the Holy Ghost, the fulfillment of prophecy has only begun. "The Church is still waiting for the Second Coming of Christ, and not before then will be seen the eternal glory which psalmody and prophecy have attributed to the Messiah-King."[26]

And the witness of our Lord points both backward to Israel and forward to the Church. "Jesus Christ . . . is the promised Son of Abraham and of David, the Messiah of Israel. And He is at the same time the Head and Lord of the Church called and assembled from Jews and Gentiles. He is as both indissolubly one. And He is as the one irremoveably both. Even as the Lord of the Church is He to be sure the Messiah of Israel and even as the Messiah of Israel is He to be sure the Lord of the Church . . . Jesus Christ is the crucified Messiah of Israel. He is as such the authentic witness of the judgment which God, in that He chooses fellowship with man, takes upon Himself. He is as such the original bearer of the Divine promise. He is as such the suffering beginner of the merciful passing away of the first human form. He is, however, even as the crucified Messiah of Israel also the secret Lord of the Church, which God has founded through this His sacrifice of Himself: for life from His mercy, for faith in His promises, as the gracious coming (and abiding) form of His Church.

"And Jesus Christ is the risen Lord of the Church. He is as such the authentic witness of the mercy in which God, in that

26. Ridderbos, J., *op. cit.*, pp. 298-299.

He chooses man for fellowship with Himself, turns His own glory (in favor) to him. He is as such the prototype of the believer. He is as such the triumphing beginner of the gracious coming of the new form of man. He is, however, even as the risen Lord of the Church also the revealed Messiah of Israel, which God has confirmed through this His sacrifice of Himself: as the manifestation of His justice, but also as the hearer of His promise, as the form of His Church determined by a gracious past."[27]

III. The Heavenly Kingdom Which He Embodied.

Since Christ is the concrete revelation of the heavenly life of the Kingdom, the Christological is the surest approach to the essential character of the Kingdom. The Wisdom of Solomon interpreted Jacob's dream as a vision of the Kingdom of God and Jesus told Nathaniel that the disciples would see heaven opened and the angels of God ascending and descending upon the Son of Man (Jn. i.51). In the Lord's Prayer He expounded the Kingdom as doing the Father's will on earth as it is done in heaven. And He who unveiled the mysteries of the Kingdom of Heaven was constantly doing the will of the Father on earth as it is done in heaven.

The requirements of the Kingdom are to deny oneself, take up one's cross, sell all that one has, pluck out one's right eye or become an eunuch if need be, hate one's own family, yea one's own life. No sermon ever measured men's conduct by so lofty a standard, or ever searched the motives and aims, the secret thoughts and desires of men with the all-seeing Eye of God as did the Sermon on the Mount. And this sermon closes with the declaration that only those who do the will of the Father shall enter into the Kingdom. Who, then, may realize these requirements? Where, among all the sons of men, is there a real citizen

---

27. Barth, K., *Kirchliche Dogmatik*, II.2.218.

of the Kingdom? Who, in such a way, is obedient to God?
Who has loved Him with all his heart, mind, soul and strength?
"No one—outside of Jesus Christ, Himself."[29] "There is no
one in whom the absolute of God's Kingdom is embodied except
the Messiah Himself." [30]

When the Word became flesh, the Kingdom of God broke
into the world in the Person of Jesus Christ. A bit of heaven
came from out the skies and entered into history in the man
Jesus of Nazareth. Through the very presence of Christ the
Kingdom had come, but in a most paradoxical way. It came
first not in the reign, but in the service of the King. He came
as the citizen before He came as the King. He first manifested
the true nature of the Kingdom in the Christlike living, the
Christlike obedience, the Christlike ministering which characterize it, before He ascended the throne of His Kingship. Our
Lord fulfilled the life of the obedient servant, the lot of the
willing subject of the Kingdom, before He mounted the throne
of the King. By doing so He drew, even in the midst of our
crooked lines, the true lineaments of the life of heaven and
offered the perfect obedience of the one citizen as the basis on
which God justly brings many sinners into the heavenly citizenship.

Consequently as the redeemed face their King, they know
that the throne is His not only by nature, but also by mediatorial
right. "It has been bought with a price—bought with the hunger
in the desert when He would not make the stones into bread;
bought with the tears He shed over the sins of men; bought
with the sweat of Gethsemane which was like great drops of
blood; bought with the bitter cross where they broke His body
in death; bought with the deathless love which through all the
years has resolutely refused to let the lost world go. The Captain of the hosts of humanity has Himself been in the ranks. He

---

29. Schmidt, K. L., *Th.W-b.z.N.T.*, I.590.
30. Dodd, C. H., *op. cit.* 137.

has endured the dicipline." He rides at the head of the hosts today, because He once walked on foot. Because His meat was to do the will of Him that sent Him, because He was obedient even unto the death of Calvary, therefore God has highly exalted Him. Unto Him who served unto the uttermost, every knee shall bow in homage and every tongue confess that He is sovereign Lord to the glory of God the Father.

The Kingdom is not a neutral magnitude, a brute fact, an impersonal thing. It is the Kingdom of God that came in the doing of God's will for the salvation of men, in a way of humiliation that only God's own grace could have wrought. It is found where hearts acclaim Him as King who for us men and for our salvation became an obedient servant of God, a willing subject of the Kingdom. For the Son of Man came not to be ministered unto but to minister, and to give His life a ransom instead of many. The Kingdom of Heaven "appears in the form of One who is proclaimed in the Gospel, in the form of Jesus. In Him, only in Him can it be observed, can it be met. The matter does *not* so stand, that the Kingdom as such, severed from Jesus who brings it, could somewhere dawn. For in that case, Jesus were only the first among men, who had seen it and so proclaimed it. The true state of the case is: Jesus has not only revealed the Kingdom of God, He has created it. He is its Prophet, but as this, its Prophet, He is at the same time and in the same person, its King. The kingdom of God is nowhere, strictly nowhere, except there where He, Jesus enters 'in the midst among us' (Lk. xvii.21). To come to the Kingdom means, therefore, exclusively and alone, to come to Jesus, to become an obedient hearer of His Gospel." [31]

This is evidenced by the way in which the New Testament represents the Kingdom of Jesus Christ as at the same time the Kingdom of God. The unbeliever has no inheritance in the Kingdom of Christ and of God (Eph. v.5). The Kingdoms of this world are to become the Kingdom of our Lord and of His

31. Thurneysen, E., *Die Bergpredigt*, p. 18.

Anointed (Rev. xi.15). "God and Christ so stand together that so soon as Christ is first mentioned, that soon is God named. Hence it should be held fast, that the Kingdom of Christ cannot be spoken of without the Kingdom of God."[32] Jesus testifies, "My Father has bequeathed me the Kingdom" (Lk. xxii.29). It is God who has translated us into the Kingdom of the Son of His love (Col. i.13). At the end of the days, Christ, who has in this way received the Kingdom from the Father, gives it back to Him (I Cor. xv.24). Since He can only give God what is already His own, the New Testament references to the Kingdom of Christ (Mt. xiii.41; xvi.28; Lk. i.33; xii.31; xxiii.42; Jn. xviii.36; II Tim. iv.1, 18; II Pet. i.11) implicitly speak of the same Kingdom of God which is explicitly ascribed to God in other places.[33]

The Gospels use the Kingdom of God reciprocally with Jesus Himself, His Name and His Message. In the triumphal entrance into Jerusalem, Mark (xi.10) records the praise to the coming Kingdom of David, while Matthew (xxi.9) and Luke (xix.38) give the praise to the Person of the Messiah. For My sake and for the sake of the Gospel (Mk. x.29) or for the sake of My name (Mt. xix.29) becomes in Luke (xxvii.29) for the sake of the Kingdom of God. The first example of this reciprocity is the Son of Man who represents the people of the saints of God (Daniel vii).[33] While Mark (ix.1) and Luke (ix.27) speak of the coming of God's Kingdom in power, the parallel passage has the coming of the Son of Man in His Kingdom (Mt. xvi.28). Accordingly Matthew as well as John "knew the reign of God in indissoluable relation with the person of Jesus, who revealed to them the mystery of God's abundant grace . . . Jesus is the Prince of Glory at whose feet the evangelists were seated."[34]

Passing through the land as the Messiah, Jesus gathered the subjects of the Kingdom about Himself.[35] He specifically

32. Schmidt, K. L., *Th.W-b.*I:582.
33. Schmidt, K. L., *Th.W-b.*, I.pp. 581, 590, 591.
34. Kolfhaus, W., *The Evangelical Quarterly*, 10:1.60.
35. Lietzmann, H., *The Beginnings of the Christian Church*, p. 62.

declared that the Father had given the Kingdom in covenant to Him even as He likewise bequeathed it in covenant to His disciples (Lk. xxii.29-30). He took the position of the Shepherd of the flock to whom the Father will give the Kingdom (Lk. xii.32; Mk. vi.34; xiv.27; Enoch 90; Psalms of Solomon xvii.45; Exe. xxxiv; Mic. v.4; Isa. xl.11).[36] He assumes the privilege of the Beloved Son who is the heir of the vineyard, the theocratic Kingdom (Mt. xxi.33-40; Mk. xii.1-12; Lk. xx.9-19), and the title of the Son of Man who gathers "the people of the saints of the Most High" and comes to sit as King upon the Throne of Glory in the final judgment (Mk. xiv.62; Matt. xxv.31ff; vii.21). "According to Enoch's apocalyptic, the Son of Man was the King of Heaven Himself and the one intended for that throne was destined to judge the enemies and adversaries of God."[37] So the Son of Man will send forth His angels and gather out of *His Kingdom* all things that offend and do evil (Mt. xiii.41). There are some standing here who shall not taste of death until they see the Son of Man coming in *His Kingdom* (Mt. xvi.28). "Of King Jesus Christ it is said: *His Kingdom* shall not end (Lk. i.33). This King promises His disciples: Ye shall eat and drink in *My Kingdom* (Lk. xxii.30). The one who is crucified with Him prays the suffering and dying Messiah-King: Remember me, when Thou comest into (or in) *Thy Kingdom* (Lk. xxiii.42). Of the character of this His Kingdom, Jesus says: My Kingdom is not of this world (Jno. xviii.36)."[38]

Thus there is a mass of Gospel testimony against the thesis that there is no place in Jesus' Gospel of the Kingdom for any messianic kingdom or for His own Kingship therein. "Critical study of the Gospels rather supports the view that He is one who claims for Himself the Kingdom (or Rule) of God which He proclaims, and speaks and acts as if in Himself that Kingdom has already come and only through Him can other men enter it."[39] "Christ was the Kingdom personalized." "He made Him-

36. Flew, R. N., *op. cit.*, pp. 29, 79, 53-54.
37. Otto, R., *op. cit.* p. 255.
38. Schmidt, K. L., *Th.W-b.*I.581.
39. Duncan, G. S., in *The Christian Faith*, p. 117.

self synonymous with the Kingdom."[40] "He Himself was there, embodying the Kingdom in His Person; and the circle gathered around Him partook of the blessings of the Kingdom."[41]

IV. THE KINGDOM GOSPEL WHICH HE PREACHED.

As the Shepherd implies the Flock, as the Servant justifies many, as the Son of Man stands for the people of the saints of the Most High, so the King embodies the Kingdom. Accordingly, when Jesus has been anointed with the Holy Spirit and acclaimed from heaven as the Messiah, the proclamation of the coming nigh of the Kingdom becomes the significant, all-comprehensive content of His preaching.[42]

The Kingdom Preached. Both John and Jesus *preached* the Kingdom. John came *preaching,* the Kingdom of Heaven is at hand (Mt. iii.1); Mk. i.4; Lk. iii.3), *crying* in the wilderness, make ready the way of the Lord (Mt. iii.3; Mk. i.3; Lk. iii.4; Jn. i.23). The Word of God came unto John so that with many exhortations he *evangelized* the people (Lk. iii.2,18). He was continually *speaking* and *saying* the things concerning Jesus (Jn. i.29,30; iii.27).

Jesus comes *preaching* the *Gospel of God* which means that the Kingdom of God is near (Mk. i.14-15). This initial statement, in many manuscripts and in parallel passages in other Gospels, is *the Gospel of the Kingdom of God* (Mt. iv.23; ix.35; xxiv.14). Jesus also *evangelizes* or preaches the good tidings of the Kingdom of God (Lk. iv.43; viii.1; vi.16) as Phillip does later (Acts viii.12). Concerning the Kingdom, our Lord and His disciples preach (Mt. iv.23; ix.35; Lk. ix.2; Acts xx.25; xxviii. 31), *bear witness* (Acts xxviii.23) *publicly proclaim* (Lk. ix.60), *persuade* (Acts xix.8), *speak* (Lk. ix.11), or *say* (Acts i.3). The Gospel of the Kingdom becomes the *mystery* of the Kingdom revealed to the disciples (Mt. xiii.11; Mk. iv.11; Lk. viii. 10). In parallel passages the Word of the Kingdom (Mt. xiii.19) is simply the Word used absolutely, or explicitly the Word of

40. Jones, E. S., *The Christian Century*, 5/3/39, p. 571; *Is the Kingdom of Heaven Realism?* pp. 58, 70-72.
41. Stalker, J., *The Kingdom of God, I.S.B.E. p.* 1807.
42. Thurneysen, E., *Die Bergpredigt,* p. 14; Dodd, C. H., *op. cit.,* p. 128.

God (Mk. iv.14-15) ; Lk. viii.11-12). The Gospel of the Kingdom is to be preached in the whole world for a testimony to all
nations (Mt. xxiv.14).

Recent studies in the New Testament reverse certain interpretations the effect of which was to minimize the value of
preaching in comparison with doing. Thurneysen's exposition
of the Sermon on the Mount shows that the contrast in the
closing section (Mt. vii.21-23) is not between the theory and the
practice of Christianity, not between lip worship and life worship.
For out of the abundance of the heart the mouth speaketh, and
the tree is known by its fruit (Lk. vi.44,51). Those who are
rejected have cast out demons and *done* many mighty *works*
in the Name of Jesus. The Lord Jesus rejects them because He
never knew them either in their profession or in their conduct.
They are servants not of God, but of men. They sought to please
men, not to please the Lord. Thus in the final judgment the
Lord decides against them and in favor of His sheep who heard
His voice and did His Word.[43] Similarly, K. L. Schmidt has
shown that the contrast in First Corinthians four, twenty is
not between word and deed, but between the mere word of *man*
and the power of *God*. "We would fully apprehend the meaning
of this passage with the paraphrase: the Kingdom of God stands
not in man's power, but in God's Word."[44]

The Preaching of the Kingdom, A Gospel. Not only is the
Gospel of the Kingdom a preaching, but also the preaching of
the Kingdom is a Gospel, a Word of Grace. The law and the
prophets were until John; from that time the *gospel* of the
Kingdom of God is preached (Lk. xvi.16). In proclaiming the
nearness of the Kingdom, John's emphasis fell upon the solemnity
of Jehovah's judgment. John evangelized only as he pointed
to the Lamb of God (Lk. iii.18; Jn. i.29, 35). On the other hand
Jesus began with the *Gospel* for the poor, the proclamation of
release for the captive, the recovery of sight for the blind, lib-

---

43. Thurneysen, E., *Die Bergpredigt*, pp. 32-42.
41. Stalker, J., *The Kingdom of God, I.S.B.E.* p. 1807.

eration for the captive, and the Lord's acceptance of sinners
(Lk. iv.18-22). Subsequently, Jesus' answer to John's doubts
reaches its climax in the words, The poor are evangelized (Mt.
xi.6; Lk. vii.22; Isa. lxi.1). Thus men wondered at the words
of grace that proceeded from Jesus' mouth (Lk. iv.22) and called
His preaching of the Kingdom a *Gospel,* the Gospel of God
(Mk. i.14-15). On His lips, the Kingdom is at hand, was not
primarily a threat concerning the day of God's vengeance, but a
promise of the acceptable year of the Lord.

Calvin catches the true note when he writes, "On account of
the inestimable plentitude of grace which has been displayed to
us in Christ, the celestial Kingdom of God is justly said to have
been erected in the earth at His Advent" (Institutes II.ix.4).
Bruce adds, "Many things in the Gospels indicate that grace was
the keynote of Christ's doctrine of the Kingdom," that it was
primarily a gift rather than a demand, an invitation not to
righteous but to sinners.[45]

Jesus came not to call the righteous, but sinners to repentance,
and the publicans and the harlots went into the Kingdom of
God before the self-righteous Pharisees (Mt. xxi.31). In the
parables of the ninety and nine, of the Pharisee and the Publican, and of the householder hiring laborers at different hours,
"Jesus' preaching of the Kingdom is directed toward sinners."[46]

Since the Kingdom is righteousness (Mt. vi.33; v.20; Rom.
xiv.17), its citizens are the penitents who hunger and thirst after
righteousness and endure persecution for righteousness' sake
(Mt. v.6, 11). Since the Kingdom is the saving power of the
Spirit (Mt. xii.28; Jn. iii.5-6), the members of the Kingdom are
those whose consciousness of their own spiritual poverty (Mt.
v.3) casts them upon God's mercy for forgiveness, acceptance
and deliverance (Lk. xviii.141iv.18-19). Its great word is, Son,
be of good cheer. Thy sins are forgiven thee (Mt. ix.2; Lk. v.
20). Its call is: Repent and believe the Gospel (Mk. i.15).

45. *Bruce, A. B.,* Apologetics, p. 374.
46. Lietzmann, H., *op. cit.* p. 66.

Since the Kingdom is God's Reign it is "a sheer gift of God"[47] not an achievement of men; it is His grace, not our merit. It is the Father's good pleasure to *give* you the Kingdom (Lk. xii.32). After pronouncing Peter blessed because of the revelation which the Father had given him, Jesus continued, I will *give* thee the keys of the Kingdom of Heaven (Mt. xvi.19). The Kingdom of God shall be taken from the obdurate Jews and *given* to a nation bringing forth the fruits thereof (Mt. xxi.43; Mal. i.10-11). To those who have been with Him in His tribulations, Christ says, I *give* to you *in covenant* the Kingdom as my Father gave it in covenant to me (Lk. xxii.29). Those on the right hand *inherit* the Kingdom prepared for them before the foundation of the world (Mt. xxv.34 cf. I Cor. vi.9-10; xv.50). God *calls* us into His Kingdom and Glory (I Th. ii.12) or *delivers* us from the power of darkness and *transplants* us into the Kingdom of the Son of His love (Col. i.13). For except a man be born from above He cannot see the Kingdom of God, except he be born of the Spirit he cannot enter it (Jno. iii.3-7).

The Gospel of the Kingdom is "not a programme for human action, but the proclamation of an act of God." ‡ According to the parables, the Word of the Kingdom comes with the preaching of the Word of God, and is spread by sowing the good seed which is the Word (Mt. xiii.19; Mk. iv.14; Lk. viii.11). In the parable of the man casting seed upon the earth, the earth bears fruit *of itself,* automatically (Mk. iv.26-28).[48] "For without any effort of his, the earth bears him fruit."[49] The seed sprouts and grows of itself. "It happens before our eyes not otherwise than as a bare miracle when without our aid, yea without our understanding, from the smallest grain of wheat it has become the fruit bearing head." [50] "In this group of parables of the Kingdom the chief lesson is the present, inward working of God's Spirit, unseen by dull or hostile eyes, a Kingdom of God which

47. Bryden, W. W., *The Christian's Knowledge of God,* p. 80.
48. Otto, R., *op. cit.,* pp 113, 117.
‡ Dodd, C. H., *op. cit.* p. 123.
49. Dibelius, *The Message of Jesus Christ,* p. 52.
50. Schmidt, K. L., *Th.W-b.*I:588, 586, 584; Lietzmann, H., *op. cit.* p. 62.

is already in the midst, silent, omnipotent, overtaking unawares those whose spiritual eyes are closed . . . (as the prophet says:) 'Not by might nor by power, but by my Spirit, saith the Lord of Hosts'."[51] The Kingdom is not within human power, but grows of itself; it is unexpectedly found, like a treasure in a field; it is not caused, produced or forced by man, but received naively, grasped intuitively as a child receives a gift. For, He who does not receive the Kingdom of God like a child shall not enter therein (Mk. x.15). The perfect example of the recipient of the Kingdom is the babe who rests in the crook of the Saviour's arms with the King's hand of blessing on his head (Mk. x.16). The Kingdom is of such as entrust themselves wholly to their King to save them unto His heavenly Kingdom (II Tim. iv.18), as Luther says, without any powers, merits or works of their own.

Since the Kingdom is "God's seed, not man's deed,"[52] our responsibility as fellow-workers of the Apostle unto the Kingdom (Col. iv.11) is to receive and preach the Word (I Peter i.23-25; Jas. i.21; II Tim. iv.2). This work calls for the most strenuous and whole-hearted endeavor, for the Kingdom of Heaven is like unto a pearl of great price or treasure hid in a field for which one is willing to sacrifice all else (Mt. xiii.44-45). God alone is Lord over every life and over all life (Mt. vi.24; vii.21-27; Lk. ix.23) and His Word speaks to social as well as individual life. However, when one is asked to accept a man-made program as the Kingdom of God, he may well remember the blessing upon those who hear the Word of God and keep it (Lk. xi.28) and the vanity of worshipping God by teaching as His doctrines the commandments of men (Mt. xv.9). And when the concrete solutions of religious socialism, whether national or international, are offered as God's Kingdom, he may further remember the characterization drawn of His Kingdom in Matthew vi.25-34 with the commentary thereon in Romans culminat-

---

51. Bacon, B. W., *The Story of Jesus Christ and the Beginnings of the Christian Church*, 1929, p. 212.
52. Otto, R., *op. cit.*, pp. 113, 117.

ing in chapter fourteen, verse seventeen. The children of the Kingdom trust their Father for food, drink and clothing (Mt. vi.30-34), while they seek and publish abroad the Kingdom of God (Lk. ix.60,62). A man's life consists not in the abundance of the things he possesses. Since the Kingdom is not of this world (Jn. xvii.36), the King as its First Citizen refused to divide an inheritance between brothers. The Kingdom of God is not meat and drink, but the righteousness of God, peace with God through our Lord Jesus Christ (cf. Rom. vi.1), and joy in the Holy Ghost.

Since the Kingdom is Divine activism, God manifested the signs thereof in the deeds as well as in the words of the Son of Man. The mighty works of mercy as well as the good news to the poor are the credentials of the Messiah both to Nazareth and to John (Lk. iv.16-30; vii.22; Mt. xi.5f), and the commission to preach the Kingdom of God is accompanied with the power to heal the sick and the authority to cast out demons (Lk. ix.1,2, 11). "The mighty works of Christ are very closely related with His message of the Kingdom."[53] In the casting out of demons Jesus sees the herald of the dawn. The miracles of the Gospels are promises of the eschatological order breaking into this fallen order, vouchers for the blessedness, health, life and wholeness of the New Day. Jesus came with "an eschatological awareness of power," the center of a "field of force" before which sickness, Satan and death wilted. His *Blitzkrieg* of mercy banished disease and death from Galilee during the days of His ministry, and brought to Judaea the first rays of that Kingdom before whose *dynamis* the *Basileia* of Satan must yield. "The Kingdom of God is the whole new activity of God which was proceeding in the life and work of Jesus."[54]

The Gospel of the Kingdom is Christ. In Christ's saving person, gracious words and works, the Father gives unto the disciples the Kingdom with its blessings of salvation, sonship and

53. Otto, R., *op. cit.* pp. 55, 290-298.
54. Flew, R. N., *op. cit.*, pp. 32, 34.

life. "The Kingdom of Heaven is Christ Jesus Himself, exhorting all men to repentance and drawing them to Himself by His grace."[55] In distinction from the lawyers who were hindering men from entering (Lk. xi.52), and from the scribes and Pharisees who were closing the Kingdom of Heaven against men (Mt. xiii.13), Jesus opened wide the door of the Kingdom. Even His solemn woes concerning the day of judgment (Mt. xi.20-24) and His majestic confession of the sovereignty of the Lord (vs. 25-26) lead to His matchless invitation of love and sympathy:

> "Come unto me, all ye that are weary and heavy laden,
> And I will refresh you.
> Take my yoke upon you and learn of me,
> For I am meek and lowly in heart,
> And ye shall find rest unto your souls.
> For my yoke is easy and my burden is light" (Mt. xi.28-30).

In place of John's sacrament of water Jesus baptized with the spiritual power of the eschatological order (Mk. i.8).[56] Referring to the Spirit which those who believed on Him were to receive after His glorification, Jesus cried,

> "If any man thirst, let him come unto me and drink.
> He that believeth on me, as the Scripture hath said,
> From within him shall flow rivers of living water."
> (Jn. vii.37-39).

In revealing to Simon the mystery of the Son of Man before His Enthronement in Power, so that he confessed the Christ, the Son of the living God, the Father made Peter a proper custodian of the keys of the Kingdom of Heaven (Mt. xvi.13-20). Since the Kingdom is God's gracious revelation of Himself in Christ, the keys are given to those who believe and confess that saving revelation. As they continue to make known God's love and forgiving grace in Christ, the Father reveals the Son "unto

---

55. Scolion attributed to Origen, Hebert, A. G., *The Throne of David*, p. 138.
56. Otto, R., *op. cit.*, pp. 68-71.

babes" (Mt. xi.25) and thus delivers them from Satan and brings them into the Kingdom of the Son of His love (Col. i.13).

The Kingdom of Heaven enters wherever the heart is born again of the Holy Spirit, united to Christ as the branch to the vine, whenever a sinner turns in faith and repentance to the Sun of Righteousness. Thus the Gospel of the Kingdom of God concerns God's saving activities for men. Its exposition stands or falls with the general exposition of soteriology in the preaching of Jesus Christ and of His Apostles. The Kingdom of God embraces the whole of the preaching of Christ and the Apostles. If the whole New Testament proclamation is the Gospel, then this whole is the Gospel of the Kingdom of God.[57]

It has already been pointed out that the Gospels use the Kingdom of God reciprocally with Jesus Christ Himself, His Name and His message, and Acts continues this parallelism (viii.12; xxviii.23,31). This parallelism between the Gospel of God's Kingdom and the preaching of the Name or of the things concerning Jesus Christ shows that the early Christian missionaries did not carry abroad disconnected fragments, but a gospel, or gospel-embryo of the Kingdom of God and a saving eschatological Redeemer in the Name of whom one obtained the Kingdom and its salvation. "For them, attaining this Kingdom was conjoined with a believing relation to the person of the Redeemer." The joyous message of peace through Jesus Christ (Acts x.36) was not an isolated saying or a single word, "rather it was the essence of this person as one who brought salvation," "a simple story of what this man had been, intended, effected and done soteriologically." "Such an embryonic Gospel is offered in Acts x.37-43." [58] In Revelation this parallelism is amplified: "Now is come the salvation and the power and the Kingdom of our God and the authority of His Christ." Thus the Reign of God is His saving power which translates us from the thralldom of Satan and brings us under the authority of His Christ, into the Kingdom of the Son of His love. And this is the Gospel, for the Gospel is the power of God unto salvation.

This means that the Gospel of the Kingdom has not fallen out of the later books of the New Testament, but has only changed its terminology. "The Apostolic and sub-apostolic Church has, to be sure, not so often spoken explicitly of the Kingdom of God, but has always repeatedly emphasized this Kingship through reference to the Lordship of Jesus Christ."[59] In the post-resurrection experience of His Lordship the belief in the Kingdom of God is held fast, for in Him even now our citizenship is in the Kingdom of Heaven (Phil. iii.20). The primitive Christian confession, *Jesus is Lord,* expressly recognizes the Reign of Christ.

According to Origen Christ is the Kingdom Himself, *auto-basileia.* For Marcion, "In the Gospel Christ Himself is the Kingdom of God."[60] "The Gospel is the Kingdom of God . . . the message and the messenger are one."[61] "For Jesus sums up in His own person that which the Kingdom of God means."[62] Luther says that the Kingdom of God is nothing else than what we learn in the Creed, that God sent His Son Jesus Christ our Lord into the world to redeem and deliver us from the power of the Devil, and to bring us to Himself, and to govern us as the King of righteousness, life and salvation against sin, death and an evil conscience. *Large Catechism.* As David delivered Israel from Goliath, so our true David has delivered us from sin, death and Satan and filled our hearts with joy and gladness. *Introduction to the New Testament.*

V. THE COMINGS OF THE KINGDOM WHICH HE ATTESTED.

The Old Testament believer who looked for the consolation of Israel, no doubt, thought of the coming Kingdom as a unit and waited for a single coming of the Messiah, although the prophets

59. Schmidt, K. L., *Th.W-b.z.NT.*I.591, 581.
60. Cited by Schmidt, K. L., *Die Polis in Kirche und Welt,* pp.31-40.
61. Clarke, W.K.L., *Divine Humanity,* pp. 96-97.
62. Hebert, A. G., *op. cit.* p. 138.

and the psalmists portrayed both His humiliation and His exaltation, both His coming as a servant and His coming on the coluds. However, as the New Testament unfolds the Old Testament eschatology, the coming of the Son of Man and of His Kingdom spreads out into stages each in its own order.

In His earthly ministry, Jesus speaks of the Son of Man as revealed not by flesh and blood but by the Father to the privileged circle of His disciples (Matt. xvi.13-16; xi.25;cf. Acts x.41). In contrast He prophesies the future coming of the Son of Man on the clouds of heaven with power and great glory, visible as immediately as lightning that flashes from one end of the heavens to the other (Matt. xxiv.27,30). Similarly, He teaches two comings of the Kingdom. Some of those standing by Him as He teaches shall not taste of death until they see the Kingdom of God come with power (Mk. ix.1; Lk. ix.27), or the Son of Man coming in His Kingdom (Mt. xvi.28). On the other hand there is a coming of the Kingdom which shall only take place after wars and rumors of wars, after nation has risen against nation and kingdom against kingdom, after the Gospel has been preached in the whole world for a testimony (Mt. xxiv. 6-13; Mk. xiii.7-10).

The Reign of Glory. Since, however, the Kingdom means the royal reign, the actual exercise of the kingship by the enthroned king, only the Second Coming of the Son of Man is exactly contemporaneous with a coming of the Kingdom. When the Son of Man comes on the clouds, comes with power and great glory, comes with His mighty angels, comes in the regeneration, then shall He sit upon the Throne of His Glory, and as Lord and Judge open the Kingdom to some and close it to others (Mt. xxv.31-46; xxvi.64; xxiv.27,30; xix.28). As He seats Himself upon the Throne of Glory and exercises the royal authority thereof the *regnum gloriae* begins. The King sends forth His angels with the sound of the resurrection trumpet to gather His elect from the four winds of heaven (Mt. xxiv.31), and to gather out of His Kingdom everything that causes offense (Mt.

xiii.41-43). Then the disciples shall sit upon twelve thrones judging the twelve tribes of Israel, for the King has appointed them a Kingdom even as the Father appointed it unto Him (Mt. xix.28; Lk. ii.29-30). The righteous shall shine as the sun in the Kingdom of their Father (Mt. xiii.41-43). In this "final consummation of the *Basileia* in the future" they shall come from the east and the west and from the north and south and shall sit down with Abraham and Isaac and Jacob in the Kingdom of God (Lk. iii.23-29; Mt. xiii.11).[63] This Kingdom of Glory appears in the Epistles when Paul charges Timothy in the sight of God and of Jesus Christ who shall judge the living and the dead, and by His Epiphany and His Reign (II Tim. iv.1), and when Peter asks the brethren to assure themselves of entrance into the eternal Reign of our Lord and Saviour Jesus Christ (II Peter i.11). And all the church fathers have the conception of a Kingdom of God or of Christ at the end of the days, a conception which is fundamentaly eschatological.[64]

The Reign of Grace. Since our Lord was enthroned not at the beginning, but at the completion of His ministry of humiliation, therefore the *regnum gratiae* strictly speaking began only with the Ascension. The Throne of Grace is only mentioned after our great High Priest has passed through the heavens (Hebrews iv.14-16). Until the King was thus enthroned the reign was only "at hand." However, "at least in a preliminary way," the Kingdom of Grace came with Jesus Himself. During His earthly ministry it was here like a tiny mustard seed which was to grow slowly (Mk. iv.30-32). In the presence of the messianic King, it was in the midst.

> "The Kingdom of God cometh not with observation: neither shall they say, Lo here! or there! for lo, the Kingdom of God is in your midst." Lk. xvii.20,21.

Accordingly there was a sense in which John was not and Jesus' disciples were in this Reign of Grace.

---

63. Flew, R. N., *Jesus and His Church*, pp. 36, 39-40; Cf. Otto, R., *The Kingdom of God and the Son of Man*, pp. 190, 274.
64. Koehler, W., *Dogmengeschichte*, p. 260.

"Verily, I say unto you, Among them that are born of
women there hath not arisen a greater than John the
Baptist; yet he that is but little in the Kingdom of Heaven
is greater than he. And from the days of John the Baptist until now the Kingdom of Heaven suffereth violence,
and men of violence take it by force. For the prophets
and the law prophecied until John." Mt. xi.11-13.

Since the Spirit is the special equipment of the messianic
King (Isa. xi.2; xlii.1; lxi.1), the characteristic of the Reign of
Grace (Rom. xiv.17), and the pervasive element and power of
the Reign of Glory (I Cor. xv.44-46), the Spirit furnishes the
best guide and analogy of the stages of the Kingdom's coming.
Having been anointed by the LORD with the Spirit (Mk. i.10),
having been given the Spirit without measure, the Messiah carried on His earthly ministry by that same Spirit.

"If I by the Spirit of God cast out demons, then is the

Kingdom of God come upon you." Mt. xii.28; Lk. xi.20.
Since the Spirit was present and was active in Him, therefore
the Reign of Heaven was pressing into the present.

In announcing the Saviour's birth, Gabriel promised the Son
of the Most High the throne of His father David (Lk. i.32).
The scribes found that out of Bethlehem should come a governor
who would shepherd His people Israel (Mt. ii.6). At His baptism, He was acclaimed by God and anointed by the Spirit as
the Messiah King. But David, also, was anointed King years
before he began to reign. The Gospel according to the Hebrews
gives the Voice at the baptism, thus: *Tu es filius meus primo-
genitus qui regnas in aeternum.* At His trial, Jesus testified that
He had been born a King (Jn. xviii.37); yea, He was born and
was crucified as King of the Jews (Mt. ii.2; xxvii.37).

However, as the Evangelist, thinking of the great coming of
the Holy Spirit at Pentecost, said that the Spirit was not yet
given, because Jesus was not yet glorified (Jn. vii.39); so also

both John and Jesus preached that the Reign of Heaven was only "at hand" until the King had been actually enthroned in His Kingship. Compared with all that went before, the Kingdom came when the King was enthroned to reign with power; compared with the age to come, the Spirit and the Kingdom are still each present in pledge, in first fruits, in anticipation of the glorious fullness of the New Jerusalem, God's reign over risen Spiritual bodies in the new heavens and the new earth.

Jesus used the one hundred and tenth Psalm to elevate the conception of the Messiah (Mk. xii.35-37). The scribes have not said enough when they recognize him as David's Son; for David speaking by inspiration of the Holy Spirit called him, Lord. And to be Lord of David, Israel's greatest King, and that a millenium before the days of His flesh, is to be Lord over much more than David, yea, to be the Lord who reigneth at the right hand of Jehovah until His enemies are made the footstool of His feet.

A little later in Passion week the High Priest solemnly appealed to Jesus, "I adjure thee by the living God, that thou tell us whether thou art the Christ, the Son of God?" According to Mark, Jesus answered, "I am; and ye shall see the Son of Man sitting at the right hand of Power and coming on the clouds of heaven." "The seat at the right hand of God is added to Daniel's picture from Psalm cx.1 which was currently interpreted of the Messiah Son of David (Mk. xii.35f)." [65] The meaning is somewhat fuller in the Matthean form of Jesus' answer which has been paraphrased thus: "Thou has said (that is to say: I am the Christ even now in my present abject condition) ; nevertheless I say unto you, henceforth ye shall see the Son-of-Man (that is to say, a wholly different form) sitting at the right hand of Power and coming on the clouds of heaven."[66] Thus, Jesus definitely identifies Himself as the Messiah, the Son of the Blessed God and claims that He shall be enthroned as

65. Moore, G. F., *Judaism*, II.336.
66. Vos, G., *The Self-Disclosure of Jesus*, p. 84.

David's Lord for His Reign of Grace and shall come as the Son-of-Man on the clouds for His Reign of Glory.

At His baptism Jesus was formally commissioned to carry on that work of Messiah which fell to the *servant* of the Lord (Isa. xl.1; Mk. i.11). Satan tempted Him to reach immediately for the power of messianic Lordship, to secure the nations of the earth by worshipping the Tempter. The Saviour chose instead the Father's will. To some extent David typefied our Lord in His suffering and conflict, humiliation and patience, as Solomon foreshadowed Him in His exaltation and reign. Even when rejection indicated the *via dolorosa,* Jesus rejoiced in the Holy Spirit and thanked the Father's will which hid the things of His glory from the wise and prudent and revealed them unto babes. The Son accepted the very difficulties of that ministry as evidence that all things had been delivered unto Him by the Father (Lk. x.21-22; Mt. xi.25f). For the joy that was set before Him, Jesus endured the Cross, despising the shame, and hath sat down at the right hand of the Throne of God (Hebr. xii.2).

As the Body of Christ the Church is commissioned to carry onward His faithful witness, to bear testimony to His grace and to His Lordship, to His present Reign at the right hand of God and to His coming Kingdom of glory. When some of us prove faithless, the Lord raises up other witnesses to proclaim the Word of His truth; for He abideth faithful, He cannot deny Himself. By His own heroic example and by the power of His Spirit, the Faithful Martyr inspires every Christian martyr with the fire charm of the courageous. The Captain of our Salvation leads onward the moving files of the children of God as they lift high His royal banner. A consciousness of this high calling is leading many of our youth to affirm that "the first duty of the Christian is expressing oneself adequately about the Gospel."[67]

---

67. Fuhrmann, P. T., *God-Centered Religion* p. 21.

CHAPTER III

THE KING UPON HIS INVISIBLE THRONE

Ps. cx.1-2.

● *"Peace, perfect peace, our future all unknown?*
   Jesus we know, and He is on the Throne."

I. THE ENTHRONEMENT OF THE KING.

> The Lord at the Right Hand of Jehovah.
> "My Father and your Father."
> Christ Received up into Glory.
> This Enthronement Hidden.

II. THE VICTORIES OF THE KING.

> A conflict of two ages.
> Christ's victories in His first coming
> His victories through His Church and Martyrs.
> His victories at His Parousia.

III. THE REIGN OF OUR INVISIBLE KING.

> "The Continuing Works of Christ"
> "A Priest upon His Throne."
> "The Word of God."
> "The Throne of Grace."

I. THE ENTHRONEMENT OF THE KING.

When the work of the first commission was finished, God gave unto our Lord a second messianic commission dating from

73

the Resurrection. By the Resurrection, God marked Him out with *power* as the Son of God, the Messiah of David's seed (Rom. i.4). At the Temptation Jesus had refused to purchase the kingdoms of the earth by bowing to Satan, now the living God whom He worshipped gave unto Him all authority in heaven and on earth (Matt. xxviii.18), and made Him ruler over the kings of the earth (Rev. i.5). God raised Him from the dead and seated Him at His own right hand in heaven, angels and principalities and powers being made subject to Him both in this age and in that which is to come (Eph. i.19-22; I Pet. iii.22). When He was thus exalted to God's right hand and had received the promised Spirit, then the King began His reign of peace, His subjects were endued with power from on High (Lk. xxiv. 49; Acts i.8; ii.4,33), and the Reign of God came with power (Mk. ix.1), for the Spirit of Jehovah is power (Mic. iii.8 ARV margin). Our Lord is the nobleman who has gone to the heavenly country and received the Kingdom, that is, the royal Throne.

As Christ had identified Himself as the Lord of Psalm cx who reigns at the right hand of Jehovah, so the New Testament, in addition to preserving this testimony in the triple Gospel tradition (Mk. xii.35-37; xiv.62; Matt. xxii.41-46; xxvi.64; Lk. xx.41-44; xxii.69) repeatedly uses the one hundred and tenth Psalm to describe Christ's exaltation, enthronement, reign and priestly intercession (Acts ii.33-36; I Cor. xv.25-26; I Pet. iii.22; Eph. i.19-22; Col. iii.1; Hebr. i.3,13; v.6,10; vi.20; vii.17,21; viii.1; x.12-13; xii.2). "This King, designated by *to kurio mou* of the Psalm . . . is according to the Messianic designation and fulfillment of this Psalm, Christ, who is Lord of David and of all the saints of the OT; and His *occupying the throne,* sit Thou on my right hand, denotes *the exaltation of Christ* to the glory and dominion of the Father, whose *sunthrones* He has become.[1]

In "the oral gospel," Peter interpreted the sixteenth and the one hundred and tenth Psalms as teaching that God had enthroned Christ at His own right hand by the Resurrection,

1. Meyer, H. W. A., *Acts*, p. 65.
Michel in *Theologisches Worterbuch*, III.1088.

Ascension and Pentecostal effusion of the Spirit, and thereby fulfilled the promise that He would seat the Messiah on David's throne (Acts ii.30). As the worship of the Tabernacle is typical of the worship in the Temple not made with hands, as the Aaronic priesthood is typical of Christ's heavenly High Priesthood (Hebrews), so the earthly throne of David in old Jerusalem is the type of the session of David's Son and Lord at the right hand of God, that is, in co-regnancy and like majesty with God.[2] Thus according to Peter, as according to the Preface to the Westminster Form of Presbyterial Church Government and the second chapter of the Book of Church Order of the Presbyterian Church, U. S., David's Lord now sits upon the Throne of David. "He is more than David or Solomon, but He is upon the throne of David and Solomon."[3]

God is fulfilling His everlasting covenant to David by enthroning David's Son and Lord to pour upon us the sure mercies of David (Acts xiii.22,34; Isa. lv.3), and by gathering in the Gentiles to rebuild the tabernacle of David (Acts xv.14-16; Amos. ix.11-12). The God of our fathers raised up Jesus from the dead and exalted Him to His own right hand to be a Prince and a Saviour to give repentance to Israel and the remission of sins (Acts v.30-32). The Wonderful Counsellor, the Mighty God, the Everlasting Father, the Prince of Peace is upon the Throne of David and upon his Kingdom, so establishing it that it cannot be shaken (Isa. xi.6-7; Hebr. xii.28). Reigning from His heavenly Throne, Christ revealed His glory to His dying martyr (Acts vii.55-56), to the exile on Patmos (Revelation), and to Saul of Tarsus.

The Resurrection and Ascension legitimized the Parousia expectation, which was included in the preaching of Jesus concerning the end, as an irremoveable part of the Christian faith. In the light of Easter and Pentecost, Calvary is not a mere cry of dereliction, but the propitiation for the sins of the world, the victory over principalities and powers and the reconciliation of

---

2. Michel in *Theologisches Worterbuch*, III.1088
3. Vischer, W., *Calvinistic Congress*, 1938, p. 256.

man to God. The certainty of Jesus' Resurrection is bound up
with the significance of His death and the certainty of His
Parousia. Without the Resurrection we have only a humanistic
Christology, the Parousia an illusion, eschatology an outworn
hull, the Cross an enigma. In the light of the Resurrection, the
life work of Jesus and His Cross are our salvation. When Pentecost changed the Reign of God from an expected to a present
reality, it established the Parousia so that it could not be dismissed as an illusion. "By these acts of God a tension between
the Parousia expectation and the present possession of the Spirit
is created."[4] Against the thesis that because Christ did not return
therefore He has not risen, we assert that because He did rise
and does reign, therefore He will return.

"The Ascension signifies the departure of Him, who in the
Spirit remains with His Church, because this is His Body, and
signifies at the same time the return home of Him who as the
exalted One goes before His Church because He is her Head.
In the Ascension, as such a double event, God, in His power
and life, greets and grips the Church of Jesus Christ which
else were in the world without power and dead, because without
future, which alone is exhibited in the exalted Christ: Jesus
Christ rules as King, all things being subject to Him, God lays
all things at His feet."[5]

"My Father and Your Father." Our Lord puts the blessed
efficacy of His Ascension in His words to Mary Magdalene:
"I ascend unto my Father and your Father, and my God and
your God." (Jn. xx.17). The greatest thing that can happen to
us is that the God and Father of our Lord Jesus Christ should
make Himself our God and our Father. This is the heart of
the whole Biblical revelation. Even the law of the Old Testament dispensation is based on this blessed fact, "I am the LORD,
thy God, who brought thee out of the land of Egypt, out of the

4. Michaelis, W., *Die Predigt Jesus vom Reiche Gottes vor und nach Pfingsten*, 1928,
cited F. H. *op. cit.* pp. 85-88.
5. Schmidt, K. L. *Die Himmelfahrt Jesu Christi.*

house of bondage," "Hear, O Israel, Jehovah is *our God,* Jehovah alone." And the new covenant has the same gracious core, "I will be their God and they shall be my people." The living God called the patriarchs and later the Israelitish nation into fellowship with Himself and thereafter was known as the God of Abraham, the Fear of Isaac, the Holy One of Israel.

Jesus found His meat and drink in the will of the Father, He drowned every disappointment and sorrow in His love, He stayed His soul through His arduous life and agonizing death on His God. Even from the darkness of Calvary the Forsaken One testified this faith, "My God, my own God." (Mt. xxvii.46). He bade us add to our faith in God, faith in Himself that we might be sure that the Father's house has mansions to receive us (Jn. xiv.1-2). His words present God to us as our Father, His meditation brings us to God our Father, the Spirit which He won for and applies to us enables us to cry from our hearts, "Abba, Father." On account of His righteousness and expiation, our sins are forgiven and we are received as the justified children of our propitiated heavenly Father. We know God as our God, the Father as our Father, only in and through the ministry of our Lord and Saviour Jesus Christ (Mt. xi.27; Lk. x.22; Jn. xiv.6; i.12; Gal. iii.26).

God has made Himself our God in giving for us His only begotten Son. God has made Himself our God in giving His Son to be the propitiation for our sins. God has made Himself our God in raising Him for our justification. God has made Himself our God in lifting Him to His own right hand to make intercession for us, so that no one may be able to lay anything to the charge of His elect. The God and Father of our Lord Jesus Christ has made Himself our Father in choosing and adopting us in the Beloved, in translating us from the Kingdom of darkness into the Kingdom of the Son of His love. The Father has made Himself our Father in forgiving our sins for Christ's name sake. His Father has made Himself our Father by giving us of His Spirit to cry in our hearts, "Abba, Father."

We are living in serious and awful days as the Four Horsemen of the Apocalypse—Conquest, Bloodshed, Starvation and Death —ride the highways of ancient civilization. But whatever the future hath of marvel or surprise, God is our God and our Father since Christ has wrought His gracious work and returned to the bosom of the Father. And whether life be easy and pleasant or tragic and terrible, there is an immeasureable gap between the holy God and guilty creatures. In ourselves we face an indignant Creator, an Almighty Judge armed for our destruction; only in Christ and through His Incarnation, Expiation, Resurrection, Ascension and Intercession does God become our God, His Father, our Father.

Christ Received Up Into Glory. The Ascension is the return of the Son to the glory which He had with the Father before the world was (Jn. xvii.5,1). The Son of Man is the living bread who came down out of heaven and, having given His flesh for the life of the world, ascended up where He was before (Jn. vi. 62,51). God, only begotten, who dwelleth in the bosom of the Father, tabernacled among us to reveal the Father and then departed out of this world to return to His Father and our Father, to His God and our God (Jn. i.14,18; xiii.1; xx.17). In the theophanies in general and in the descriptions of the Son of Man in Daniel and in the Gospels the clouds indicate the divine glory. As the disciples were looking at the risen Lord, He was taken up and a cloud received Him out of their sight, and angels said: "This Jesus who was received up from you into heaven, shall so come in like manner as ye beheld him going into heaven" (Acts i.9-11). Thus was He seen of angels (I Tim. iii.16), for the angels desired to look into the sufferings of Christ and the glories that shall follow (I Peter i.11-12).

And the Church of the ages has beheld choirs of angels upon the battlements of glory welcoming the Lord of glory ascending to the Throne of His Father (Rev. iii.21) with the words the psalmist wrote to welcome into Zion the Ark, the Throne of the King of Israel:

> "Lift up your heads, O ye gates;
> And be ye lift up, ye everlasting doors:
> And the King of Glory shall come in
>
> * * * * *
>
> Who is this King of Glory?
> The Lord of hosts,
> He is the King of glory."

In *the Passing of Arther* as Sir Bedivere watches the receding barge. there comes to him across the waters, faint and far off, as from beyond the limit of the world,

> "Sounds as if some fair city were one voice,
> Around a King returning from his wars."

"Does not the poet's fancy convey to us a suggestion, however faint and inadequate, of the sounds which filled the realm of glory, and went echoing among the stars, when Jesus went in through the everlasting doors of Heaven and sat down on His mediatorial Throne? The fair city of Zion was then one voice around her King returning from His wars."[6]

As that reception into Heaven is revealed we behold a Lamb standing as it had been slain in the midst of the Throne and of the four living ones and of the elders, taking the book out of the right hand of Him that sitteth upon the Throne, and opening the seals thereof, while all creation hymns His praise. "Worthy is the Lamb that hath been slain to receive the power and riches and wisdom and might and honor and blessing."

The exaltation of Christ is the proper reward for His humiliation and the due recognition of His perfect life of obedience and unbroken fellowship with the Father. Being fundamentally in the form of God, He thought the being on an equality with God not the prize to be greedily grasped, but emptied Himself of all thought of self by taking the form of a servant, being made in the likeness of men, and being found in fashion as a man He became obedient as far as death, and that the death of the Cross, wherefore God also hath highly exalted Him (Phil. ii.5-9). His meat was to do the will of Him that sent Him.

---

6. Stewart, A. *Shoes for the Road*, pp. 50-51.

He drew His breath in the fear of the Lord (cf. Isa. xi 3). Though He was tempted in all points like as we are, though He suffered being tempted, yet was He without sin. "He alone needs not like the rest of us to return as a lost son from a distant place to the Father's house. He has never fallen away from His Sonship. He is, even from eternity, the Son. And in the storm of all the temptations of the world He has maintained this relation of Sonship." "According to the biblical view, the fullness of power, glory and blessedness corresponds to the perfect fellowship with God." That the Father should leave this One helpless and forsaken after His mission was finished were unthinkable. Here no delay is possible. "Exaltation must follow humiliation and with it the fullness of power that corresponds to the Sonship."[7] Thou hast loved righteousness and hated iniquity. Therefore, O God, Thy God hath anointed Thee with the oil of gladness above Thy fellows (Heb. i.9). The God of our fathers hath glorified His holy child Jesus (Acts iii.13).

This Enthronement Hidden. In exalting Christ to His own right hand God has declared that eventually every enemy shall be put beneath His feet and every tongue shall confess that He is Lord to the glory of God, the Father. Referring to this full vindication of the Christian faith, to the public establishment of the Kingdom in glory Professor Heim says: "The King of the Future has mounted His throne, but His Kingdom will be established first in the coming aeon."** However, at His Resurrection all authority was given unto Christ in heaven and on earth (Mt. xxviii.18), and at His Ascension He was enthroned above every principality, power, lordship, and name, not only in the age which is to come, but also in this age (Eph. i.20f). Invested with the Spirit, seated at the right hand of Power, holding the plan of the ages in His nail-pierced hand, gird with all the panoply of glory, the Redeemer is now administering the counsels of redemption for the salvation of His people, the Conqueror of death is pressing the mission which spreads God's

---

7. Heim, K., *Jesus der Weltvollender*, pp. 178-179.
** Heim, *supra,* p. 180.

kingdom from sea to rolling sea. What will be manifest in the
age to come is true today: Jesus Christ is the one and only
true King of kings and Lord of lords. Here and now we owe
allegiance to that King whose glory shall be manifest in the
Coming Age.

The Ascension is "the hidden enthronement of the crucified
Son of Man" and the Parousia is "the public, universally visible
laying hold of power by the secret King of the world."[8] In the
New Testament this is the age of faith, the Coming Age is the
age of sight. Blessed are the pure in heart for they shall see
God in the age of glory. For this age the final beatitude is,
Blessed are those that have not seen and yet have believed (Jn.
xx.29). Now we walk by faith not by sight, only when sight
replaces faith shall we see face to face (I Cor. xiii.12; II Cor.
v.7). Now we live in the sphere of faith, the faith of the hidden
Son of God who loved us and gave Himself up for us, with
the eternal things invisible to us. Here we enjoy the firstfruits
of the Spirit as a foretaste of a closer communion with God, as a
pledge of a vision of Christ as He is. Our hearts turn to Him
whom not having seen we love, on whom though now we see
Him not, yet believing we rejoice with joy unspeakable and full
of glory, for our hope is set upon the grace which will be brought
at the *Revelation* of Jesus Christ (I Peter i.8,13). The Apostle
Paul was not unaware of the idea of mystic vision, but carefully
weighing his religious possessions and his hope for the eternal
future he described this as the age of faith, that as the age of
sight.[9]

The two ages appear in both the teachings of Jesus and of
Paul. The sin against the Holy Ghost shall be forgiven neither
in this age nor in that which is to come (Mt. xii.32); those who
have forsaken loved ones for Christ shall receive a hundredfold
more now and in the coming age, life eternal (Mk. x.30). The
children of this age are wiser than the children of light (Lk.

8. Deissner, K., *Paulus und die Mystik seiner Zeit*, p. 97f.; Baudissin, W., *"Gott schauen"*
in her altestament-Religion; Nygren, *Agape and Eros*, I.180.
9. Deissner, K., *Paulus und die Mystik Seiner Zeit*, p. 97f.

xvi.8). The children of this age marry, those that attain unto
that age and the resurrection neither marry nor die; being children of the resurrection they are children of God (Lk. xx.34-36)
Paul reckons Satan the god of this age (II Cor. iv.4) and condemns the disputer of this age (I Cor. i.20). We formerly
walked according to the age of this world (Eph. ii.2), and
Demas has forsaken the Apostle for this present evil age (II
Tim. iv.10). Since Christ has delivered us from this age (Gal.
i.4) we ought not to fashion according to it (Rom. xii.2). We
have already been translated from the kingdom of darkness
and our citizenship is now in heaven whence also we look for a
Saviour (Phil. iii.20).

Plato sees one order, a sensual, above another, an intellectual.
The New Testament sees one age succeeding another. But the
break is not a clean break. In principle the resurrection age begins
with the Resurrection of Christ while the old age does not end
until the final resurrection. Thus the two ages strive for the
mastery today; the old age of Adam and Satan against the new
age of Christ and the Spirit. The gift we have received is the
earnest of the fullness of the new age which will come at our
resurrection in Spiritual bodies. But even now we are tasting
the powers of the age to come, the blessed winds from that
glory age are blowing from the ascended Christ into our present
evil age.[10] The dawn of that age has broken into this age in
Christ's Resurrection and the present Reign of His grace foreshadows His future Reign of glory. The age of Adam shall end
with the last trumpet, the age of Christ shall manifest its glory
then, for the age of the Spirit is the age that knows no end.

II. THE VICTORIES OF THE KING.

In the period between the first and the second comings of
Christ there is a conflict of the two ages. The age which began
with the Fall still continues to exist under the Prince of the
Powers of this Aeon; but the new age has entered with the Res-

---

10. Cf Enoch. In the name of the future world, for peace has gone forth from thence
since the foundation of the world." Otto, R., *op. cit.* p. 209.

urrection of Christ, so that, here and now, we taste the powers of that age which shall be manifest in glory at His Second Coming. In this intermediate period between the reconciliation of the world by the death of Christ and its final redemption or deliverance from evil at His return, the anti-God power has been deprived of his right, but not yet of his might. This is not the period in which the opposing Power has complete authority over the world, else the very existence of the Church would be impossible; and neither is it the period in which the world has been purified of all demons, else the world would be the Church.[11]

Since evil is essentially irrational, one must accept certain statements thereon even though a completely rational integration be not evident. Satan is in the God of this aeon; yet God worketh all things, He worketh even in Satan. Since the power to work against God has been given Satan by God, the rights of the omnipotent God are not thereby curtailed.[11] Satan is God's Devil and Christ is ruling in the midst of His enemies. Hence, "The Christian life is one of peace within chaos, of forgiveness within sin, of light within darkness." [12]

In the fullness of time God sent forth His Son to redeem His people from bondage to the elements of the world. The fullness of time indicates a period when the prince of this world seemed to have both the heathen and much of the Jewish world under his sway, when the powers of darkness were threatening the very existence of mankind. The entrance of the Lord of Glory into history is the turning point of history and the proper center from which time is dated. He was manifested to destroy the powers of the Old Aeon and introduce the New Aeon. He came to fight against the Satanic powers, to break their domination and to introduce new factors into history.

In the temptation Jesus met His great antagonist and resolutely refused to prostitute His messianic Sonship to exhibitions which Satan suggested. Though Satan tried our Lord, he found nothing in Him. Tempted in all points like as we are, Christ showed that

11. Heim, K., *Jesus der Weltvollender*, pp. 229f.
12. Homrighausen, E. G., *Theological Schools Viewing the World Task*.

a free spirit can obey God in the lot and limitations of a creature. Though Satan returned with the offer of a kingship following the feeding of the five thousand and pressed Him to take some other way than the cup the Father offered in Gethsemane, Christ kept His obedience spotless even unto death that its unsullied holiness might be a robe of righteousness for sinners. Accordingly, as the work of the Redeemer progressed, He beheld Satan fallen as lightning from heaven (Lk. x.18). His work was binding Satan and despoiling his goods (Mt. xii.29; Mk. iii.27), and the prince of this world would be cast down out of heaven (Jn. xii.31; Rev. xii.10).

How can God be a just God and a Saviour? "The problem of guilt is the problem of power." "Jesus first forgave the paralytic: then He gave him the power to walk." (Heim). As long as sin was not expiated Satan accused God for the passing over of sins done aforetime in the forbearance of God. The discordant voice of the Adversary broke upon the chant of heavenly praise. He insisted on the infliction of death on the same eternal principles of justice by which he himself was ruined as a sinner, and consequently invested the deathbed of sinners with fearful lookings for of judgment and fiery indignation. But when Christ was set forth in His own blood as a propitiation for sins, He blotted out the bond written in ordinances that was against us and took it away, thus triumphing over principalities and powers in the Cross. When Christ was delivered up to death for our offenses and raised for our justification, He vindicated God's justice in forgiving sinners. Thus when the ascended Christ appears in heaven as the Lamb that hath been slain for the sins of the world, Michael and his angels prevail against Satan:

"Now is come the salvation and the power and the kingdom of our God and the authority of His Christ; for the accuser of our brethren is cast down, who accuseth them before our God . . . and they overcame him because of the blood of the Lamb and the word of their testimony (Rev. xii.10-11)."

Consequently the Apostle hurls the challenge: "Who shall lay anything to the charge of God's elect? It is God that justifieth. Who is he that condemeth? It is Christ that died, yea rather, that is risen again, who is even at the right hand of God, who also maketh intercession for us (Rom. viii.33-34)." When Satan appeared in a dream with a list of Luther's sins, the Reformer was able to answer, "One thing thou hast forgotten: 'The blood of Jesus Christ cleanseth us from all sin.'" Because He bore our sins in His own body on the Tree, God is just in justifying sinners and,

> "I may my fierce accuser meet
> And tell him, Thou hast died."

All the efficacy of His Incarnation and Atonement Christ carried with Him to the right hand of the Father. God manifested in the flesh was justified in the Spirit, so that whenever we sin we have an Advocate with the Father, Jesus Christ the righteous (I Tim. iii.16; I Jn. ii.1). Thus we look backward to the mercy-seat where His expiation is set forth and upward to the glorified existence of Christ in heaven wherein all the merit of the Cross is made available. By rising for our justification and becoming the life-giving Spirit He is the living witness of righteousness for us in the presence of God. Our righteousness is a living, flawless, accepted fountain of justification from which a believer may ever draw. For our righteousness is Jesus Christ, the same yesterday, today and forever. Since the exalted Christ is righteousness incarnate, we may be found in Him clothed, not in the filthy rags of our own self-righteousness but in the flaming righteousness of the LORD (Phil. iii.9; Jer. xxiii.6). Taking refuge 'neath the shield of His righteousness and under the covert of His heavenly intercession we come by the new and living way to the Throne whence the streams of grace and help do flow. In the Resurrection of Christ, the New Aeon in principle began; in His Ascension endowment with the Spirit, He is our righteousness in the presence of God; in His session at God's right hand, He enrolls our citizenship in heaven.

By His first coming and by making satisfaction for sin, Christ in principle defeated Satan. The working out of this victory is taking place on the field of history and will be consummated at the return of Christ. He shall reign until every enemy is destroyed and the last enemy that shall be destroyed is death (I Cor. xv. 25-26). And Christ is now reigning in the midst of His enemies (Ps. cx.2) as He subdues us unto Himself by the Spirit. Thus God works faith in the hearts of sinners and translates them into the Kingdom of the Son of His love. And yet this all-important, this real change in a man's life is a hidden change. All about us are men still walking according to the aeon of this world, according to the prince of the powers of the air (Eph. ii.2). And even those who are made partakers of the Holy Spirit only *taste* the good word of God and the powers of the age to come (Heb. vi.5).

"For since the end of the world and its judgment has not yet arrived with His appearing, we live, from the Christian and eschatological point of view, in the interim period; thus, as a matter of fact, a new historical epoch did actually begin with Jesus, the special mark of which is the fact of the church, and the history of the church, in the midst of and interwoven with secular history. God having revealed Himself as Three in One, the existence of the Church is the deepest meaning of history, and even the solution of the problem of history as such. Such language is not the illusion of an orthodox absolutism, turning a blind eye to the sinful form in which the church appears. Nor is it the ecclesiastical conservatism which regards the existence of the church as practically the fulfillment of history (Tillich). It is sober deduction from the eschatological gospel of the Kingdom; in and through the coming of God's sovereignty, through repentance and the forgiveness of sins the community of the last days, which waits till God's new world be made complete, comes into being.

"Of course this interim period is to be distinguished from God's sovereignty when it is consummated, when sin, death and

all abominations of this world will have disappeared. And yet
it is the 'day of salvation' in which the gospel is proclaimed, the
divine Spirit enlightens men's hearts and moves them to faith;
it is the period of the history of the Christian church. To be
sure, it is also the period in which unbelief opposes faith and
saving history operates secretly and paradoxically, under the
history of Christianity and the church which is full of sin and
apostasy from divine truth." [13]

The conquests of the Christ are not limited to His personal
victories, He also conquers through His confessors. "The facts
prove that the primary agent in church history is Jesus Christ
Himself." "It is Christ, who through the Church makes Himself
Lord of History and He succeeds in His endeavors because by
His love He becomes master of human hearts." Thus, "He imposes His truth upon men," and "the disclosure of Christ's truth
becomes the judgment of history." [14] Second only to our Lord's
individual victory in His obedience unto death stands the victory
of His primitive Church. Not with sword's loud clashing, or roar
of stirring drums, but with deeds of love and mercy, with lives of
faith and hope, and with martyrdoms of courage and constancy,
that ancient Christian Church conquered the pagan, persecuting
Roman Empire. In less than three centuries the despised Christians rose from the Cross to the Crown. From being the off-
scouring of the earth the Church became the mistress of imperial
culture, the favored of kings, the queen of the Mediterranean
world. And more generally, one finds that as the Church has
spread the blood of the martyrs has ever been the seed of the
Church. After a period of heroic martyrdom, the Christian faith
has been received with toleration and with favor. The children
have built monuments to those their fathers stoned. So the confessors and martyrs reign in the victory of the things for which
they suffer, in the domination they exercise through their lives,
their words, their teachings, their faith. More than all, the Christ
for whom they love not their lives unto the death conquers

13. Wendland, H. D., *op. cit.*, pp. 148-149.
14. Piper, O., *God in History*, pp. 140, 141, 147, 144.

through them, as the people for whom the martyrs suffer wash their robes and make them white in the blood of the Lamb.

Now while we do not wish to be too definite in setting the times or the seasons that the Father has left in His own power, we would modestly add our voice to those who interpret the nineteenth chapter of Revelation in accord with these historical facts. This book was written during the Domitian persecution to comfort and strengthen the martyrs. In the seventh series of the Seven Visions (xix.11-xxii.5), the King of kings appears on a white horse smiting the nations by the sword which proceeds out of His mouth, for His Name is the Word of God. Earlier in Revelation the heavenly Christ is portrayed as the Lamb who has overcome His enemies and is set down with the Father in His Throne, for He is King of kings and Lord of lords (iii.21; xvii.14). Accordingly, we understand the figure in xix.11-16 to be a symbolic description of our ascended King ruling from heaven by the Word of God and enabling His witnesses to overcome by the blood of the Lamb and the word of their testimony.

As the stone cut out without hands smites the image and becomes a great mountain filling the whole earth (Dan. ii34-35, 44-45), so the Hero of Calvary leads His host of martyrs against the pagan power of Rome until He overthrows those who opposed God's Anointed and persecute His disciples. The period of Roman persecutions is the Church's battle with the beast. However, after the short period, symbolized by three and a half years, this battle is over. The system of Roman imperial might and persecution is overthrown. This mighty effort of Satan to crush the Church, which led to the persecution of Christians because they were Christians, is soon to end. The Prophet sees an angel coming down to bind Satan so that he can deceive *the nations* no more for a period described in the symbol as a thousand years. By the word of Christian testimony sealed in martyrdom, the cruel Roman beast that required men to worship him was overthrown and the martyrs lived and reigned with Christ in white-robed glory while their words, testimony, faith and love dominated the Church of the Ages.

However, "when the thousand years are finished," Satan is to be loosened so that he can deceive the nations once more for a little time. Then shall Nero and the rest of the dead persecutors live again in the sense that nations will again take up their task of persecuting Christians because they are Christians. "As the age in which we are living draws near to the end there will be an intensifying of the forces of evil. The opposition to the Church and its work will be world-wide; and the powers of paganism and ungodliness will combine in a concerted effort to overcome the Kingdom of Christ." [15] ',The New Testament sees the most frightful concentration of Satanic power take place just before the end." [17] Serious students are wondering whether such a time is not facing us today. "The period in which we live is undoubtedly one in which Satan is allowed to concentrate his attacks on the Church, more intensely than for any time past." [16] Possibly the revival of the conflict with paganism may be seen in the godless opposition in Russia, the pagan proposal to restore the old gods in Germany, and the shrine worship of Shinto in Japan.

The enemies of Christ have been fettered by His death and exaltation, but they still exist, and their attacks against His body would crush the Church except for her Head. In spite of Satan, death and sin, the mighty Conqueror of them all reigns.

> "Satan: so call him now, his former name
> Is heard no more in heaven."—Milton
>
> * * * * *
>
> "Thou madest Death; and lo, Thy foot
> Is on the skull which Thou hast made."—Tennyson.

Though they are not yet annihilated, Christ looks to the advent of the new age at His Parousia when all power shall be taken from His enemies (I Cor. xv.24ff). "Yet the decisive victory has been won already; Christ has asummed His power and reigns till at last His enemies are subject to Him." [18] At His command

15. Richardson, D. W., *The Revelation of Jesus Christ*, p. 170.
16. Piper, O., *op. cit.*, p. 166.
17. Wendland, H. D., *op. cit.*, p. 63.
18. Aulen, G., *Christus Victor*, p. 87.

are all the reserves necessary to bring the task to its glorious consummation. He shall continue to reign in the midst of His enemies until He returns for the final resurrection victory. "Believe on Him who has raised our Lord Jesus Christ from the dead, and given Him glory and a seat at His own right hand, to whom everything is subject, of things in Heaven and things on Earth, to whom all life ministers, who comes as a Judge of the living and the dead, whose blood God will demand of those who are disobedient to Him" (Polycarp).

Meanwhile let us take a realistic view of life. Jesus predicted wars and rumors of wars. Our Adversary did deceive even the Rock Disciple into becoming his mouthpiece (Mt. xvi.23). He desires to sift the disciples as wheat (Lk. xxii.31) or to devour them as a roaring loin (I Peter v.8). Though Christ's heel is on Satan's head, he still "swinges the scaly horror of his tail." We need constantly to resist him that he may flee from us, and look to the God of peace to bruise him under our feet (Rom. xvi.20).

> "Did we in our own strength confide,
>   Our striving would be losing;
> Were not the right man on our side,
>   The man of God's own choosing:
>
> Dost ask who that may be?
>   Christ Jesus, it is He;
> Lord Saboath His Name,
>   From age to age the same,
> And He must win the battle."

III. THE REIGN OF THE INVISIBLE KING.

At His trial, our Lord testified that henceforth He, the Son of Man, would be seated at the right hand of power (Lk. xxii. 69). With Luther and Calvin we understand this expression as meaning that Christ shares fully the Divine Majesty, Almightiness and Transcendence. We do not think of Christ's work as ending with His earthly ministry, that was only what Jesus began to do and to teach. Acts tells us what the risen, living Christ continued to do through His Apostles.

> "Hail, Son of the Most High, heir of both worlds,
> Queller of Satan! On Thy glorious work
> Now enter; and begin to save mankind." Paradise Regained.

By the foolishness of preaching *God saves* those that believe, a sacrament is a visible sign by which *the Lord seals* upon our consciences His promises of salvation. The whole work of the Church is the great work of God, for Paul, Apollos, Peter and other ministers are only fellow-workers employed by God, who alone gives the increase (I Cor. iii.4-9). Christ is not a mere historical figure at our disposal, we are His servants at His disposal. In the plentitude of His power and Divine fullness, He does not stand in need of us.| He calls us and uses us as His instruments, but as Luther said, He may shatter and reject the instruments He has employed. We have our commission from Him who is the light of the world, but He has other wicks upon whom He can set up His light as on a candlestick.[19] God takes the Kingdom from a fruitless nation (Mt. xxi.43; Mal. i.11-12), if we fail Him deliverances shall arise from another source (Esther iv.11), and whosoever loves father or mother more than the Christ is unworthy of Him (Mt. x.37ff). Clothed with all authority in heaven and on earth, Christ, the Lord of hosts, has other hands than our hands to do His work. The decisive question with each one of us is how Christ places Himself in relation to us, whether He receives us and enrolls us in the picked troops with which He fights His battles or rejects us as unfit. And the highest honor which can come to any man is for Christ to accept Him for His service, give him the Cross to bear and call him to lose his life under the banner of Christ in the decisive battle of world history.[20] The living Son of God leads onward the hosts of God and ultimately determines the course and the consummation of history. *Vexilla Dei prodeunt.*

---

19. Niemoller, M., *God is My Fuehrer*, p. 278.
20. Heim, *op. cit.* pp. 252, 253.

At the Resurrection Christ became the life-giving Spirit (I Cor. xv.45) ; at His Ascension He was enthroned for His reign of grace, at Pentecost He began to pour forth the Spirit as the life of the Church. "Being therefore to the right hand of God exalted, He hath poured forth this, which ye see and hear" (Acts ii.33). According to the genuine, ancient Christian conception, the Spirit is the supramundane gift of the new age, the eschatological Kingdom itself working as *dynamis*.[21] Several of the fathers and one of the cursives have "Thy Holy Spirit come and cleanse us" for "Thy Kingdom come" in the Lukan text, thus showing that for the early church the Kingdom of God as an inward power is identical with the inward working of the Spirit. "Christ's Ascension into Heaven was the real commencement of His reign," for "the Kingdom of Christ consists in the Spirit." *(Institutes* II.xvi. 5,14)

At the Passover the Jews brought the firstfruits of the new harvest to the Lord, at Pentecost they offered loaves of the completed harvest. At the Passover season Christ completed His atoning work for us, at Pentecost the Spirit was given to turn the riches of Christ's purchased redemption from being a treasure laid up in heaven to a treasure received by God's people. The firstfruits of the Spirit having been assuredly given at Pentecost, God will not withdraw His hand until the whole inheritance is enjoyed. And this enjoyment comes from the Lord who has become the life-giving Spirit. As the Head of a new people, Christ's humanity became, as it were, a reservoir filled by the fountain of Deity from which streams of life-giving water continually flow for the spiritual creation and sustentation of His people. At Pentecost the Spirit came organically from the Head to the Body; He came upon every member, not merely the leaders; He came to be the life, the light, the guide of the Church until the return of her Lord. From the Throne of David Christ governs the Church by the Spirit speaking through the Word. Receiving the Spirit without measure, the Messiah baptizeth

---

21. Otto, R., *op. cit.* p. 80.

with the Spirit. From Christ's ascending into heaven we reap a threefold benefit: in that He maketh intercession in heaven unto His Father for us; in that we have our flesh in heaven as a certain pledge that our Head will lift His members up unto Himself, and in that He sendeth us His Spirit, as a pledge between us, by the powerful working whereof we seek not things on earth but things that are above, where He sitteth at the right hand of God.[22]

The work of Christ in His exaltation as well as in His humiliation has been traditionally presented under the form of the three offices of Prophet, Priest and King. In the one hundredth and tenth psalm He reigns as Lord in the Divine Majesty and ministers as priest of the order of Melchizedek; in Zechariah the Branch is a priest upon His throne (vi.12-13); in the ninth of Isaiah He is the Mighty God, the Wonderful Counsellor, the Everlasting Father, the Prince of Peace. In the Great Commission, Jesus asserts His kingly authority, His prophetic words and His priestly presence. In the oral gospel He is exalted to God's right hand, a Prince and a Saviour, to give repentance to Israel and remission of sins (Acts v.31). In the three great visions of Christ in the Book of Revelation the three offices continually intertwine. As He walks in the midst of the churches, the Son of Man is clothed in the long priestly robes, out of His mouth proceedeth the sharp two-edged sword of His prophetic Word, while the glory shining from His countenance and the keys of death and of Hades at His girdle indicate His royal reign. In the fifth chapter, the slain Lamb is priestly, the place in the midst of the Throne, the Lion of Judah and the root of David are kingly, the opening of the book is prophetic. Of the four names given the Divine horseman in the nineteenth chapter, two are prophetic, one is kingly and one is probably priestly. Thus the offices of Christ may be distinguished and the truth thereby brought home to us, but they cannot be separated. As we cannot take an incident from His earthly ministry and say

---

22. *Heidelberg Catechism,* answer 49.

this is the work of one office to the exclusion of the other two, so neither can we parcel out the heavenly ministrations. But a meditation on these three aspects of His gracious work may quicken our apprehension of His work in His body the Church.

A. *"A Priest Upon His Throne."* The same Christ who came not as a judge but as a lover, who loved His own that were in the world unto the end, reveals Himself in heavenly glory as the One who still loveth us (Rev. i.5 b ARV) and who ever liveth to intercede for us (Hebr. vii.25). He, who was delivered for our offenses and raised for our justification, also maketh intercession for us (Rom. viii.34). He who is the propitiation for our sins is also our Advocate with the Father (I John ii.1-2). Made a High Priest by the power of an endless life, He ever appears in the presence of God to save unto the uttermost those who come unto God by Him and to secure for them grace and help in time of need. Having made one sacrifice for sins forever, He sat down on the right hand of the Throne of the Majesty in the heavens, waiting till His enemies be made the footstool of His feet (Hebr. viii.1; x.12-13).

"The scene is laid in the holiest of all where the High Priest stood in front of the mercy-seat, presenting himself as it were 'before the Throne' (Rev. viii.3). In other words, He is represented as 'at the right hand of God' where, on His Ascension, the Father had bidden Him 'sit down,' to intimate that His intercession is no suppliant petitioning for undeserved favours, but the expression of claims recognized ere they are uttered or signified. It is in acknowledgement of these claims that He receives the Spirit, that is to say, authority from the Throne to employ His agency in the actual salvation of each of His people. Thus, this department of Christ's priestly work holds at once of the purchase and of the application of redemption. The actual salvation of any soul, as it is by virtue of His meritorious death which His intercession pleads, so it is through the agency of His Spirit which that intercession procures. In this intercession the merit of His death and the might of His Spirit find their legal connection, and by means of it the one passes into the other." [23] In the midst of the Throne the Lamb stands as it had been slain, His continuous presentation of His sacrifice securing the grace of the Holy Spirit for His people.

There are three appearances of Christ in the Epistle to the Hebrews. He *appeared* once at the end of the ages to put away sin by the sacrifice of Himself (ix.26) ; thereafter He entered into the holy place to *appear* before the face of God for us (ix. 24) ; finally He shall *appear* a second time apart from sin unto the salvation of those that wait for him (ix.28). The period of His personal, visible absence from us is just the period of His appearing before God for us, the period of His priestly intercession in heaven. As the old High Priest left the people to intercede for them in the Holy of Holies, so our High Priest must remain within the heavenly tabernacle as long as there is "grace merited by His death to be pleaded, to be obtained, and to be dispensed by Him." According to this imagery, Jesus Christ will cease His great work of intercession at God's right hand only when the whole number of His elect are converted; He shall appear a second time unto the glorification of the redeemed only when the mystical body of Christ is completed.

As the Minister of the true Tabernacle, the heavenly High Priest applies the benefits of His atonement, the efficacy of His intercession according to His promises:

"For this is the covenant that I will make with the house of Israel after
    those days, saith the Lord:
  I will put my laws into their mind,
  And on their heart also I will write them;
  And I will be to them a God,
  And they shall be to me a people:
  And they shall not teach every man his fellow-citizen,
  And every man his brother, saying, Know the Lord:
  For all shall know me,
  From the least to the greatest of them.
  And I will be merciful to their iniquities,
  And their sins will I remember no more." (Hebr. viii. 10-12;x.16-17)

23. Brown, David, *op. cit.*, pp. 91-92.

In this ministry of grace God is so bountiful that no saved sinner ever stands in a merely legal relationship to Him. Those whose sins He forgives are His people upon whose heart He writes His laws. Only those who are regenerated can stand in the blessed state of forgiveness, for justifying faith is the act of only regenerated hearts.

While idealism proclaims an immediate access to God in this age, the Epistles see the ban of separation from God removed only in Christ.[24] There is no immediate access for sinners, we have boldness to enter into the holy place by the new and freshly sacrificed way He has dedicated for us. Christ alone has preserved His fellowship with the Father, and it is only as we are incorporated into His body and form constituent parts of His person that we are admitted into this fellowship. The passengers on an ocean liner are preserved from sinking into the deep ocean only by their incorporation into that ship. "As the ship has the power not to sink, so has the perfected Christ the power to remain in God and not to sink into the depths of distance from God. We have not this power. We can, therefore, only keep ourselves above the water on this journey through the world in that we become constituent parts of His Person, which will be moved wholly by Himself." [25] The deepest confession of the Christian heart runs: "I sought a way of acquiring strength sufficient to enjoy Thee; but I found it not until I embraced that 'Mediator between God and man, the man Christ Jesus,' 'who is over all God blessed forever' calling unto me and saying, 'I am the way, the truth and the life'." [26] Through the efficacy of His work for us which He gathered unto Himself and took to the altar of Heaven at His Ascension, and the effectual fervent prayers of His present intercession for us, His God becomes our God, His Father, our Father.

B. *"The Word of God."* Our King is a Prophet (Acts iii.22) and His sword (Psa. xlv.3) is a sword coming out of His mouth

---

24. Cf. Schweitzer, A., *The Mysticism of the Apostle Paul.*
25. Heim, K., *Jesus der Weltvollender*, pp. 244-245.
26. Augustine, *Confessions*, VII.xviii.

(Rev. i.16; xix.21) and His Name is called the Word of God (Rev. xix.13,16).[27] Christ promised that where two or three were gathered in His Name there He would be in the midst. His Great Commission closes, "Lo, I am with you always." Where the Head is there is the Body, where Christ is there is the Catholic Church. He is the living and active Lord who is present in His Word and Spirit to found, establish, and maintain His Body, the Church, in every generation. Christ executeth the office of a Prophet in revealing to us by His Word and Spirit the will of God for our salvation.

Since no one knoweth the Father save the Son and he to whom the Son willeth to reveal Him (Mt. xi.27; Lk. x.22), the Only-begotten, who dwelleth in the bosom of the Father has declared Him (Jn. 1.18). In order to continue His work of revealing the grace and truth of God, Christ committed the revelation He made unto writing. Christ Himself is the theme and meaning of Scripture, and every part thereof is a sector not a segment of the whole, the ultimate meaning of which must be found in Jesus Christ. Since this is the only saving revelation of Himself God has given, it is most necessary. "Faith cometh by hearing and hearing by the Word of Christ." (Rom. x.17).

The heavenly King wields the instrument of His own forging, the sword of the Spirit which is the Word of God, for the salvation of sinners. "Belief in Christ on the authority of Scripture is belief in Him on His own authority, being in fact the living flash of identification between the word as written and the living voice of Him whose word it is." [28] The spiritual secret of Hudson Taylor's life can be found in the conviction that, "The living God still lives, and the living Word *is* a living word, and we may depend upon it. We may hang upon any word God ever spoke or caused by His Holy Spirit to be written." [29]

---

27. Peck, T. E., *Miscellanies*, III.80.
28. Martin, Hugh, *The Westminster Doctrine of the Inspiration of Scripture*.
29. Taylor, Howard, *Hudson Taylor's Spiritual Secret*, p. 178.

"Oh, make but trial of His love;
    Experience will decide
How blest are they, and they alone,
    Who in His truth confide.

Fear Him, ye saints, and you will then
    Have nothing else to fear;
Make but His service your delight
    Your wants shall be His care."

The Word of God is with power because it is accompanied by
the Spirit. The bonds of the covenant by which God unites His
people to Himself are His Spirit which He has put upon them
and His Word which He has placed in their mouths (Isa. lix.21).
For clear vision one needs light and seeing eyes. The eyes of our
sin-darkened hearts are enlightened by the Spirit that in the
light of the Word they may behold the Father's face. God has
established a kind of mutual connection between the certainty of
His Word and of His Spirit, so that our minds are filled with a
solid reverence for the Word when by the light of the Spirit
we are enabled therein to behold the Divine countenance, and
on the other hand we gladly receive the Spirit when we recognize
Him in His image, that is, in the Word. *(Institutes* I.ix.3).
"The *sole* agent of real faith in Christ is the Holy Spirit." [30]

This way of governing His people is an eminently gracious
way. "No longer do I call you servants; for the servant knoweth
not what his lord doeth; but I have called you friends, for all
things that I have heard from my Father I have made known
unto you." His authority is the power of truth, and we accept
the obedience of faith believing that the truth shall make you
free. By His Word which is truth and His Spirit who is truth,
Christ, the truth, implants His truths in men. "It is Christ Who,
through the Church, makes Himself Lord of History, and He
succeeds in His endeavors because by His love He becomes master of human hearts." [31] As the primary agent in church history,
He is the Lord of secular history. By the truth of Christ, the
love of Christ and the wisdom of Christ, the Church moves

---

30. Kraemer, H., *op. cit.* p. 132.

history. Christian truth enforces issues and brings about judgment.[31] *Magna est veritas et praevalebit.*

The heavenly Teacher reveals God unto men by fulfilling His earlier promise, "And I, if I be lifted up will draw all men unto myself." This promise has special reference to His death which is the heart of the Gospel, but not to the exclusion of His Resurrection and Return. Thus, the Church has found the liturgy of the Word in terms of the Gospel and the Epistle,[32] the one setting forth the concrete events in our Lord's ministry, the other the total evaluation of His work, the saving significance of His person. And thus the Church year revolves around Christ as the earth around the sun. Both the Apostles' Creed and the best hymns cluster around the great acts of God for our salvation. The Lord's Supper, which shows forth His death till He come, is a memorial of a departed Friend, a parable of a present Friend, a prophecy of a coming Friend. As Christ gave His disciples bread to assure them a share in the coming Kingdom, so He commanded that they be given the baptismal seal by which they should be known as belonging to the people of God in the coming Judgment. The holy ordinance of marriage is repeatedly used as an image of the union of Christ with His people which is to be consummated at His Appearing.

The keeping bright of the Christian hope is necessary as an encouragement in the dark days when Satan seems to be dominant in this period of Christ's invisible reign. "Only when the Church in quiet confidence without any emotional excitement reckons with the coming of the Kingdom of God in power as an outstanding event, only then can she bear the present world situation without her breaking." [33] Because she looks forward to a coming condition in which this frightful dissonance is dissolved, because she knows that God has the battle in His hand however much He may hold back the full power of His might until His own time and season arrives, she endures as seeing

---

31. Piper, O., *op. cit.* pp. 134, 135, 130, 144.
32. Davidson, Principal R., *Common Worship in the Reformed Churches.*
33. Heim, K., *Jesus der Weltvollender*, p. 234.

Him who is invisible. Looking forward to the glory of His Coming she sees the whole mountain filled with the horses and chariots of the Lord and realizes that those that are for us are more than those that be against us. The living Christ calls us by His Word and His Spirit, and He Himself is the theme of that Word — Christ in the grace of His first, and in the glory of His second Coming.

> "He rules the world with truth and grace,
>   And makes the nations prove
> The glories of His righteousness,
>   And wonders of His love."

C. *"The Throne of Grace."* God raised from the dead His Holy Child, Jesus, and exalted Him to His own majesty and power that as a Prince and a Saviour He might give repentance and the remission of sins (Acts v.31). By virtue of His priestly meditation there is a THONE OF GRACE at which all those who come unto God by Him may receive grace and mercy. By His finished sacrifice Christ removed the guilt which stood between the holy God and sinners, by His intercession He secured the regenerating gift of the Spirit, and His royal work of grace is the ministration of the Spirit. By pouring upon us the Spirit of grace and supplication He causes us to behold the Lamb of God that taketh away the sins of the world. Under His mediatorial sway His people take of the cup of salvation, learn the preciousness of the Lord, and find rest for their souls. And ever and anon when the enemy comes in like a flood, He sends forth His Spirit to lift up a standard against him.

The rest which Christ gives is found "in the bands of saving authority and the cords of believing subjection," under an easy yoke and a light burden. The Throne of Grace is a throne, a reign. "The Messiah is the incarnate representation of that divine authoritativeness which is so characteristic of Biblical religion." [34] The ruler's staff shall belong to Judah and the obedience of the people unto Shiloh (Gen. xli.10), the star out

---

34. Vos, G., *The Self-Disclosure of Jesus*, p. 10.

of Jacob shall yield the sceptre of power (Num. xxiv.17), out of Bethlehem comes the governor who is to shepherd Israel (Mic. v.2; Mt. ii.6), even as the King of Kings ruleth with a rod of iron (Rev. xix.15-16) and as every thought is to be brought into captivity to the obedience of Christ (II Cor. x.5).

Through the Sermon on the Mount one hears the shout of a King, a King whose "I say unto you" stands as the Word of God upon which men must build if they would stand in the flood of mortal ills prevailing. In this sermon, Jesus brought the whole moral and ethical conduct under the eye of the heavenly Father. The standard and promise is the Father's perfection, the motive His glory, and the reach of the Divine requirement as far as the all-seeing eye can penetrate. Our conduct is not measured by any form of heteronomy, be it human value, tribal custom, or philosophical universal, but by the revealed will of God. The Saviour removed the law of God as far as possible from mere custom, norm or abstract legality by presenting the heavenly Father at its every point of impact upon the soul. Following in the path of Isaiah, He condemned the placing of the traditions of men above the Word of God (Mt. xv.1-9), and taught His disciples to obey God rather than man (Acts v.29-32; Mt. vi.24, vii.21). Accordingly, discipleship is not absolute freedom of thought but the obedience of faith, not unlimited liberty of conscience but God alone as the Lord of conscience, not every man a law unto himself but slavery to Christ alone as the true and only freedom of the human soul. "If ye abide in my word, then are ye truly my disciples; and ye shall know the truth and the truth shall make you free." Against both the autonomy of the Enlightenment and the heteronomy of current totalitarianism we lift as our banner, the Theonomy of the Throne of Grace.

Both overarching and undergirding Christ's revelation of the Father's will are those assurances of His grace which make His yoke easy and His burden light. In the greatness of His saving sufficiency there is the blessing of the Kingdom for those who are destitute of spiritual wealth, and the promised fullness for those who hunger and thirst for righteousness. Ye shall be perfect is the promise in the law, the inviolable Word of the King of love. The gates of Mansoul are stout barred against every effort to crash an entrance. But when the nail-pierced hands of love gently knock, when the Holy Ghost sheds abroad His redeeming love, the gates of that soul, in its first knightly act, rise like the castle gates of yore and receive the King of glory. "We can only be free in so far as we think and feel and act in terms of what is not ourselves." He that saveth his life shall lose it, he that loseth his life for the Son of Man's sake shall find it.

> "My will is not my own,
>   Till Thou hast made it Thine.
> If it would reach a monarch's Throne
>   It must its crown resign."

This authority of Christ calls for corporate as well as for individual recognition. "Protestantism does not consist in asserting man's liberty against the authoritative claims of Romanism, but in asserting the Authority of Christ over against all those who try to erect their Catholic or Humanistic kingdom of heaven, which may be nothing but the Tower of Babel." The Pope set himself up as lord of the treasury of merits and ecclesiastical tradition and monarch of the Church, while Humanism acknowledged reason or religious feeling or socialism as authorities beside the Revelation of God, even as it is now acknowledging the new political principles of National Socialism.[35] Calvin recognized that the Church is founded on the eternal throne of Christ and that since Christ is the only King, the Church ought to be governed only by the law of Christ. While Rome ascribed authority to the clergy as such, Calvin held that the authority of the ministry is joined inseparably to the Word. It belongs to Christ's Majesty to rule and teach the Church, through His Word and Spirit, by the ministry of men; thus mediately exercising His own authority, and enforcing His own laws, unto the edification and establishment of His own Kingdom. When even the Lord said,

---

35. Hesse, T., *The Church of the Reformation, The Evangelical Quarterly*, 7.4.415-518.

"My doctrine is not mine, but His that sent me," certainly His servants ought to recognize that the authority of everyone is subject to the control of the Word of God (Institutes, iv.viii.2, 4,9). While Melanchthon in the Smalkaldic Articles accepted the Pope *de jure humano,* and Luther said that the princes were chief members in the Church, the Reformed Faith holds that "Christ is the head, the chief of the Church; no one else can be; every elevated position of any man in the Church is incompatible with the honor of Christ; the headship of any man suppresses the Headship of Christ. . . . The headship of Christ is not only spiritual and moral, it is political and juridical." "Christ is the only head, the only chief, the only universal bishop." [36]

The sole Headship of Christ over against Erastianism and clericalism was vindicated by the Scottish Assembly of 1638 when Alexander Henderson, preaching from Psalm cx.1, declared the pretended bishops and archbishop of the Church of Scotland deposed and excommunicated. The Form of Presbyterial Church Government agreed upon by the Westminster Assembly presents as its preface and cornerstone:

"Jesus Christ, upon whose shoulders the government is, whose name is called Wonderful, Counsellor, the mighty God, the everlasting Father, the Prince of Peace, of the increase of whose government and peace there shall be no end, who sits upon the throne of David and upon his king-dom, to order it, and to establish it . . . having all power given unto Him by the Father who . . . set Him at His own right hand . . . and gave Him to be head over all things to the Church, which is His body."

James H. Thornwell sought to give the Throne of Christ sole authority in the Church by placing the Kingship of Christ over against any allegiance due by the Church to any state or nation, by insisting that the Church confine her activities and worship to those things that are warranted in the Word, by limiting her

---

36. Doumergue, E., *Jean Calvin,* V. pp. 5, 6, 141, citing Rieker, *Grundsatze der reformier-ten Kirchenverfassung,* pp. 68-9, 108-9; Zwingli *Confessio gallicana; Confessio belgica,* et.al.

definition of an ecclesiastical offense to that which is contrary to the Holy Scriptures, and by recognizing that all the officers of the Church are the appointment and institution of Christ, the King.[37] In the Gifford Lectures, Barth points out that the great thing which is done in the Church is what Christ does, blessing His Word, His sacraments and the testimony of Christian faith and love by the power of the Holy Spirit. Hence, the first duty of the Church is to *inquire* of her Lord what things He would have in her worship, and then wholeheartedly to obey her invisible King. "For Jesus Christ, whose life is the Christian life, does live in God, and does sit at the right hand of the Father in His everlasting Kingdom and hence in measureless exaltation over His Church, as her heavenly and invisible Head." [38]

The Throne of Grace is a throne of victory. The final overthrow of evil is to take place at the culmination of Christ's mediatorial reign. But even now He reigns in the midst of His enemies and they are being subdued under Him. As the Confessional Synod of Barmen declared, He does conquer us and all His other enemies and rules over and defends His own. He is mighty to the pulling down of strongholds, so that every plant that His Father has not planted shall be rooted out. According to God's hidden method Christ overcomes all the machinations of the evil one. Often the kings of the earth take counsel against the Lord and against His Anointed, but "He that sitteth in the heavens shall laugh: the Lord will have them in derision." "Thou shalt break them with a rod of iron; Thou shalt dash them in pieces like a potter's vessel."

Christ must reign until He has put all enemies under His feet, and the last enemy that shall be destroyed is death (I Cor. xv. 25-28). As His own victory over death in His Resurrection was, in a special sense, the beginning of His mediatorial reign, so the working out of this victory in the raising of His people from the dead and the demolition of death is the completion of the reign of

37. *Thornwell's Collected Writings*, IV; Peck, T. E. *Ecclesiology;* Robinson, S. *The Church of God; Book of Church Order,* Presbyterian Church, U.S., pars. 9, 10, 173.
38. Barth, K., *The Knowledge of God and the Service of God,* p. 153.

grace. "The first act of Christ's mediatorial kingship was His ascension . . . the last act of His reign will be the last judgment at His return when He will return the administration of the Kingdom to God the Father." (Institutes II.xv.5).

The rendering up of the Kingdom to God the Father does not mean that Christ is not to reign in the Kingdom of glory. The mediatorial stewardship will be completed, but the state of glory is the Kingdom of Christ and of God (Eph. v.5). We look for the appearing of Jesus Christ and His Kingdom (II Tim. iv.1), for "the everlasting Kingdom of our Lord and Saviour Jesus Christ" (II Peter i.11) when "He shall reign forever and ever" (Rev. xi.15). "The eschatological gospel of the Kingdom is of necessity itself Trinitarian in character; it is the Kingdom of the Father, the Kingdom of the Son and the Kingdom of the Holy Ghost." [39] However, the mediatorial kingdom is in a special sense the Reign of Christ, since the Trinity has invested the Mediator with all authority in heaven and on earth to apply the redemption He has purchased and carry onward to its consummation the Kingdom of Grace.

A Scottish minister, known for piety, said that as he looked into his own heart he could see nothing there but darkness, guilt and pride. "Then," said he, "I remembered that Christ is a Prophet who can enlighten my darkness; Christ is a Priest who can remove my guilt; Christ is a King who can humble my pride. And I said it were good that Christ and I should meet."

> "Lo the incarnate God, ascended
>   Pleads the merits of His blood.
> Venture on Him, venture wholly,
>   Let no other trust intrude.
> None but Jesus, can do the guilty sinner good."

---

39. Wendland, H. D., *op. cit.* p. 147.

CHAPTER IV.

LORD BOTH OF THE DEAD AND OF THE LIVING

ROM. XIV.9

● *"My knowledge of that life is small,*
The eye of faith is dim,
But 'tis enough that Christ knows all,
And I shall be with Him."

I. FACING DEATH.

Death speaks a language that everyone understands and obeys. The way in which individuals and nations face death molds history.

> The German Myth of the Twentieth Century
> The Scottish National War Memorial

Invictus - as written by William Henley.
> as adapted by D. R. Davies for England's travail.
> as answered by Dorothea Day in *My Captain*.

The Stirrup Cup - by Hon. John Hay
> by Gen. E. P. Alexander.
> by Dr. J. P. Smith.

God has made Himself our God in Christ.
> The Word brings Christ to the soul.

II. FROM DEATH TO THE RESSURRECTION.

The Church in Paradise and the Church on earth are one Flock.

A. *The Role of the Intermediate State in Christian Thought.*
When Christian thinking is dominated by the Word of the emphasis is on the Resurrection; when dominated by human philosophy it is on the intermediate state. *Purgatory.* Human moralism vs. Divine grace. "The knowledge of original sin is the end of moralism." The sufficiency of Christ's one satisfaction for sins.

B. *The Intermediate State in Scripture.* Hope of a blessed hereafter in a God-given fellowship, rather than in a natural immortality. Texts that are ambiguous on the intermediate state. Texts that are definite concerning the intermediate state. The sleep of death. Memory. Mind. Love. Worship.

"Afraid?"

I. FACING DEATH.

There is one truth given for all times, classes and generations. Death speaks a language that everyone understands in his own tongue, and everyone obeys—peasant and scholar, soldier and sailor, mother and child, banker and miner. "Death is the Divine command—STOP!—and we cannot disobey it." [1] The king that saith in his heart, I will exalt my throne above the stars of God, and I will sit upon the mount of congregation in the uttermost parts of the North, shall be brought down to Sheol, to the uttermost parts of the pit (Isa. xiv.3-21; Cf. Eze. xxxii.17-32). "For death is the king of terrors, and the terror of kings." The prosperous farmer who plans to build larger barns and crowd them with grain that he may say to his soul, "Soul, thou hast much goods laid up for many years; take thine ease, eat drink and be merry," will hear God say, "Thou fool, this night is thy soul required of thee, whose then shall the things be that thou hast

---

1. Barth, K., *The Epistle to the Romans*, p. 169.

prepared?" (Lk. xii.16-20). "It may be said that philosophy, for
the first time, is concerned with death as a primary, fundamental
problem." [2] We may not be able to predict the time as exactly
as did Alan Seegar; but otherwise it is as true of each of us as
it was of him,

> "I have a rendezvous with Death
> At some disputed barricade;
> When Spring comes back with rustling shade
> And apple blossoms fill the air,
> And I, to my plighted word, am true,
> I shall not fail that rendezvous."

"The world has one central point—death." "Therein we stand
together like children in a great circle, hand in hand." "It is no
small matter to have death as the centrum of life, death and his
premise, sin and sorrow." [3]

Since death is such a universal truth, the way in which each
individual faces the grim reaper makes a tremendous difference
in his life, and the way in which a group or a nation face this
heritage of the human race molds history. Perhaps the most
impressive illustration of the last statement is the contrast
between the way in which two of the great European peoples
have memorialized their soldiers who died in the First World
War.

Germany has witnessed a recrudescense of paganism which has
banished the biblical hope of eternal life, and with Frau Luden-
dorf has substituted faith "in the immortality of the Nordic
man." The Myth of the Twentieth Century is built on the
idealistic thought structure of Hegel and Fichte, according to
which the state is "the real god" and the German people "a divine
good." It is held that those who died in battle sacrificed themselves for the honor of the race and the greatness of the nation.
At death, they returned to the sacred soil, to the eternal rhythm
of death and birth. Rosenberg's aim is the creation of a *Volks-
kirche* to preserve the honor of the nation for which so many
sacrificed themselves. Those who wish to see Christianity rest-

2. Davies, D. R., *The Two Humanities*, p. 59.
3. Barth, K., and Thurneysen, E., *Come Holy Spirit*, 1934, p. 176.

ing upon "the religious consciousness" or "Christian experience" rather than upon the Word might remember that Hauer of Tubingen thanks Schleiermacher and the "liberal" theology of the nineteenth century for freeing Christianity from its Asiatic-Semitic (Biblical) form and for founding it anew upon the Germanic-Deutsch spirit, thus preparing the way for a Germanized Christianity which rests on the race myth rather than on the Gospel. The *Deutsche Christen* seek a German Church to serve the myth of race, blood and soil, believing with Reinhardt Krause that "service of our people is Cottesdienst." [4]

On the other hand, Scotland is dotted as thick with shafts commemorating those who fell bravely in the World War as our Southland is with monuments to the Confederate dead. On the Castle Rock in Edinburgh by St. Margaret's Chapel stands Scotia's magnificent memorial to these dead. There is a sacred hush about its walls. The guide explains it before one arrives and remains outside as the visitor reverently ponders this symbol in stone and bronze of the ongoing of those who gave their lives in the great encounter. On the outer walls there are sculptured figures of the cardinal virtues, signifying the challenge to the living which Scotland draws from her heroic dead. Somehow one feels the solemnizing power of that Scottish Memorial in binding Church and people to the hope of eternal life which "is the very main spring of religion." [5] Thus Scotland lives with the gaze of her heroes fixed upon her, knowing that they died in the confidence that she would carry on. Some of the meaning of that memorial may be expressed in the word of a French Christian student who died beside so many of his Scottish allies, "All together, in the shadow of our glorious dead, we shall throng with calm and assured tread the foot-paths of the future." [6]

Here in America our leading Calvinistic preacher, Dr. C. E. Macartney, has taken up the call for a message concerning the hereafter. "In the last ten years I have emphasized more and

---

4. Frey, Arthur, *Der Kamf der Evangelischen Kirche in Deutschland.*
5. Taylor, A. E., *The Christian Hope of Immortality.*
6. Grauss, Charles, cited by Captain Pierre Maury, *Students and World Advance,* 1920, p. 107.

more the doctrine of immortality and the future life. I feel that all of us, of whatever school of theology, have neglected sadly and without excuse this great doctrine. Sometime before his death I read that interesting sketch of his boyhood days by the late Clarence Darrow, *Fairfield*. He tells of his early association with the little church in Ohio and how he visited, in his last years, the church yard. This naturally led him to speak of death and he wondered at 'the general conspiracy to keep silent about that event which awaits us all.' Certainly in the church today there seems to be a general conspiracy to keep silent about the future life, and about that 'honor and glory and immortality' which St. Paul says is the end of our Christian Faith. The failure to sound the note of the future life has made much of our preaching secular and commonplace. The less we think and speak about the life to come, the worse will this life become. This has been a growing conviction of the past years, and more and more I find myself, and with profit to myself and, I hope, with profit and comfort to those to whom I preach, striking the note of the life everlasting. The final article of the Apostles' Creed, is, I believe, the greatest article: 'and in the life everlasting.' For without belief in that article, the great affirmations of the creed which go before it are left without meaning." [7]

How then shall we face death? What comforts are there for the fatal hour? What anchors for the soul within the veil? Perhaps we shall find that we can answer these questions together; that in answering one we are answering them all.

Invictus. In the bold words of *Invictus,* William Henley faced death.

> "Out of the night that covers me,
> Black as the pit from pole to pole,
> I thank whatever gods may be
> For my unconquerable soul.
>
> In the fell clutch of circumstance
> I have not winced, nor cried aloud.
> Under the bludgeoning of chance
> My head is bloody, but unbowed.

7. Macartney, C. E., *Warm Hearts and Steady Faith, The Christian Century*, 3.8.39., p. 319.

> Beyond this place of wrath and tears
> Looms but the horror of the shade;
> And yet the menace of the years
> Finds, and shall find, me unafraid.
>
> It matters not how strait the gate,
> How charged with punishment the scroll,
> I am the master of my fate;
> I am the captain of my soul."

However, it may well be doubted whether those who so glibly quote these lines in the days of their strength, remember them in the solemn hour when the approach of death has swept away the illusions of sense and worldliness and the soul returns "from its chase of vanities to the thought of its sins and their dread punishment." When a man faces "the fundamental truth that sin intrinsically deserves and must receive its due penalty," he realizes that it is a fearful thing to fall into the hands of the living God.[8] Indeed, D. R. Davies finds Henley's bravado insufficient for Britain's present travail. Instead he offers the faith in God which is necessary for the transformation of despair *when everything* has gone, thus:

> "Out of the night that covers me,
> Black as the pit from pole to pole,
> I thank the Bible God who is
> For my conquered, battered soul.
>
> In the fell clutch of circumstance,
> I both winced and cried aloud,
> Under the bludgeonings of chance,
> My heart was bloody and bowed down.
>
> It matters not how strait the gate,
> How charged with punishments the scroll,
> Christ has saved me from my fate,
> God is the Captain of my soul."[9]

Somewhat earlier, Dorothea Day answered Henley's bold paganism with a Christian confession, *My Captain*:

8. Dabney, R. L., *Discussions*, I.475.
9. Davies, D. R., *The Two Humanities*, pp. 182-183.

"Out of the light that dazzles me,
Bright as the sun from pole to pole,
I thank the God I know to be
For Christ the conquerer of my soul.

Since His the sway of circumstance
I would not wince nor cry aloud.
Under that rule which men call chance
My head with joy is humbly bowed.

Beyond this place of sin and tears—
That life with Him and His the aid,
That, spite the menace of the years,
Keeps, and shall keep, me unafraid.

I have no fear though strait the gate;
He cleared from punishment the scroll.
Christ is the Master of my fate;
Christ is the Captain of my soul."

Miss Day found her comfort in the fact that Christ had cleared from punishment the scroll. By one draught He drank damnation dry! The same anchor held in the life of William Mills Halsted, an elder in the Union Place Presbyterian Church and one of the founders of the Union Theological Seminary of New York. Under date of November the tenth, 1845, Mr. Halsted wrote to his son on the solemn subjects of sickness and death: "The only preparation we can have is an interest in the atonement which has been offered for sin. Jesus came into the world and died to save sinners: the salvation provided will not avail any who do not truly repent of their sins and exercise faith in Jesus as their Savior, trusting in his merits for pardon and acceptance. Have you seen yourself to be in the sight of God an unworthy, guilty sinner? Lost and under condemnation? Felt that there is no hope for you but in the atonement of Christ, and have you been enabled to look unto Him for salvation? If not, as you value true peace of mind here and happiness hereafter, I would urge that you delay not to look unto Him who alone can give them to you." [10]

10. Cited by MacCullum, W. G., *Life of Wm. Steward Halsted, Surgeon*, 1930, pp. 4-5.

Death is the penalty of sin, but Christ delivered us from the curse of the law by being made a curse for us as He hung upon the tree (Gal. iii.13). He took the bond that was against us out of the way by nailing it to His Cross (Col. ii.14). By tasting death for every man He destroyed him that had the power of death, that is, the Devil, and delivered them who through fear of death were all their lifetime subject to bondage (Heb. ii.9, 14, 15). As a result, the Living One, who was dead and is alive, carries the keys of death and Hades (Rev. i.18). By dying for our sins and rising again He has robbed death of its sting (I Cor. xv.3,55). By obeying the precept and enduring the penalty of the law, He has robbed death of its victory. He and He alone speaks the forgiveness and peace which softens the sinner's death-bed. Only His "Son, be of good cheer, thy sins be forgiven thee!" can supply the faith that speaks thus,

> "In peace let me resign my breath
> And Thy salvation see;
> My sins deserved eternal death,
> But Jesus died for me."

The Stirrup Cup. How shall we face death? One of the most interesting and instructive contrasts or series of contrasts is found in the portrayal of death as *the Stirrup Cup*. The imagery is drawn from the cavalry-man's custom of drinking a cup as he mounted his steed and from the apocalyptic symbol of death as the pale horse. With rare literary skill, the Honorable John Hay, sometime Secretary of State, used this figure to express his attitude toward death.

> "My short and happy day is done,
> The long and lonely night comes on;
> And at my door the pale horse stands
> To bear me forth to unknown lands.
>
> His whinny shrill, his pawing hoof
> Sound dreadful as the gathering storm,
> And must I leave this shelt'ring roof
> And joys of life, so soft and warm?

> Oh, joys of life, so soft and warm,
> Kind friends so faithful and so true,
> My rosy children, and my wife
> So sweet to kiss, so fair to view.
>
> So sweet to kiss, so fair to view;
> The night comes on, the light burns blue;
> And at my door, the pale horse stands
> To bear me forth to unknown lands."

Through the beauty of these lines shimmer the lights and delights of this life, and over them broods the fear of death as a strange adventure, terrifying, abhorrent, but unavoidable. General E. P. Alexander, Longstreet's chief of artillery, disliked this note and under the same imagery of drinking the stirrup cup wrote other lines to express the dauntless heart and unfaltering hand with which he would mount the steed of Death.

> "But storm and gloom and mystery
> Shall only nerve my courage high
> Who thro' life's scenes hath borne his part
> May face its close with tranquil heart.
>
> No trembling hand will grasp the rein,
> No craven soul the path will trace;
> This life has not been mine in vain,
> In unknown lands I'll seek my place.
>
> I drain the cup and boldly face
> The heritage of the human race,
> Whose birthright 'tis to pierce the gloom
> And solve the mystery of the tomb.
>
> I follow some, and others lead
> From whom my soul would ne'er divide.
> One fate for all. Where moves the great
> Procession, there let me abide."

Both of these poems came into the hands of James Powers Smith, a distinguished minister of the Synod of Virginia, who as an aide-de-camp to Stonewall Jackson had gallantly ridden through the valley of the shadow of many a death. Feeling that something was needed to dispel the fear expressed by Colonel Hay and provide the tranquil heart desired by General Alexander, Dr. Smith wrote:

> "The pale horse stands and will not bide,
> The night has come and I must ride;
> But not alone to unknown lands,
> My Friend goes with me holding hands.
>
> I've fought the fight; I've run the race.
> I now shall see Him face to face,
> Who called me to Him long ago
> And bade me trust and follow.
>
> The joys of life have been His gift,
> My friends I'll find when clouds shall lift;
> I leave my home and all its store
> To dwell with Him forevermore.
>
> What does He give? His cup of love;
> Until with Him I rest above!
> I'll mount and ride, no more to roam,
> The pale horse bears me to my home!"[11]

Dr. Smith had put His trust in Him who by His own death for us abolished death; and found his comfort in the living Friend who was to go with him even through Death. When he died alone, he was not alone; his Friend went with him holding hands.

A college girl in my congregation died one summer with tuberculosis. Before her death she said that she would not get well, but that Christ had assured her, "Lo, I am with you always." When he knew the end was coming fast, my father repeated in quiet confidence, "Yea, though I walk through the valley of the shadow of death I will fear no evil, for Thou are with me."

All Christian history is redolent with the testimony of His presence in that eventful hour. Stephen saw such a vision of the Son of Man as he received the crown of martyrdom that his face shone like the face of an angel. Polycarp needed not to be tied to the stake, but drew strength to endure the flame from the King he had served eighty and six years. To steady her in the approaching ordeal a triumphant vision was vouchsafed to that heroic young mother, Perpetua. When Walter Milne, the last and oldest of the Martyrs of St. Andrews, was drawn up

---

11. *The Presbyterian of the South.*

from the bottle dungeon he was too weak to stand. Men said
he would be unable to testify. But God so strengthened His witness with His grace and with the refreshing air providentially
permitted between the dungeon and cathedral, that Milne made
the arches of that vast edifice ring with his testimony. John
Owen welcomed death as the long-wished-for day in which he
should see the glory of Christ in a manner in which he was
incapable of doing in this world; Alexander Henderson said
"there was never a school boy more desirous to have the play
than I am to leave this world;" Robert Bruce breakfasted with
his children and went to sup with the Lord Jesus Christ. Grim-
shaw grieved that he had done so *little* for Christ, and rejoiced
that Christ had done so *much* for him. For Andrew Fuller there
was no rapture, no despondency, but this word of a calm mind,
"My hope is such that I am not afraid to plunge into eternity." [12]
And time would fail me to tell of Hus and Hamilton, of Ridley
and Cranmer, of Wesley, of Erskine and the Stamms.

> "For all the saints who from their labors rest,
> Who Thee by faith before the world confessed,
> Thy name, O Jesus, be forever blest,
> Alleluia, Alleluia."

There were two old men that "Rabbi" Duncan, the beloved
sage of the Free Kirk of Scotland desired to imitate. One "a
theological professor of Pesth who, when in his dotage was
oblivious to everything. But troops of children used to follow
him, and laying his hands on their heads, all he could say was
'*Iesous Christos*' (Jesus Christ). The other is of the old man
who was dying and his memory quite gone. His own name was
mentioned: 'Don't know that man.' His grandchildren's names:
He shook his head. The Saviour's name — when leaping up with
energy he said, 'Ah, Jesus Christ, my Saviour, my God'." [13]
Through nineteen hundred years of Christian history

---

12. Cited, Plumer W. S., *The Grace of Christ*, pp. 341, 342, 346.
13. Brown, David, *Memoirs of John Duncan*, p. 446.

> "The last low whispers of our dead
> Are burdened with His Name."

From Christ's dying, rising and interceding for us, Romans brings us the assurance that neither life nor death shall separate us from the love of God in Christ Jesus, our Lord. To these great assurances, Hebrews adds the comfort of His sympathy and solidarity with us, even in the fear of death. He Himself likewise took the nature of man, of the seed of Abraham, and passed through the whole curriculum of temptation, obedience, patience and death which is our lot. Since He suffered being tempted, He is able to succor them that are tempted. Our High Priest can bear gently with the ignorant and erring, for in the days of His flesh He offered up strong cryings and tears unto Him who was able to save Him from death. Yea, He *tasted* death to its bitterest dregs that He might deliver us from its sting of sin, its fear of Satan. In place of the curse of the law, we have redemption through His blood, even the forgiveness of sins; in lieu of the leer of Satan, we have His Word, "I will never leave thee, nor forsake thee." We go through no darker room than He has gone through before us; and the darkness of Calvary makes it light about us as we enter the valley of the shadow. Resting on the promises of God, we are strong and of good courage.

> "The soul that on Jesus hath leaned for repose
> I will not, I will not desert to His foes,
> That soul, tho' all hell shall endeavor to shake,
> I'll never, no never, no never forsake."

When Jackson, Mississippi, mourned the death of her first citizen, Dr. J. B. Hutton, she remembered his testimony to the sufficiency of God for life's most tragic moment. On that former day he was seated with his sorrowing loved ones in the front pew of the church he had so long and faithfully served. In front of the pulpit from which his many eloquent messages had been uttered was a sombre casket holding the cold and silent form of his first-born son, a boy whom he passionately loved because a physical infirmity deprived him of a fair chance in life. Humanly speaking, the death of that young man had been a tragic blunder. The doctor had given the antitetanic serum to a patient suffering with asthma, without making a preliminary test; and death had ensued instantaneously. The choir was softly singing the final stanza of "Lead, Kindly Light," when Dr. Hutton slipped quietly from the pew, placed his hand tenderly on the casket, and in a voice choked with emotion, said:

> "My friends, what I have been telling you through all these years is true. Only faith in God can bring us consolation in hours of deepest sorrow. I have preached this to you from this pulpit many times, I have been with you in your own hours of grief and bereavement, and I now know that my Redeemer liveth and He is able to keep that which I have committed unto Him against this day." [14]

As Dr. Hutton preached Christ, God bore in upon the preacher's soul the assurance that the Captain of our salvation will lead on till,

> "The night is gone
> And with the morn
> Those angel faces smile
> Which I have loved long since and lost awhile!"

In Jesus Christ, God's everlasting arms are beneath this transitory life; behind death is the Prince of Life; beyond the grave is the Resurrection. "For," says the Apostle Paul, "whether we live, we live unto the Lord, or whether we die, we die unto the Lord. Whether, therefore, we live or die, we are the Lord's. For to this end Christ died and lived, that He might be Lord of both the dead and the living" (Rom. xiv.8-9). In these words the Apostle states the very heart of the Christian faith: namely, that *we are the Lord's* and He is our Lord whether we live or die. Because God has made Himself our God and made us His people, therefore, there is comfort and forgiveness, life has

---

14. Sullens, Major Frederick, in *The Jackson* (Miss.) *Daily News*, September 23, 1940, p. 4.

a purpose and a meaning, and there is a light in the valley of the shadow.

The substance of the Old Testament is that God is the God of Abraham and of His seed after him; of the New that He is the God and Father of our Lord Jesus Christ and, in Him, our God and our Father. This is the great message of the covenant theology. Our fathers confessed a voluntary condescension on God's part by which He graciously entered into covenant fellowship with us. This is the kernel of the famous Heidelberg Catechism:

"Q. What is your only consolation in life and in death?

A. It is that, with my body and with my soul, whether in life or in death, I am not my own, but I belong to my faithful Saviour, Jesus Christ."

I am the Lord's, blessed condition! I, the sinner, belong to my faithful Saviour, grace abounding! If we live, we live unto the Lord. If we die, we die unto Him. Hence "to live is Christ and to die is gain."

Christ Jesus is our hope, our anchor reaching within the veil of heaven's glory. Christ hath bound us to Himself by His Word and His Spirit. In the struggle of death, when there is no strength in us and the Accuser attacks us night and day, Luther tells us to cling ever closer to the Word, as a man climbing down a cliff clings to a rope that is thrown to him and which alone can save him from the cliff below. We cling fast to its great promises. Faith is nothing else than that movement which we must always make, away from ourselves and from our feelings and variable moods, to the Word.[15]

Among the many testimonies to the power of that Word which brings Christ to the souls of men for their comfort in the hour of death, there is this interesting one from the Reverend Marcus Dods, the elder, of Belford, Northumberland. After stating that his faith was not rashly formed nor lightly adopted on the opin-

---

15. Cited by Heim, K., *The Gospel of the Cross,* pp. 107-108.

ions of other men but that he had won his way painfully out of doubts to his acceptance of the Bible, Mr. Dods continued:

"My own experience abundantly testifies the power of the Bible to afford the most effectual support in that hour when support is most urgently needed and most difficult to be found. Few have passed so far into the domain of death and been permitted to return. I have felt the breath leaving me, that I expected not again to inhale. I have counted the dull, heavy throb of my heart as it grew fainter and fainter, fully anticipating at every pulsation that it would 'heave but once more and forever be still!' I have gazed on the faces of those dearest to me till my eye grew dim in the blackness of death, and I could no longer see; and I have listened to the soothing voice of affection till my ear grew torpid in the apathy of death, and I could no longer hear; and I have felt the icy chilliness of death shooting through my veins, arresting the current of life in its course, till sensation itself forsook me, and I could no longer feel. And while thus placed on the very line that separates time from eternity, what was it that, under a deep consciousness of manifold guilt, enabled me to look forward in that momentary expectation of finally passing that line, calm and tranquil as I am now? Gentlemen, it was just that Bible of whose Divine inspiration I once as foolishly maintained the low view that prevails, as I thank God I have now long and cordially renounced it. I consider the opportunity afforded me of bringing it to so severe a test as one of the richest blessings of my life. And recalled as I have been to longer days, I wish to consider every day lost, which does not add to my knowledge of its contents, or deepen my experience of its value." [16]

II. FROM DEATH TO THE RESSURRECTION.

Our text and theme indicate that Christ is Lord not only of life and its last hurdle, dying, but as well of death and all that lies beyond. In this chapter we wish to limit our consideration

---

16. Dods, M., *Remarks on the Bible*, Edinburgh, 1828.

of the great BEYOND to the fact that He is Lord over those who sleep in Him from their death to the Resurrection. Other phases of what lies on the other side of dying are reserved for the following chapters.

In an earlier chapter we considered Christ as the invisible King of the Church militant; here we notice His reign over "the Elect that be departed, commonlie called the Kirk Triumphant;"[17] in later chapters we shall look to that day of triumph when as King of Kings and Lord of Lords He shall present unto Himself the Church Glorious, without spot or wrinkle or any such thing. At the present, the Church toiling and struggling here below is half the story; the Church gathered above is the other half:

> "Blessed that flock safe penned in Paradise;
> Blessed this flock which tramps in weary ways:
> All form one flock, God's flock; all yield Him praise
> By joy or pain, still tending towards the prize."

Yea, since both halves have one Lord—Christ—they are one Flock.

> "Ye say, we hear, that yonder,
> Thou goest and we stay!
> And yet Christ's mystic body
> Is one eternally."

A. *The Role of the Intermediate State in Christian Thought.* The biblical emphasis is neither upon the intermediate state, nor upon what happens to individual souls at death, but rather upon the resurrection, the final judgment, the Kingdom of glory and the cosmic consummation. The texts dealing with the intermediate state are few, and neither Jesus nor the New Testament writers ever suggest that man is by nature immortal.[18] Accordingly, whenever Christian thinking is dominated by the Word of God, the stress is on the Resurrection. "Wherever the natural immortality of the soul is an accepted dogma, we can be confident that we are in a sphere of thought dominated by Eros," [19] that is, by human speculation.

17. *Scots' Confession*, XVI.
18. Findlay, J. A., *The British Weekly*, 1/23/41, p. 170.
19. Nygren, A., *op. cit.*, I:176-177.

Justin Martyr held that souls were not essentially immortal. The relative emphases of the Christian rule of faith are well represented in the Apostles' Creed which affirms both the Resurrection of Christ and our resurrection, but has nothing to say about the immortality of the soul or the intermediate state. The Reformers agreed in anchoring their hope in the resurrection at the last day, while Luther and Tindale who protested most against beginning with Aristotle, were not sure whether the few texts dealing with the intermediate state were to be taken as setting forth the usual condition of the dead, or represented exceptional cases.[20]

With the current movement away from speculation back to a theology of the Word, the emphasis on the hope after death is taken from the nature of man and placed upon the character of God, from the guilty sinner to the gracious covenant of God. Thus, the *anima immortalis* is often rejected, and with it a number of "the theologians of the Word" are affirming that, "Death is God's judgment on the whole man, body and soul, and resurrection is the raising of the whole man to life by the act of God's Agape." [21]

Barth affirms death as separation of the immortal soul from the mortal body but places the emphasis on the Resurrection.[22] The emphasis among the Biblical theologians falls on the Resurrection with the intermediate state treated briefly as a mere parentheses. Thus, Vos gives the intermediate state four pages in two lengthy articles on the Resurrection.[23] In a long article on the Resurrection, Cameron of the Free Church remarks that the immortality of the soul, in its separate abstract form, is not found in Scripture.[24] Stuart Robinson shows that as a dependent existence the soul may cease to exist, if God please, that sin entitles the soul to an immortal hell, and that the separation of

20. Althaus, *D.L.D.*, v.a.pp. 139-141.
21. Nygren, A., *op. cit.* I:176-177; Brunner, *Der Mensch im Widerspruch*, p. 375; Stange, Dunkmann cited Holmstrom, *op. cit.* pp. 298-299; Klieforth, Althaus, *op. cit.* 135-152; K. L. Schmidt Notes on Eschatology; Cf. John Miller, *Are Souls Immortal?*
22. Barth, *Credo*, p. 168.
23. Vos, G., *PTR*, xxvii:1-35; 193-226.
24. Cameron, J. K., *Evangelical Quarterly*, 6:2:158.

the physical from the spiritual is a temporary incident in the creature's existence. The temporary suspension of the bodily functions of the spirit is somewhat analogous to the quiescence of the psychical nature during infancy. The form of eternal existence shall be according to the original type.[25]

With the coming of Platonic speculation into Christian thinking the emphasis shifted to the intermediate state. Origen, whose speculative temperament was like a captive balloon held to earth only by the rule of faith, posited autonomous souls with plenary power of contrary choice both in the pre-temporal and in their post-temporal states. Accordingly, souls fell before they were placed in bodies and continue to rise and to fall hereafter. Augustine regarded a purgatorial fire as not improbable. Gregory the Great made purgatory a dogma to share with penance in atoning for post-baptismal sins.

The Reformation rejected Purgatory, but the Enlightenment and Kant have introduced its equivalent into Neo-Protestantism. For the Deist, Christianity is only the republication of the natural revelation, and whatever in it is new is not true and whatever is true is not new. Accordingly, philosophy perennially finds arguments for the immortality of the soul, but rejects the Resurrection of Christ, since it is a new distinct event, not a mere republication of old truths. Kant reasoned that if I *ought,* then I *can,* but in view of my radical evil it will take an immortality to enable me to become what I ought to be. "Through the work of Ritschl, Kant's interpretation came to play a great and disasterous role in theology." [26] So much so that, "The belief in individual immortality was the only eschatalogy to which one held fast in the nineteenth century." [27] Indeed, leading British theologians of this century tell us that the Reformation erred in surrendering Purgatory and retaining Hell, that irresistible grace implies universal restorationism, or even that, "The resurrection

25. Robinson, S., *Discourses on Redemption,* pp. 383-414
26. Nygren, A., *op. cit.* 1:74.
27. Holmstrom, *op. cit.,* p. 35.

of the body takes place at death, when the spiritual body is liberated from the earthly house of this tabernacle." [28]

Professor A. E. Taylor of Edinburgh shows that the Platonic doctrine of the immortality of the soul is based on the inherent nature of the soul rather than on the character of God, that for it man wins the crown by his own effort rather than by God's gift of grace and that it is "dangerously like a doctrine of the survival of half a personality." [29] Against the universal restorationism of this Neo-Protestant Purgatory, Professor G. T. Thomson of New College has coined this provocative phrase,. "A Church without a Hell isn't worth a damn." [30]

Purgatory. In one form or another Purgatory is affirmed as a part of Catholic eschatology, of Swedenborgian thought, of the Enlightenment moralism, of idealistic evolutionism and of anthroposophic doctrine. Against the doctrine of Purgatory the theology of the Reformation teaches the completion of salvation by the *creative* acts of God, at death and through the Resurrection. Professor Althaus has laid bare the roots of this difference in the great distinctions between Romanist and Reformation theology; in the question of the primacy of God or of man, of theology or of psychology; in the doctrine of a mere kingdom of sin or of original sin, that is, the question of the freedom or of the slavery of the will; and of the meaning of justification.[31]

To the charge of the Romanists that death is "Presbyterian Purgatory," one might reply that even Karl Adam, the leading Romanist theologian on the Continent, admits the possibility of a sanctifying power in the perfect act of love to the Father, with which some die.[32] But such an answer would place one on the Romanist ground of psychology; whereas the Protestant answer is founded not in the psychological, but in the theological, understanding of death. We hold to an objective significance of death,

28. Paterson, W. P., *The Nature of Religion,* p. 481, The Rule of Faith, pp. 321, 353; Hughes, H. M., *Basic Beliefs,* pp. 187, 189, 198; Pilcher C. V., *The Hereafter,* pp. 184-185.
29. Taylor, A. E., *The Christian Hope of Immortality,* p. 16.
30. Cited, *The Calvin Forum,* VI.7.143.
31. Althaus, P., *DLD.*4.204-222.
32. *ibid,* p. 207, citing Adam, K., *Wesen des Kathol,* p. 118.

to a change which occurs at death wrought, not by magic, but by the creative act of God. Purgatory is based on the supposition of a gradual evolution of moral personality wrought by the power and acts of the human will. It sets up a man-made concept of moralism and insists that God limit himself by this moral world order. This "moralistic emphasis upon the central importance of man's strivings and standards really corresponds to the old Ptolemaic astronomy, which made the earth the axle of the universe, all heavenly bodies revolving around it in their courses. . . . When Christianity sounds the note of grace, it is upholding the new and true astronomy of religion." [33]

Moralism begins in a concept of the human personality purifying, lifting, educating itself by acts of the will, perhaps assisted by grace, reaching onward and upward toward the goal of a perfect moral personality. The theological understanding of death recognizes that God's mighty acts of grace are not conformable to the measure erected by man's moral reason, that, as Luther put it, they are "against all reason." It sets up the doctrine of the Word that God is not limited by the slow processes of evolution, but in a moment, in the twinkling of an eye we shall be changed from the old body of carnal subjection and death and made like unto His glorious body (I Cor. xv.52). God can call men in the twelfth hour to a new life of service. He can call the wholly imperfect, like the thief on the Cross, and sovereignly give him at one stroke the full freedom and power for the heavenly life. Further, theology understands that the change at death has for its goal not primarily the perfecting of human personality but the making an end of our rebellious life-will, the putting to final death of the old man of sin that God's will may be perfectly done.

This further means that the difference between a gradual change in Purgatory by man's will and instantaneous changes at death and the resurrection by God's creative acts is rooted in the different understandings of man and his sin. Catholic and

---

33. Moffatt, James, *Grace in the New Testament*, pp. 397-398.

crypto-catholic theories are rooted in individual and social moralism, in the free self-activity of the individual, completed, however, by his ingrafting into a kingdom of sin. Puratory is conceived as a place where the individual is freed at death from
the earthly inheritance and the collective will of other sinners
and carried to a fellowship of those who will help him. But my
sinfulness is deeper than the removal of the body and the social
milieu. Moral evolutionism breaks on the reality of original sin.
Original sin says more than the Kingdom of Sin. "Kingdom of
Sin means: there is a history of sin in the individual and corporate life, a sinful becoming. Original sin means: all history of
sin is only an expression of an already, ever more real, original
sinfulness; all sinful becoming only occurs on the ground of an
original sinful being. Kingdom of Sin means: I must be what
I have become in my own becoming and through my super-
individual becoming. Original sin means: I must be what I
originally am. Kingdom of Sin: through our doing comes a
becoming that establishes a nature. Original sin: our doing
and being is grounded in an original nature. Kingdom of Sin
means: historical connection of humanity in its sinfulness."[34]
Origial sin signifies that I am carnal sold under sin (Rom. vii.14).
I am not, as a free personality, Lord of my sinful being but just
its slave. Moral evolutionism can never lead me out beyond the
limits of this slavery. "Indeed the knowledge of original sin is
the end of moralism." [34] Conversely, in defending Purgatory,
Mohler condemns the Protestant doctrine of original sin with its
servum arbitrium and maintains the "free moral point of view."

Thus the doctrine of Purgatory drives one back ultimately to
the question of the extent of human depravity as a result of the
fall and to the nature of regeneration. The Augustinian holds
that fallen man does not obtain grace by freedom, but freedom
by grace. When Erasmus attacked Luther on his doctrine of
the bondage of the will, Luther said, "I must acknowledge that
in this great controversy you alone have taken the bull by the

---

34. Althaus, P., *DLD*.4.211.

horns." Similarly, Calvin held that the slavery of the will was
the greatest difference separating the Romanists and the Reformers.[35] It is scarcely an accident that the three best theological
minds of the Reformation period found here the crucial distinction. Nor is it an accident that our penetrating thinker, James
Henley Thornwell, describes free-will in fallen man as either
tautology or error and grace as the antithesis of the sovereignty
of man.[36] Coming to this century, Dean Doumergue recognized
the slavery of the will as "the center of the center of the Reformation theology;"[37] President George W. Richards holds "that
the cardinal issue in the Reformation was the conception of the
will of man, whether it is free or bound;"[78] Karl Barth, in his
celebrated *Nein!* finds the architectonic distinction between the
Vatican and the Reformation in the doctrine of human depravity;
and now Althaus in tracing the question of Purgatory to its
ultimate lair comes to *Erbsunde.*[39]

Here we need not human but Divine activism. Only "God's
action through the Gospel places me beyond this my inseparably
sinful reality. In that He awakens faith in me, in that I surrender to the judgment of His grace in Jesus Christ I am no
more I myself, but beyond myself, a new man. This is my salvation: that I believe, in faith I confess myself wholly sinful
and lost and surrender ever again to God's sentence of death."[40]
Faith involves the acceptance of God's gracious judgment of
death over me as the old man (Rom. viii.13; Col. ii.5). All
through the process of sanctification I am called to die unto sin
and to live unto God. I find, however, Satan ever builds up the
old man. As a result "sins can be overcome, but not sin."
According to the original sinfulness of man, he lives not from
God and gives not to God the honor of His God-head. Thus,
in breaking any commandment one is breaking the first com-

---

35. Doumergue, E., *op. cit.* iv.155 with citations from Calvin, Luther and Erasmus.
36. *Thornwell's Collected Writings*, II.381.
37. Doumergue, *ibid.*
38. Richards, G. W., *Creative Controversies in Christianity*, p. 189.
39. Althaus, *D.L.D.*, 4.211.
40. Althaus, *DLD*.4.211.

mandment to honor and love God; and, even in keeping other commandments, the old man is transgressing the first commadment in not giving God the honor and glory of obedience.

Our Christianity is continually derogating from the glory of God the Holy Spirit in applying to man the blessings of Christ's atonement. We are continually taking to ourselves the honor and glory of work that God has done in us. "Because we are something through God, we wish to be something before God instead of being nothing before Him." "The hands of faith are merely receptive hands." Faith is the empty hand which the beggar lifteth to Christ for justification, and this faith is the gift of God. "Faith has no merit in it, for it gives nothing to the God of salvation. It is only a taking. Calvin says that 'faith brings a man empty to God that he may be filled with the blessings of Christ'." [41] But even down to death the old Adam lives and thus the full conversion, the total break, lies behind us only in the sense that it also lies before us.

Two years ago I had the privilege of staying in a very pious Scottish home. When I ventured to comment on this fact, my host promptly assured me that he was not pious, but that his wife had been. He told me something of the period of deep concern followed by several years lived on the flood-tide of Divine assurance vouchsafed to this godly woman, and of the later years marked by a close walk with God. However, when the end came this saint of old Scotia described her soul as leprous all through, waiting the touch of the Great Physician.

In the face of the world, the flesh and the Devil, the old Adam is never destroyed in this life. Here the Christian still cries, "O Wretched man that I am, who shall deliver me from this body of death?" (Rom. vii.24). In accepting Christ we acknowledge that our old man needs to be done away, and in daily repentance we repeat this confession. We are baptized into Christ's death that the body of sin might be done away (Rom. vi.3). Death and the resurrection make evident what has been hidden with Christ in God (Col. iii.3). Death removes the old

41. Ross, *Proceedings of the Calvinistic Congress,* p. 22.

man that is not subject to the law of God, neither indeed can be. As such, Luther called on the Christian to be ready to die that he might cease from sinning, and John L. Giradeau said that the happy thing about dying was that one could not sin any more. James Woodrow remarked that it meant one could not play the fool any more. All three were right. At death, freedom from the fetters of that old man who could not be subject to God breaks into the soul, not through the power of death, but by the might of God on the occasion of death. When we are raised with Christ, the Spirit of Him that raised Jesus, our Lord, gives our whole being the likeness of Jesus Christ.

The most and the best things that we have, said Spurgeon, are these things that are given us by God. The Christian looks for his salvation, not to the power of his will, not to the forces of evolution, but to the free acts of the living God—to Christ's intervention for us, to His heavenly intercession, to the Spirit's work of faith in applying to us that redemption, to the Father's forgiveness and justification of sinners solely for Christ's sake. Accordingly, Althaus properly parallels these *leaps* wrought by God's grace in this life with the instantaneous changes at death and the resurrection. "The redemption from our sinfulness through God's mighty acts in death and the resurrection is for the moralistic consciousness just such an offense as the justification of the sinner through God's 'synthetic judgment,' no more and no less." Logically "the one who will teach Purgatory in some form must also impugn justification; that is clearly possible through a moralistic reinterpretation of its strict meaning." But "he who has understood what justification really is will not affirm the heresy of Purgatory." The same God who justifies the ungodly (Rom. iv.5) does not wait on us to be fitted for Heaven by human, organic, moral purification, but with sovereign grace breaks through our chains when He will.[42]

Since both original sin and actual transgressions involve guilt, the aspect of Purgatory which caused deepest concern to Calvin

42. Althaus, *DLD*.4.221.

and his successors among the Reformed dogmaticians was the doctrine that it was a satisfaction for sins paid after death by the souls of the deceased.[43] The whole thought that fallen man makes satisfaction for his sins either here or hereafter introduces the conception of our merit and places there, rather than in the mercy of God and the work of Christ, the ground of our forgiveness. Indeed, merit is the antithesis of mercy, and human merit the denial of the gratuitous forgiveness of sins *(Institutes* III.iv.25). The rejection of merit and the gracious nature of God's dealings with us are illustrated in the parable of the householder who employed laborers at sundry times a day and paid those who labored only an hour the same as those who had borne the heat of the day. The Father's blessings are of mercy, not merit.

Further, any place for human merits is a derogation from the honor of Christ, whose atonement "is the only satisfaction, expiation and purgation of the sins of the faithful" *(Institutes* III.v. vi). Indeed, "there is nothing more absolutely incompatible with the nature of the Gospel than the idea that man can 'satisfy Divine justice' for his sins." [44] Since this error is at the foundation of the doctrine of Purgatory, Calvin denounces it as a pernicious fiction of Satan that makes void the cross of Christ, insults the divine mercy and weakens our faith. If we are to give Christ the entire and undiminished honour of saving sinners, by transferring to Himself the whole punishment we deserve and thus obliterating our guilt before the throne of God, we must reject Purgatory. Our sins are forgiven *for His Name's sake* (I Jn. ii.12).

B. *The Intermediate State in Scripture.* Since the biblical point of view is corporate rather than individual, eschatological rather than temporal, there are not many texts definitely dealing with the intermediate state; but there are some, and their testimony comforts our hearts in Christ as we stand beside the silent sea.

---

43. *Institutes,* III.vi.vi.; *Thornwell's ollected Writings,* I.423-424.
43. *Institutes,* III.vi.vi.; *Thornwell's Collected Writings,* 1.423-424.

The foundation of all our Christian hope is the gracious Father and the fellowship which He has been pleased to establish with us in Jesus Christ. "God hath given unto us eternal life, and this life is in His Son. He that hath the Son hath the life" (I Jn. v.11-12). God is not a mere Artificer ready to throw away a tool as soon as it is worn, nor a callous militarist concerned only that the ranks be filled. "He is love, that is, He gives Himself, His 'heart' and seeks us, ourselves, not something from us, but us, our 'heart.' He gives Himself as our Father and calls us as His sons. This signifies an indestructible fellowship. In that God gives Himself to me as 'my' God, He raises me to imperishable life." [45] "The certainty of the believer's standing in fellowship with Christ presses on to the thought that this fellowship will not be broken. On the other side of the hour of death, however he may otherwise think his condition may be, the believer expects in any case no separation from Christ."[46] He has been made certain that neither life nor death shall separate him from the love of God which is in Christ Jesus (Rom. viii. 38). Those who hear the Saviour's voice and believe on Him have eternal life (Jn. v.24; vi.47-54; xi.26).

However, when it is shown that fellowship with God reaches beyond death, it is not necessarily evident that the intermediate state is one of conscious life. Some of the texts on which abundant life immediately after death has been posited refer to the Resurrection or are ambiguous. For example, the references to friends receiving one into the eternal tabernacles (Lk. xvi.9) and of reclining with Abraham, Isaac and Jacob in the Kingdom of God (Mt. viii.11; Lk. xiii.28, 29) have been used to prove recognition in the intermediate state;[47] whereas both references are to the final state following the Resurrection.

The God of the Living. (Mt. xxii.32). The Old Testament never conceives of death as natural, but as the punishment for sin. "It conceives man as a unit, and death—the sundering of

---

45. Althaus, *D.L.D.*, v.a.106.
46. Doumergue, E., *Jean Calvin*, IV.344.
47. Smyth, J., *The Gospel of the Hereafter*, p. 125.

soul and body — as the most dreadfully unnatural thing that can befall him." "The body is laid in the grave, and the soul departs to Sheol; but every soul that departs to Sheol is a dead soul as truly as the body that is laid in the grave is a dead body." [48] The Old Testament throws the eye of hope not upon the shades of Sheol, but upon the resurrection of the body. This eschatological view is the key to Jesus' exegesis of God's Word to Moses, " 'I am the God of Abraham, and the God of Isaac, and the God of Jacob.' God is not the God of the dead, but of the living." Too often this is interpreted as meaning that God is the God of the living, since their souls live in the great beyond, and the argument diverted to the immortality of the soul, rather than the resurrection of the body. "But that is simply because we have preferred to be taught by Plato rather than by the Scripture. From the standpoint of the Bible the souls separated from the bodies, though living, are *dead;* they are under the power of death. They are dead, because still enduring the penalty threatened against sin. The Living God is the God of the living, not of the dead; he cannot have proclaimed himself the God of those hopelessly under the power of death, suffering the penalty of sin. If he proclaims himself, therefore, the God of Abraham and Isaac and Jacob, this is proof beyond cavil that Abraham and Isaac and Jacob, whatever temporarily may be their state, belong fundamentally to the realm of the living, not to the realm of the dead, and cannot therefore be permanently held by the bonds of death. And the realm of the living is not the realm where dead souls are, but where living souls are, i.e., souls not suffering disabilities through death. Death cannot have permanent dominion over those whose God is the Living Lord: in the very nature of the case they belong to the Kingdom of Life. They must, therefore, emerge from Sheol and return to the light of life—body and soul alike partaking of the undivided life that belongs to human nature." The Living God has nothing in com-

48. Warfield, B. B., *The Old Testament and Immortality, in The Bible Student,* v.5.246-248, May, 1902.

mon with the shades of Sheol; the God of the living is the fountain of life.[48] The four-fold repetition of the promise, "I will
raise him up at the last day," in the sixth of John (39, 40,44, 54)
shows that our Lord's gaze was fixed upon the Resurrection when
He spoke of eternal life.

The Psalms. Hoping in God the Psalmist looked beyond death
to a future life wrought by his Rock, his Redeemer and the Lifter-
up-of-his-head. One who has learned the way of the heavenly
Shepherd, who has trusted His goodness and mercy through all
the days of this life, cannot conceive of His care ceasing at
death. Beyond the days of this life the sweet singer of Israel
expected to dwell in the house of the Lord forever (Ps. xxiii.6).
Into the empty places in our hearts and homes the words of comfort steal, "Thy lovingkindness is better than life."

Several of the psalms specifically breathe the faith that God
will not leave the psalmist's soul in Sheol.

> "God will redeem my soul from the hand of Sheol;
> For He will receive me." (xlix.15)

> "Nevertheless I am continually with thee:
> Thou hast holden my right hand.
> Thou wilt guide me with thy counsel
> And afterward receive me into glory." (lxxiii.23-24).

> "For thou wilt not leave my soul to Sheol;
> Neither wilt thou suffer thy holy one to see corruption.
> Thou wilt show me the path of life:
> In thy presence is fulness of joy;
> At thy right hand there are pleasures for evermore." (xvi.10-11)

Some scholars apply these passages to the intermediate state,
thus: "It is most probable that in Ps. xlix.15 and lxxiii.24 and
xvi.10, the faith is expressed that the righteous one is received
after death into blessed fellowship with God." [49] However, since
the clearest of these is applied by Peter (Acts ii.25-28) and by
Paul (Acts xiii.35) to the Resurrection of Christ with a conse-

---

49. Otto, R., *op. cit.* p. 240, citing Volz, P., *Die Eschatologie der judischen Gemeinde,*
z.a. p. 117.

quent implication of our Resurrection, it is not certain to the
writer whether these promises of the future life apply exclusively to the Resurrection or both to the Resurrection and to
the intermediate state.

Uranochiliasm. The millenium account of the souls of the
martyrs living and reigning with Christ (Rev. xx.1-20) has been
interpreted by several of the most highly esteemed Presbyterian
scholars as the intermediate state of the righteous dead. It is
held that this vision brings before us the spectacle of the peace
of God's saints gathered in heaven. "The millenium of the
Apocalypse is the blessedness of the saints who have gone away
from the body to be at home with the Lord." [50]

"No better description of it can be framed than in the stately
and majestic language of our Catechism: 'The souls of believers
are at their death made perfect in holiness and do immediately
pass into glory; and their bodies, being still united to Christ do
rest in their graves till the resurrection." [51] This heavenly mil-
lenialism may be described as Uranochiliasm. Modesty is certainly becoming in interpreting the twentieth chapter of Revelation, and particularly in differing with the esteemed scholars who
support this exegesis. However, since the writer has elsewhere
offered a different tentative interpretation of this passage, he
here places it also in the group of passages, whose testimony to the
intermediate state is ambiguous.

The Souls Under The Altar. Earlier in Revelation there is a
vision of the souls of the martyrs underneath the altar, crying
unto the Lord for vengeance upon their persecutors and receiving white robes (vi.9-10). Two things seem to stamp this as a
vision of the intermediate state. The martyrs pray for the coming
of Christ, the final judgment and the perfect blessedness which
they will then receive. In answer they are told to wait until their
fellow servants have also been martyred; meanwhile they are

50. Warfield, B. B., *The Millenium and the Apocalypse*, pp. 22, 18:cf. Richardson, D. W., *The Revelation of Jesus Christ*, pp.170ff.
51. Caldwell, E. C., *The Millenium*, p. 23.

given white robes and a rest which falls short of the consummation.

In Rev. vi.9, the souls are *beneath* the altar as in Rev. vii.15, He that sitteth on the throne spreads his tabernacle *over* them. In the final state the Tabernacle of God is with men (Rev. xxi.3).[52] Crying with a loud voice, praying, hearing the Lord's reply and being clothed with white garments scarcely fits a wholly unconscious state.

Preaching unto the Spirits in Prison. Calvin and Barth find a testimony to the conscious state of the dead in First Peter iii. 18-20. "St. Peter said that Christ preached to those who were in prison for the instruction of the spirits, and not only to the spirits of the believers, to whom he announced forgiveness of sins, but also to the unbelievers to whom he announced confusion." "Whatever may have been the sense, the import of the preaching of Christ, those who heard it, understood; that is, they were not sleeping."[53] Some scholars have sought support for the descent of Christ to the spirits of the departed in I Peter iv.6; Acts ii.31; Eph. iv.9; Rom. x.7; Rev. i.9; Isa. xxiv.22.[54] On the other hand other scholars, such as Hodge, have interpreted the main passage as a preaching of the Spirit of Christ through His prophet Noah. Accordingly, some will classify this as an ambiguous passage. The writer accepts Calvin's intepretation of I Peter iii.18-20, but is not sure of the application of the other passages alleged in support.

However, there are several New Testament passages about which there can be no reasonable ground for ambiguity. Even Althaus admits that Lk. xvi.19-21; xxiii.43; II Cor. v.6; Phil. i.23 represent dying as departing to be immediately with Christ.[55]

Dives and Lazarus. The parable of Dives and Lazarus and the answer to the thief on the Cross furnish specific evidence that Christ's preaching also contains the idea of the individual's

52. Lohmeyer, E., *op. cit.*, pp. 61, 69.
53. Doumergue, E., *Jean Calvin*, IV.344.
54. Smyth, J., *op. cit.* pp. 73ff.; Schmidt, K. L., *Lectures on Romans*, 1938.
55. Althaus, P., *op. cit.*, p. 137

entrance into a conscious state after death. "Immediately after death, Lazarus goes to Abraham's bosom, and the rich man to hell." [56] While his brethren were still living, Dives was in torment and Lazarus in the blessedness of Abraham's bosom. Whether with the ancient doctors one understands this as history, or with more recent commentators as parable, the story represents the souls as living, remembering, speaking, carrying on conversation. By the repose of Abraham's bosom, Calvin understood not idleness, or sleep, but a tranquility and a good assurance of conscience.[57]

The Dying Thief. When the dying thief appealed to the Lord to be remembered when He came in His Kingdom, the Saviour could easily and naturally have passed over the intervening period and promised him a share in the final eschatological order with the coming of the Kingdom of glory. The fact that Jesus' answer goes over and beyond the question and directs attention to the immediacy of Paradise makes the declaration all the more pointed. And the introduction of the statement by the word, *Verily, Truly, Amen,* throws a tremendous emphasis upon it.[56]

"Verily, I say unto thee,

Today shalt thou be with me in Paradise" (Lk. xxiii.43).
Here the new convert is promised fellowship with His Lord not only in some distant age in which the Kingdom shall come in glory but on the day of his death. The penitent thief went immediately to be with Christ in Paradise. "How gloriously it is therefore transfigured with the bliss of heaven where he is." [59]

Departing to be With Christ. For Paul's death means overcoming the separation from Christ which the fleshly existence signifies and coming to Christ (II Cor. v.6ff; Phil. i.23). In the paragraph containing the former of these passages Paul compares the three possible states of the Christian. He would rather live

---

56. Otto, R., *op. cit.* p. 52.
57. Doumergue, E., *op. cit.*, IV.344.
58. The *Amen-Logia* of the Gospels furnish an interesting parallel to *the Faithful Sayings* of the Pastoral Epistles.
59. Warfield, B. B., *The Bible Student* v. 5. 247

until the Parousia of Christ and receive His resurrection body, the building from God, put on over his present body. The thought is the same as that in I Cor. xv.53, where Paul speaks of the corruptible body putting on incorruption, only there the subject of the act is the present earthly body, here the subject is the incorporeal part of the believer (II Cor. v.2). The believer who is living at the return of Christ will *put on* his heavenly tabernacle *over* his earthly house, or his earthly corruptible body will be *clothed upon* by his incorruptible body.[60] However, Paul fears that this blessed lot may not be his. He fears dying before the Parousia since it will mean the loss of his body and a consequent condition of nakedness. If he cannot have the superlative thing of putting on his eschatological body over the present one, then Paul is willing to take the second best and to endure being absent from the body, because that means being at home with the Lord. Thus in Paul's scale of values the Parousia with the glorified body is first; the condition to which he goes through death and the burial of this body is second, for the nakedness from death to the Parousia is more than compensated by being at home with the Lord. Similarly, in Philippians he says that to depart and be with Christ is much better for him than to abide in the flesh; however, it may be more needful for the Church at Philippi for him to continue his life work (Phil. i.21-24).

"In II Cor. v. the whole train of Paul's reasoning is based on the thought that there will be a differentiation in feeling (that is, a perceptible difference in the self-reflective consciousness) in the state after death. Whether he feels clothed with a body or feels naked will be an object of perception to him. To the unconscious dead there is not and cannot be any distinction between the one state and the other: all things are alike to them. Even though only the minimum of what appears desirable to Paul, i.e., to die before the Parousia, is in store for him, still he expresses the assurance that to be in an 'unclothed' (naked) state at home with the Lord will be a cause of contentment, and

60. Vos, G., *PTR.*, xxvii.210.

the looking forward to this provisional minimum a reason for good courage, which it could not be without the expectation of consciousness in the post-mortem state. Similiarly, in Phil. i.23 the having departed and being with Christ is estimated as 'very far better.' To be sure, the estimate is formed in his present mind, but the whole contrast of 'worse' or 'better' loses its significance if consciousness, the only standard of difference in appraisal, be denied." [61] The anxiety concerning the loss of his body is pressed into the background through the certainty that dying brings him in any case to be with Christ, and union with Christ is an addition to life incomparably outweighing the loss of life in the laying aside of the body.[62] For me to live is Christ, said Paul, and to die is gain, for to depart and be with Christ is very far better. Christ is the life (Jn. xiv.6), the Living One (Rev. i.18), who hath life in Himself (Jn. v.26) and in whom is life (Jn. i.4). He came that we might have life and have it more abundantly (Jn. x.10'. Accordingly, being at home with Him must mean life even in death.

The Sleep of Death. How then shall one interpret the frequent descriptions of the dead, especially of the departed believers, as a sleep? The Old Testament commonly speaks of the dead as asleep with their fathers, a phrase that perhaps rests on a conception of compartments in Sheol. In Daniel those asleep are to awake, some to everlasting life and some to everlasting shame and contempt. In the apocrypha and apocalypses, sleep is used of the righteous dead with the implication that they will awake to a blessed resurrection. The New Testament describes the dead in Christ as having fallen asleep in Jesus with the connotation that they will wake to a blessed resurrection (Acts vii.60; I Thess. iv.13,14,15; I Cor. viii.39; xi.30; xv.6,20,51).

In view of the paucity of bibical examples of conscious life after death, Luther interpreted the condition of the dead generally as a deep, dreamless sleep without consciousness or appre-

61. Vos, *P.T.R.* xxvii.9.
62. Althaus, P., *op. cit.*, p. 137.

hension. The death sleep, though deeper than earthly sleep, is like it in that in sleep we are not living and yet living. "We shall sleep until He comes and knocks on the grave and speaks: 'Doctor Martin, stand up.' Then in a moment I shall be raised up and be eternally happy with Him." To this general conception of awakening in the morning without knowing what has occurred during his night's sleep, Luther admits exceptions. God can awaken the sleepers as He did Moses and Elijah who appeared at the Transfiguration, and the story of Lazarus shows that the souls of the dead are not always asleep.[63]

On the other hand Calvin interprets the several cases of biblical record not as exceptional, but as typical, written for our admonition. For him, the word sleeping is only applicable to the body, from which also comes the word *dormitory,* a place for sleeping and *cemetery* a place for burial. "When one accompanies the human corpse to the *cemetery,* he speaks Greek. If he speaks Latin, he ought to say he carries it to the *dormitory* to sleep." [64] The figure of sleeping is a description of what happens to the person in terms of the body. So far as the earthly bodily life is concerned the dead are asleep, out of contact with the world. The original coloring of the words for sleep has largely been lost by attrition and has come to mean little more than to be placed in the recumbent position in the grave. "When even pre-Christian paganism does not universally ascribe to *koimenos* or *kekoimenos* a sleep or rest, in the sense of *unconsciousness,* we may not assume that this ancient term was saved out of semi-oblivion into a new literalness for the Christian faith." [65] The texts cited show that the state of death is a state of consciousness capable of the sensation of comfort or discomfort according to the presence or absence of the body and thus differs from an absolute quiescence.

---

63. Althaus, P., *op. cit.* 139-41.
64. Doumergue, E., *op. cit.,* p. 343.
65. Vos, G., *PTR,* xxvii.8-9.

The figure of repose indicates peace, security, confidence, blessed rest. Christ is present with the souls of the pious and receives them into paradise where they enjoy consolation. "The blessed assemblage of holy spirits being called the bosom of Abraham teaches us that it is enough for us at the close of this pilgrimage to be received by the common father of the faithful and to participate with him in the fruit of his faith." [66]

Further, Calvin holds that sepulture is not a mere human invention but has been introduced by God as a testimony to life eternal and the resurrection. "When men are buried they are put into the earth, as in a ward, until they are raised at the last day; thus the sepulchre is to us like a mirror of the resurrection." [66] The martyr who is burned at the stake gives his body as a testimony to Christ; the Christian who dies in a quiet bed ought to commend his body to loved ones that his sepulchre may testify his hope of the Resurrection. Hence cremation is ordinarily to be rejected, not because it is beyond the power of God to raise the body that has been incinerated, but because it destroys the imagery of the resurrection.

Again the imagery of sleep carries a special sense of tenderness reminiscent of the ordinary act of putting a child to bed with loving hands.

> "And, friends, dear friends,—when it shall be
> That this low breath is gone from me,
> And round my bier ye come to weep,
> Let one, most loving of you all,
> Say 'Not a tear must o'er her fall!
> He giveth His beloved, sleep."
>   —Elizabeth Barrett Browning.

In how much detail, then, do the Scriptures and necessary inferences therefrom illumine the present condition of those whom God giveth sleep? The first thing signalized is memory. The dying thief appealed to the Saviour to remember him. Abraham said to Dives, "Son, remember." Dives remembered both his thoughtless brothers and his own thoughtlessness of Lazarus.

---

66. *Institutes* III.xxv.6; Doumergue, *op. cit.* p. 344.

The saints under the altar remember their persecutors. Thus, man carries his memories with him into the life beyond, to comfort or to plague him.

Augustine associated intellect and love with memory as the three great functions of the soul. Dives exhibits reasoning power and concern for his brethren as he pleads for one to be sent to them from the dead, to do what Moses and the prophets have not done for them. One cannot think of Moses and Elijah conversing with the Saviour on the Mount about the decease which He was shortly to accomplish at Jerusalem without attributing to them some intellectual apprehension of the importance of the Redeemer's work and a profound love to Him on that account.

God is the Father of whom every family in heaven and earth is named, and His is the Father's house. He has quickened us with Christ that in the ages to come He may unfold to us the grace of His fatherly kindness in Christ Jesus (Eph. ii.4-7). We go to be with Christ, and one can at least infer that, in proportion as we see Him as He is, we shall love Him as we ought.

> "O Christ, He is the fountain,
>   The deep, sweet well of love.
> The streams of earth I've tasted;
>   More deep I'll drink above."

And since death was to gather the dying saint to his people, it may be inferred that the tenderness of the Father's love includes in the home above some spiritual recognition of those ties which mean so much to us here.

The promise of the dying thief and Paul's assurance that he would go to be with Christ include the recognition of the Saviour. On the Mount of Transfiguration, Moses and Elijah were recognized. Hebrews speaks of our coming to the spirits of just men made perfect (xii. 22-23). References to Moses and to the Patriarchs being gathered each *unto his people* and of David's going to be with his departed son have been understood as indications that the dying believers go to be especially with their

departed loved ones, or even that these loved ones may often
be God's messengers to take them "to Abraham's bosom." As a
pastor, I witnessed a death at which, amid signs of God's sanctifying and forgiving grace, the dying saint spoke of the presence of departed loved ones in radiant glory. The late S. J.
Cartledge looked for "Reunion and recognition of friends and
loved ones gone before." [67] Fanny Lorrester wrote,

> "There loving eyes are to the portals straying;
> There arms extend a wanderer to fold."

The Son of Man speaks of the hosts of heaven as *his angels*
(Mt. xiii.41; xvi.27) and Hebrews (i.14) describes them as ministering spirits doing service for the heirs of salvation. The
angels carry Lazarus to Abraham's bosom (Lk. xvi.22). Since
angels rejoice over the sinner that repenteth (Lk. xv.10) and witness the believer's fidelity to his charge (I Tim. v.21), it is easy
to infer that they often welcome the pilgrim of the night into the
gates of light. As the Reverend William Ross was preaching in
Glasgow for a friend who was being married, he suddenly
declared, "The hosts of God are twenty thousand. This room is
full of angels, I see them all around. The Lord has laid His
hand on me." And so this man of God died and was buried in
Edinburgh.[68]

Whether or not the spirits of loved ones that have gone on
before or the angels of God be so employed in a particular case,
one remembers the Saviour's promise to the dying thief, His
assurance that He would come again and receive His disciples
finally into the many mansions and the Apostle's conviction that
he would depart to be with Christ. We believe that He is the
Lord of the dead as well as of the living and that we go to be
with Him.

> "War, far away, like bells at ev'ning pealing,
> The voice of Jesus sounds o'er land and sea,
> And laden souls by thousands meekly stealing,
> Kind Shepherd, turn their weary steps to Thee."

67. Cartledge, S. J., *The Drama of Redemption*, p. 124.
68. Account given by Principal John Macleod of Edinburgh.

The Revelation given to John shows the four and twenty elders worshipping Him that sitteth upon the Throne and the Lamb (iv.10-11; v.8-10). The souls of the martyrs are beneath the altar as though their martyrdoms were a sacrifice of praise and thanksgiving, and clothed in robes whitened in the blood of the Lamb they offer worship service in the temple of God night and day (vi.9-11; vii.14-15). The worship of their spirits is a worship in spirit and in truth. Nor is it reasonable to assume that the heavenly visitants failed to worship the majesty of the Lord Jesus when He received from God the Father honor and glory in the holy mount (II Peter i.16-18).

One might summarize this discussion of Christ's Lordship over both the dead and the living by a series of theses, but a better testimony to our faith is to be found in the words with which Rev. E. H. Hamilton of Suchowfu, China, has described the martyrdom of Rev. John Vinson of Haichow, November 3, 1931.

> "Afraid? Of what?
> To feel the spirit's glad release?
> To pass from pain to perfect peace,
> The strife and strain of life to cease?
>   Afraid — of that?
>
> "Afraid? Of what?
> Afraid to see the Saviour's face,
> To hear His welcome, and to trace
> The glory gleam from wounds of grace?
>   Afraid — of that?
>
> "Afraid? Of what?
> A flash — a crash — a pierced heart;
> Darkness — light — O Heaven's art!
> A wound of His a counterpart!
>   Afraid — of that?
>
> "Afraid? Of what?
> To do by death what life could not —
> Baptize with blood a stony plot,
> Till souls shall blossom from the spot?
>   Afraid — of that?"

CHAPTER V.

CHRIST'S RESURRECTION AND OURS

II Cor. iv.14.

● *"The Gospel of the Resurrection is alike the token of our apostleship and the test of our sincerity."* S. M. Zwemer.

I Cor. xv.20; II Cor. iv.14. Acts iv.2.

I. The Ressurection in the Primitive Preaching.

Nothing is more characteristic of the primitive preaching than its emphasis upon the Resurrection.

Paul's major epistles, imprisonment epistles, evangelistic appeal.

Primitive preaching prior to Paul.

Our Lord's own teaching.

II. The Resurrection in the Divine Revelation.

The Resurrection is a revealed doctrine, the credibility of which is vindicated by integrating it into the whole of revealed truth.

The Resurrection and the age to come.

The Resurrection and the Incarnation.

The Resurrection and Justification.

The Resurrection and the Spirit.

The Resurrection and Christian Theism.

III. The Resurrection in Nature and Attestation.

No a priori doctrine of the Resurrection, its nature revealed in its attestation.

A. The Resurrection is objective. Witnesses were not believers in the Resurrection, but were driven from unbelief to faith. The Empty Tomb. The Gospel of the Forty Days.

B. The Resurrection is corporeal.
  Christ's body according to the Gospels and Acts.
  Paul a Pharisee not a Platonist.
  The Spiritual body distinguished from the natural not from the physical. The Spiritual man not a ghost. I Cor. ii.14-15.
  The risen Christ exists "in the body of His glory."
  God does not capitulate to Satan even in the things of the body.

C. The Resurrection is glorious.
  A Change as mighty as the Resurrection.
  Raised in Glory. Raised in Incorruption. Raised in Power. Raised a Spiritual Body.

I. THE RESURRECTION IN THE PRIMITIVE PREACHING.

Nothing is more characteristic of the primitive preaching than its emphasis on the Resurrection of Christ. Second only to this emphasis on His Resurrection is the connection of His with the believers' Resurrection. "Paul ever speaks of the Resurrection of Christ in connection with our Resurrection." [1] When Paul faced doubts as to our Resurrection, he answered them by appeal to the first principles of the Christian preaching. "If Christ is preached that he hath been raised from the dead, how say some among you that there is no resurrection of the dead?" (I Cor. xv.12). Christ was not only delivered up for our offenses, He was also raised for our justification (Rom. iv.25). At the heart of Paul's great doctrine of the indwelling of the Holy Spirit is his conviction that if the Spirit of Him that raised up Jesus Himself from the dead dwell in you, then He that raised up Jesus, the Messiah, the representative of His people, from the dead will make the indwelling Spirit accomplish for you what

---

1. Schmidt, K. L., Lectures on Eschatology, University of Basel, Winter Semester, 1937-38.

He did for Jesus in His Resurrection. What God did for Jesus He will do for the believer (Rom. viii.-11).[2] "Christ's Resurrection is the same in character as that of His people." [3]

The imprisonment epistles teach that regeneration is being raised with Christ (Eph. ii.1-6), that knowing the power of His Resurrection is the way to attain unto our Resurrection from the dead (Phil. iii.10-11), and that our being bound up with Christ in His Resurrection is the basis for admonition to high thinking and holy living (Col. iii:1-2). Galatians begins by defining God the Father with reference to Jesus Christ and His Resurrection, somewhat as First Peter attributes our faith and hope to the instrumentality of His Resurrection (i.3, 21).

When Paul trims his evangelistic appeal down to its bare bones, it is a call to believe in the heart that God hath raised Jesus from the dead and to confess His lordship with the lips (Rom. x.9-10); I Cor. xii.3). The ABC's of the Christian Gospel are that Christ died for our sins according to the Scriptures and that He hath been raised on the third day according to the Scriptures (I Cor. xv.1-8). This is the message Paul preached first of all to the Corinthians, even as it is the message he also received (vs. 1-2). The repetition of the same verb to describe the reception of the Gospel by the Corinthians and by the Apostle and the close parallelism of the thought carries the implication that this summary of the Gospel was the Creed of the Damascus Church which was imparted to Paul at his baptism. It seems to have been the pre-Pauline creed of the Church in Rome (Rom. vi.3-4). Its Aramaic denotation of Peter as Cephas, and its listing of the responsible apostolic and mass-disciple testimony suggest that it is the primitive Jerusalem creed. Both in the Corinthian and in the Roman passage Paul is connecting Christ's Resurrection with ours.

Paul's reference to his reception of this Gospel shows that the Resurrection of Christ was central in the primitive preaching prior to Paul's conversion, as is abundantly clear in Acts. In appointing a successor to Judas Iscariot the prime requirement

---

2. Vos, G., *The Pauline Doctrine of the Resurrection, PTR,* XXVII, p. 28.
3. Cameron, J. K., *The Evangelical Quarterly,* 6:2:149.

for an Apostle is that he be a witness to the Resurrection of Jesus (Acts i.22; cf. I Cor. ix.1-2; xv.8-9). The fact and the attestation of the Resurrection of Christ is the great message of Pentecost (Acts ii.24-32), as it was in the sermons following (x.40; xiii.30-37). The Sanhedrin was troubled because the Apostles proclaimed in Jesus the Resurrection from the dead (iv.2). Before the Jerusalem Council, Peter maintained that he was mainly called in question for his proclamation of the Resurrection of the dead; and later declared that it was in the name of the crucified Jesus whom God had raised from the dead that they performed the miracle of healing the cripple at the Beautiful Gate of the Temple (Acts iv.2, 10, 33;v.30). Somewhat later Paul defended himself at Athens for preaching this doctrine (Acts xvii.18, 31-32). Indeed, a comprehensive summary of the "oral gospel" is this: "with great power gave the apostles witness of the Resurrection of the Lord Jesus; and great grace was upon them all" (iv.33).

The Gospels carry this preaching of the Resurrection back to our Lord, Himself. They not only give the cryptic word about destroying this Temple and raising it again in three days (Jn. ii. 19-22; Mt. xxvi.61; Mk. xiv.58); and the sign of the prophet Jonas (Mt. xii.39-41; Lk. xi.29-32; cf. Mt. xvi.4); but as well Jesus' explicit teaching of His sufferings, death and rising again. There are four such accounts in Mark in the period following Peter's confession (viii.31; ix.9; ix.31; x.34) and a reference thereto by the young man in white at the tomb (xvi.6-7). Four of these references are repeated in Matthew (xvi.21; xvii.23; xx.19; xxviii.6) and three of them in Luke (ix.32; xviii.33; xxiv.6-8), the last being a peculiarly clear reminder of the Galilean testimony that the Son of Man would be crucified and the third day rise again. Each of the Gospel endings and the opening of Acts presents Jesus' appearing to, conversing with His disciples, and by the many infallible proofs of His risen presence leading them from unbelief to acceptance of His Resurrection. Indeed, these summaries in the Gospels both before and after the Resurrection, the sermons in Acts, and Paul's accounts of "the

148 Christ — The Hope of Glory

oral gospel" (1 Cor. xv.3-4;12;i.17, 18, 23; I Thess. i.10; II Tim. ii.8; Gal. iii.1) have convinced the critics that the Passion and Resurrection Preaching was the most primitive form in use in the early Church and constitutes the longest and the most primitive unit in the Gospels.

The Saviour did not isolate Himself and His Resurrection from that of His people. In comforting Martha and Mary on the death of Lazarus, Jesus said, "thy brother shall rise again." Martha answered, "I know that he shall rise again in the Resurrection at the last day." Jesus said to her, "I am the resurrection and the life, he that believeth in me, even though he were dead, yet shall he live, and whosoever liveth and believeth on me shall never die." (Jn. xi.23-26). On another occasion He testified: "All that the Father giveth me shall come unto me, and him that cometh to me I will in no wise cast out. For I came down from heaven, not to do mine own will, but the will of Him that sent me, and this is the Father's will which hath sent me that of all which He hath given me I should lose nothing, but should raise it up again at the last day. And this is the will of Him that sent me, that every one which seeth the Son, and believeth on Him, may have everlasting life: and I will raise him up at the last day" (Jn. vi.37-40). Jesus referred to the Resurrection in refutation of the Sadducees who disbelieved it, in comforting Martha and Mary on the death of their brother, in sending out His disciples to "the lost sheep of the house of Israel," in preparing the disciples for His death and departure from them, in assuring John the Baptist of His being the long-expected Messiah, and in His announcement of the final judgment and the end of the world.[4] This great resurrection emphasis is likewise characteristic of First Peter (i.3, 21), of the benediction in Hebrews (xiii.20), and of the Revelation which the Lord Jesus Christ made of Himself from Heaven (Rev. i.18; ii.8).

Thus, "the fact of the Resurrection assumed vast importance in the estimation of the founders of the Christian Church."[5] If

---

4. Cameron, J. K., *The Resurrection of Christ, Evangelical Quarterly*, 6.2.152.
5. *Ibid*, p. 151.

Christ be not risen, Christian preaching and Christian faith are both vain, Christian testimony is false, believers are still in unforgiven sins, loved ones who have fallen asleep in Christ have perished (I Cor. xv.14-18). Finding in the Resurrection a central theme of the Bible and a point of crystallization for its theology, Professor Walter Kunneth presented Christian theology as the Theology of the Resurrection.[6] President Francis L. Patton says, "It is upon this cornerstone of Resurrection fact that men have built the cathedral of Christian faith" [7] Canon Gore "cannot find anything which can justify the belief that the Catholic faith in Jesus, as St. Paul and St. John first taught it, could be maintained apart from the belief in His corporal Resurrection." [8] Professor Karl Barth thanks God that the old Scots Confession of 1560 was a good confession at this point, for "a confession that was weak at this point would not be a Christian confession." [9]

In the hands of men like Irenaeus the Resurrection kept the Christian or theocentric viewpoint from being swept into a flood of Hellenic anthropocentricity — preserved God's great *agape* from degenerating into a Platonic *eros*.*

II. The Resurrection in the Divine Revelation.

A. *Doctrine of Revelation*. The prominence of the Resurrection in Christian preaching suggests that it is definitely a doctrine of Revelation. It is a doctrine which our Lord found in God's Revelation of Himself to Moses at the burning bush (Mt. xxii. 31-32; Mk. xii.26-27; Lk. xx.37-38) and which every part of the New Testament sounds in our ears. On the other hand, "It is a matter also that is almost unknown among the heathen. A few passages have been discovered which may seem to discountenance universal ignorance of it among them. There are common to men glimmerings of light as to the immortality of the soul, but such in regard to the reviving of the dead body are wanting.

---

6. Kunneth, W., *Theologie der Auferstehung,* 1933.
7. Patton, F. L., *Fundamental Christianity*, p. 240.
8. Gore, Charles, in *A New Commentary on Holy Scripture.*
9. Barth, K., *The Knowledge of God and the Service of God.* p. 88.
* Nygren, A., *Agape and Eros.*

What exceptions there may appear to be may be due to tradition, or some rays of the light of Revelation that may have penetrated the general darkness. Resurrection is a fact that unassisted reason could not have discovered. There is much, indeed, connected with the matter that might seem to warrant unbelief in it on the part of men who are not in possession of Revelation." [10] Apart from Revelation, "This truth is too difficult to command the assent of the human mind. To enable faith to surmount so great an obstacle, the Scripture supplies us with two assistances; one consists in the similitude of Christ, the other in the omnipotence of God." [11] So great is the opposition of natural reason to the Resurrection, that the difficulties of accepting it appear insuperable, unless and until it is presented in its true context as an essential and integral part of revealed truth. In the Temple of Rationalism, the Resurrection has ever appeared as an extraneous piece of furniture; in the house of Naturalism it is an alien child; only in the Church of the Word is it the head of the corner; only in the household of Christian faith is it *das liebestes Kind*.

The Kantian approaches the study of the Resurrection of Jesus with the assumption that knowledge within the limits of pure reason is only of phenomena. Under this limitation "the only facts in question are the empty tomb and the appearances," or, the report of the appearances. In interpreting these phenomena, the historian of this school explains them in terms of ordinary life which means he explains the Resurrection away. The Enlightenment philosophers who banish the supernatural from history and present man and his development in absolute contrast to the Biblico-theological view,[12] frankly admit that the evidence for the Resurrection of Jesus is very strong; and then declare that were it a hundred times stronger any hypothesis were better than the acceptance of an actual Resurrection since that

10. Cameron, J. K., *ibid*, p. 160.

11. *Institutes*, III.xxv.3.

12. Troelsch E., Article *Enlightenment*, in *New Schaff-Herzog Encyclopedia;* Article *Historiography* in Hastings' *Encyclopedia of Religion and Ethics.*

contradicts their conceptions of the laws of physics and chemistry.[13]

From the Christian standpoint we cannot agree that the Resurrection is to be rejected because it does not fit the naturalistic canons of human reason, for man as a totality is fallen, and his reason is no perfect criterion. Even in the realm of general knowledge, the Enlightenment may not boast, "We are the people, and wisdom will die with us." According to the Gestalt Psychology, the total configuration is to interpret the part, and the consummation the earlier stages. Thus any element in the Christian picture such as the Resurrection is not an isolated segment, but a sector of the whole circle, and the resurrection world of God is to illumine the present age. According to the Phenomenological Psychology one needs primarily to strip off the excrescences until one grips the essence of the matter. To the Christian believer, "the essence of Christianity is in the Resurrection," [14] for the Creator has shined in his heart to give the light of the knowledge of His glory in the face of the Risen Christ. Since, "In His light we see light," "the Resurrection like the Atonement, is a fact which may be apprehended only by Revelation" and "the knowledge of the Resurrection is the knowledge of the Risen Lord." [15]

Hence, properly to weigh the Resurrection one ought to integrate it into the warp and woof of the Biblical structure and see how this integration affects each and every part and parcel of the Christian revelation. Then having seen in the Resurrection a deed of God in truly Divine dimensions that is of the essence of the Christian configuration let him evaluate the Christian revelation as a whole, compare it with every other great world and life view and thus Decide. The Resurrection cannot be fairly rejected because it does not fit a world and life view based on premises antagonistic to the Christian picture. Let it be seen in its own context and principle arrayed against principle. It

13. Lake and Rashdall as cited by Orr, J., *The Resurrection of Jesus*, p. 46. cf. D. C. Macintosh in Harvard Register, XXXIX:14:36.
14. Kraemer, H., in I.M.C., 1:283.
15. Bromily, G. W., *The Evangelical Quarterly*, 12:2:107-108.

is our confidence that to those who will to do the will of the God
of truth, the resurrected Christ will reveal Himself as He did
to Paul, to Gilbert West, to Lord Lyttleton, to Paul E. More,
and to a host of others.

In particular, the Resurrection of Christ should be integrated
with the new Divine eschatological order with a Biblical theism
which envisages the regeneration of soul, body and nature, and
with the Christian plan of salvation.

The Resurrection and the Age to Come. The miracles of the
Bible are not isolated phenomena. They are the first rays of the
eschatological dawn, the breaking into this evil age of the age
which is to come. In this present world they show by way of
model or example the might and extent of Christ's power of
palingenesis. Moreover the Resurrection is the centrum through
which this organic re-creation is to be accomplished.[16] "The
Resurrection, with which the new eternal world breaks in, has
already begun: Christ is risen." [17]

In tasting death for every man and in rising from the dead
Christ destroyed him that had the power of death, that is, the
Devil, delivered men from the fear of death, and brought them
into a new world and life view in which the final word is not
DEATH, but LIFE. Since Christ has shown Himself stronger
than the rushing avalanche of death, all that are in Christ shall
be made alive. Even now the power of His Resurrection is
pressing into the arena of time, as the winds from that coming
aeon of holiness fan our sin-scorched brows.

The primitive apostles proclaimed the Resurrection of Jesus
as the guarantee of the Resurrection of believers (Acts iv.2).
For Paul, Christ's Resurrection is the first-fruits, the beginning
of the one Resurrection process. Since all things are summed up
in Christ, the Head, the Christian has been raised with Christ
and his citizenship is even now in heaven. In principle, the Body
is even now what it will be in the age to come, but the living
Christian is in heaven wholly and entirely in the risen Christ, his

---

16. Kuyper, A., *Encyclopedia of Sacred Theology*, pp. 422-424.
17. Althaus, *D.L.D.*, v.a.17.

Head (Phil. i.6; ii.16; iii.20; Eph. i.14, 21; iv.15, 30; ii.6, 13).

The Resurrection is the key to the Christian chart of the ages. The Greek sees two worlds side by side or one above another, the world of flesh or flux and the world of idea, spirit, or reason. In distinction from this static and non-successive view, the Old Testament is dynamic, consecutive, historical, a present age to be succeeded by an age to come. The Greek is vertical, the Jewish is horizontal. "The time factor is essential in Judaism's view." [18] However, as the New Testament unfolded the Old Testament view, the eschatological age began with the Resurrection of Christ and co-exists with the old age. This adds a vertical to the horizontal conception, but does not make it static. The Risen Christ, as Lord of the Spirit, is projecting the future age into this age, claiming for it the domination of the Christian's life and preparing for the realization of the age to come.

THE TWO WORLDS, AGES OR AEONS

(1) Greek Conception
World of the Spirit or Reason

World of Flesh or Matter

---

(2) The Old Testament Perspective
This age or world   The age or world to come

---

(3) The New Testament Presentation
The world to come
realized in principle

Fall | Resurrection of Christ | (in Heaven) | Parousia | New Heaven and New Earth Future age and world realized in solid existence.

This age or world   (on earth)

---

18. Flew, R. N., *Jesus and His Church*, p. 43.
cf. Vos, G., P.T.R. xxvii. p. 440; Hodge, C. W., Jr., Lectures on *History of Doctrine of the Holy Spirit*.

Thus the Resurrection is "the living bond of union between this and the coming age," "the center which gives meaning to the whole occurence of saving history." "As connected links in a chain which mutually condition and define one another, the great acts of salvation are united *sub specie resurrectionis*: the forgiveness of sins and salvation, reconciliation and renewal, Creation and the Parousia, the original condition and the Resurrection life." [19] When these acts are so linked, they cannot easily be changed into a timeless symbol of a constant intention on God's part in the sense of idealism. Hence, the Resurrection becomes the hallmark of a Christian theology.

The Resurrection and The Incarnation. In 1906 Albert Schweitzer isolated the Resurrection from the Parousia and dismissed the Resurrection as a mere illusion and the historical Jesus as mere man. In 1928, Wilhelm Michaelis, fitting together the Messiahship, the Parousia, the Resurrection and Pentecost, freed the eschatological character of salvation from the limits imposed by the Enlightenment and legitimized the Parousia expectation in Christian faith and hope. When the proclamation of the Resurrection was valued as unreal, an eschatological Jesus appeared either as unhistorical or as deluded. When the Resurrection signifies the breaking in of a new dimension of reality, the risen, living Lord becomes the warrant for all the ultimate significance of life.

Christ can never be rightly understood as a mere child of history, as the emergence of just another term in the historical series, within and explicable by the processes of the world. He can never be smuggled in under Evolution. "It is nonsense to suggest that the world itself can produce its Lord. The world can produce only what is like it, not one who stands above it." [20] Instead of moving from History to Revelation one ought to come from Revelation to History, for only in the light of Revelation does life cease to be a cyclic process and become a meaningful movement to a goal. "The understanding of history has its

19. Kunneth, W., *ThdAuferst* summarized by F. H. *op. cit.* 385.
20. Schaeder, E

ground not in history, but in Christ." "Through the central significance of the Resurrection of Jesus, history is qualified as
saving history." [21] In the fact that the Risen One is the Crucified lies the saving significance of the Cross, in fellowship with
the Risen Lord the saving effect of the death on Golgotha becomes
a present reality, and the Parousia a legitimate hope of glory.

Thus the question of the Resurrection is, *What think ye of
Christ?* Because one cannot believe in the Resurrection of an
ordinary man, it does not follow that he cannot believe in the
Resurrection of Christ. Since He was like no other person, the
presumption against miracle in His case is reversed. "Far from
its being inconceivable that He should have been raised, it is
inconceivable that He should not have been raised; such a one
as He could not possibly have been holden of death." [22] The
saving significance of *the Word made flesh* carries with it the
actuality and the saving significance of His Resurrection. The
Easter Message "ascribes the fact that Jesus Christ has risen
from the dead entirely to His divinity." [23] "Jesus Christ is the
colossal stumbling-block, the colossal miracle, beside whom
everything else is light as the dust of the balance." [24] Every
Christian fact proceeds from and is authenticated by the central
miracle of the Incarnation. From the Incarnation as the centrum
of this entire central action the Resurrection is an immediate
result. The Resurrection is not the Resurrection of a mere man
but of the Lord Jesus Christ, the Saviour in whom alone our
souls find pardon and peace. A thousand miracles attest His
Divine person. Death may not be the end of that human nature
which He has assumed. When He, the Eternal, has entered the
arena of Time, the issue cannot be in doubt. Life, life eternal,
not death, must triumph. And, blessed be His Name, He is the
Messiah, the head and representative of a people given Him of
the Lord. Thus His Resurrection is the sign of a power which

21. Kunneth, W., *op. cit.;* cf. Barth, *K. D.* I.2.64.
22. Machen, J. G., *What is Faith?* p. 133.
23. Barth, K., *The Knowledge of God and the Service of God.,* p. 88.
24. Thomson, G. T., *Calvinistic Congress,* 1938, p. 76-77.

shall ultimately establish a society of persons in which the moral law will shine as resplendent in righteousness as the starry hosts shine with celestial brightness.

The Resurrection and Justification. The Christ whose Resurrection is presented in the Bible is that One who alone may be expected to bridge the awful gap between the Holy One of Israel and guilty man. A realization of His justice, His righteousness and His holiness, and of our wicked violation of His law, our rebellion against His sovereign majesty requires precisely this Mediator if God is to be just and justify the ungodly. The Resurrection of Christ is immediately related to and directly integrated with the working out of this great salvation. Paul presents Christ's Resurrection and His death for sin as forming two constituent and indissoluably connected parts of the work of Redemption. The simple meaning of Rom. iv.24 is that Christ was delivered up to death on account of our trespasses and raised on account of our justification. Our penalty was completely laid on Him and in His completed death our justification was virtually secured so that "it needed only the passing of death from off Him and the consequent substitution of life for death to declare this." By suspending the forces of death operating on Him, God declared that the full penalty of death had been paid; by His Resurrection God annulled the sentence of condemnation. In the fifteenth of First Corinthians the Apostle begins: "If Christ be not raised, your faith is vain; ye are yet in your sins;" but in the light of Resurrection as the final removal of the penalty for sin imposed by the Law, he concludes, "O death, where is thy sting, O grave, where is thy victory? Thanks be unto God who giveth us the victory through Jesus Christ our Lord." The problem of the Divine righteousness is the great question with Paul. In Rom. iv.24, 25, justifying faith is directed toward God as the one who raised Christ from the dead. In Rom. viii.33-34, it is God who justifies His elect on the ground of Christ's death, and on the stronger ground of His Resurrection. In the tenth chapter of this epistle all doubts whether an adequate righteousness has been provided are resolved in the question of the Incarnation and of the Resurrection. Who shall ascend into heaven for the purpose of bringing Christ down to earth, as if His life of humiliation had not taken place? Or, who shall descend into the abyss for the purpose of bringing Christ up from the dead, as if His Resurrection, as the firstfruits of the justifying harvest, had not taken place? Accordingly, to believe in thy heart that God has raised Christ from the dead is to appropriate the righteousness of faith.

The Jews placed the act of justification at the end of the age, at the general Resurrection and the Judgment, so that in this life one could never be certain that the balance would be in his favour. Paul agreed with the Jews in the fundamental importance of justification, but he clothed the anticipated judgment in terms of the present. He read their future justification back into this life by the raising of Christ for our justification. In so doing he made this element of eschatology into soteriology; or better, the Resurrection of Christ makes the final justification — an eschatological blessing — to be also a present possession. Accordingly, the New Testament eschatology is both a *having* and a hoping, and it is this *sub specie resurrectionis*.

"How is God's full justification possible, since those who are justified before Him are still sinners? Only so that God's judgment of justification belongs together with the full freeing from the power of sin to which He leads on His children through judgment into eternity. When God's forgiveness treats us as innocent, that is the same as an anticipation of that which He will make of us entirely first through death or beyond death." [25] And it is the risen Christ who binds together our present justification and our final glorification. Easter is the assurance of forgiveness and the guarantee of eternal life. Even now we have a righteousness in heaven that is perfect and unchangeable. For Christ is our Righteousness and Jesus Christ is the same yesterday, today and forever.

---
25. Althaus, P., *D.L.D.*

"Look, Father, look on His anointed face
 And look on us as found in Him.
Look not on our misusings of Thy grace,
 Our prayer so languid and our faith so dim.
For lo, between our sins and their reward
 We set the passion of Thy Son, our Lord."

God's act in raising Christ testifies to His justification. Thus
His Resurrection comes out of His justification, and our justification comes out of the Resurrection of Christ. "In the justification of Christ lies the certainty and root of the Christian's
justification. For the supreme fruit of Christ's justification, on
the basis of passive and active obedience, is nothing else than
the Spirit (cf. Gal. iii.14), and in turn the Spirit bears in Himself the efficacious principle of all transformation to come, the
resurrection with its entire compass included." [26] For our salvation "a Living Saviour is needed, but a living Saviour, who as
a sin-bearer, had been dead and buried, but had triumphed" [27]
over sin, death, Hell and the grave, a Saviour who was *justified
in the Spirit* (I Tim. iii.16). "For the very same reason that the
Resurrection of Jesus is in a very real sense the justification of
the Christ, this can likewise be affirmed of the resurrection-life
which since that moment Christ lives." In his resurrection state
Christ is righteousness incarnate." [28] "A risen Christ at God's
right hand is the measure and pledge of the believer's acceptance." [29]

The Resurrection and the Spirit. As the living Witness of
righteousness for us in the sight of God, the risen Christ is the
life-giving Spirit. The vital relation is dependent upon and
flows out of the forensic one.

The Holy Spirit is fundamentally related both to the Resurrection of Christ and to the Resurrection of His people. The
present possession of the Spirit is a seal, a promise, a pledge and
a firstfruits or first installment of His possession of us in the
life to come (II Cor. i.22; Eph. i.13, 14; iv.30; Gal. iii.14; I Cor.

---

26. Vos, G., *PTR* xxvii.1.pp.15-17.
27. Cameron, J. K., *TEQ*, 6.2p.152.
28. Vos, G., Princeton *Biblical and Theological Studies*, p. 236.
29. *Brooks.*

v.5; Rom. vii.23). Thus life in the Spirit here issues in the Resurrection, and that because the Spirit is both the fundamental characteristic of the Resurrection and its Author. "The Spirit appears as the substratum, the element, as it were, in which, as in a circumambient atmosphere the life of the coming aeon shall be lived. He produces the event and continually underlies the state which is the result of it. He is Creator and Sustainer at once, the *Creator Spiritus* and the Providence of the supernatural state of the future life in one." [30]

As Christ was raised a life-giving Spirit, our bodies shall be raised Spiritual bodies. The Holy Spirit is the permanent and determining power of the resurrection body. Since the Spiritual order is to succeed the natural, to be Spiritual is to belong to the world to come. By His Resurrection Christ became the center of this new order, so that our citizenship is even now with Him in the eschatological order, in the heavenlies (Phil. iii.20; Eph. i.3; cf. I Cor. x.3-4). The Spirit's proper sphere is the resurrection age which began with the Resurrection of Christ. From the risen Christ the Spirit projects Himself into the present life of the believer, and this is a prophecy of His echatological operations in the believer's resurrection. Or orienting the thought, at the Resurrection Christ became the life-giving Spirit and so the last Adam, the progenitor of a new race (I Cor. xv.45).

From the thought of the Spirit as the determining element of the life to come, the Apostle easily moves to the thought of Him as the author of the resurrection act, or the instrument through whom God affects this in Jesus and in believers. If one accepts the textual reading preferred by the translators, this is clearly brought out in Romans eight eleven. "But if the Spirit of Him that raised up Jesus from the dead dwelleth in you, He that raised up the Messiah Jesus from the dead shall give life also to your mortal bodies through His Spirit that dwelleth in you." As God's instrument the Spirit manifested resurrection power in raising Jesus, and so God will make the indwelling Spirit

30. Vos, G., *PTR,* xxvii.27.

accomplish for His people that which He has already accomplished in the Resurrection of their Messiah. By His Resurrection the Saviour was equipped to carry on His mediatorial work of Lord and Messiah by endowment with the Holy Spirit, the supernatural power and the essential element of the resurrection life. The Spirit became His subjective possession, the source of His own glorified theanthropic life which He communicates to work a creative renewal of life in man's spirit, and so to unite the believer in a mystical vital union with Himself. In this soteriological, eschatological sense *the Lord is the Spirit* and *the Lord of the Spirit* (II Cor. iii.17-18). "The Lord of the Spirit is Christ so far as He is exalted to a condition in which Spirit expresses the character of His essence" (Gloel). Thus the Resurrection of Christ becomes a source of new life for us. We who were dead in trespasses and sins are quickened together with Him and raised up together with Him (Eph. ii.1). And by being so actually joined with the Lord as to be one Spirit with Him (I Cor. vi.17) the members receive new gifts of grace and strength from the Head.

The Resurrection and Christian Theism. In proportion as the Incarnation has been related to the Parousia, as Christ's Resurrection has been related to ours, as the miracles of His ministry have been seen as the signs of the Kingdom of Glory, in proportion as Christianity has been heard as the herald of a new Divine order it has won new consideration. We need to carry these integrating thoughts concerning the Resurrection into the whole light of Christian theism which ever moves from God, the Original, to man, the copy. We need to see this miracle not as an isolated phenomenon, but as a mighty movement of life going out from God to recreate the cosmos and to lead it to its final consummation. When we place the Resurrection in its true theistic context we find that it is best represented neither as antagonizing nature nor as violating natural law nor as transcending nature, but as springing from the same counsel of God from which nature sprang and as organically united with nature.

"If you take the cosmos as a product wrought by God, which henceforth stands outside of Him, has become disordered, and now is being restored by Him from without, with such a mechanical-deistical representation you must make mention of something that is *against* or *above* nature; but as the penalty of never understanding miracle. This is the way the watchmaker does, who makes the watch and winds it, and, when it is out of order, repairs it with his instruments; but such is not the method pursued in the *re-creation*. God stands not deistically over against the world, but by the *immanent* power of God and the will of God immanently upholding this power, while both of these depend upon His transcendent counsel . . . The creation took place in such a way that in itself it carried the possibility of re-creation . . . Man is not first created as a unity that cannot be broken, then by sin and death disjointed into parts of soul and corpse, and now by an act of power mechanically applied from without, restored to unity; but in the creation of man itself lay the possibility of this break and the possibility of the reunion of our nature. Without sin, soul and body would never have been disjointed by death; yet in the creation of man in two parts lay the possibility of this breach." "The miracle, therefore, in its concrete form is not from nature, but from the root from which nature sprang. It is not mechanically added to nature, but is organically united to it. This is the reason why, after the Parousia, all action of the principium of grace flows back into the natural principium, brings this to its consummation, and thus, as such, itself disappears." [31]

In considering the Resurrection the eye focuses upon God. The Christian faith knows nothing of an immortality of the person based on the inherent power of the soul to attain for itself a blessed hereafter. That would be to deny death or to fail to appreciate it as the judgment of God. Rather Christian hope looks to the character and saving intervention of God, the Giver of eternal life. "The Resurrection is the miracle of God, with which He in Christ through His Spirit removes the man from

31. Kuyper, A., *Encyclopedia of Sacred Knowledge*, pp. 425-428.

the dead into the new eternal life." [32] By giving the largest place to *egeirein* in the active voice, Paul places the Father as the active voice, Paul places the Father as the subject and the creative aspect of His act in raising the dead in the foreground. On the other hand, Christ is passive, the terminus upon which God's resurrection power acts, that through Him it may work on others (Rom. iv.24, 25; vi.9; viii.11, 34; x.9; I Cor. vi.14; xv.12-17, 20; II Cor. iv.14; v.15). It is God who raises Christ, even as God will quicken our mortal bodies (Rom. viii.11), and as the new tabernacle is of God's own making, *ek Theou* (II Cor. v.1). The Resurrection is a truly creative act of God, the act of Him who calls the things that are not and they come to be (Rom. iv.17). It streams from the richness of God's resources in the bestowal of form and from His sovereignty in choosing from the available forms in each case what seems most fitting to Him (I Cor. xv).

The God upon whom the eye focuses for faith in the Resurrection is the God who reveals Himself in His Word. A Naturalism which rests on either a deistic, a pantheistic or a dualistic basis excludes such a miracle. The God of Platonism may not be expected to quicken a mortal body, since matter is an eternal entity not of his making. The Resurrection is only credible then as an integral part and parcel of Biblical theism. The living God did call on Abraham to offer Isaac, the only son of the promise, and to believe that God would raise Isaac from the dead and so fulfill His promises through Isaac (Rom. iv.17; Heb.xi.19). And God calls upon us to have the faith of Abraham, who staggered not at the promises of God but waxed strong through faith, giving glory to God and accounting Him able to do that which He had promised, even though it be through Resurrection. When we believe in Him who raised Jesus our Lord from the dead, our faith and our hope are in a God who is sufficient for every need of His people. The Lord who conquered death is mighty above every physical force; the Father who raised Him for our justification is sufficient for every problem which even sin can

---

32. Althaus, *D.L.D.* v.a.109-110.

raise. It is His to say: "I, even I, am He, and there is no God with me; I kill, and I make alive; I wound and I heal; and there is none that can deliver out of my hand." (Deut. xxxii.39).

III. THE RESSURECTION IN NATURE AND ATTESTATION.

The theme of this section is so stated as to bring together the two questions of the nature and attestation of the Resurrection. The purpose in treating the two themes together is to keep the discussion of the character of the Resurrection in line with the evidence attesting it. We have no *a priori* view of the Resurrection to set forth. We desire to present the Resurrection which is attested in the New Testament. It is not good apologetics to discredit some or all of the evidence in order to set forth a view of the Resurrection which may be less objectionable to certain minds; nor is it good theology for human reason to veto elements in God's revelation or to call God or His Word to the bar of human judgment. Thus, the question of the nature of the Resurrection coalesces with that of the attestation of the Resurrection in the Word.

In many respects, "The Resurrection belongs with many other objects of eschatological faith to the region which eye saw not, and ear heard not, and which entered not into the heart of man." [33] We dare not define the characteristics of the Resurrection more exactly than the record warrants lest the shadow of puny man place limits upon the inexhaustible fullness of life and forms which God has power to create. The terms suggested, even by theologians of the Word, are not always helpful.[34] While the Scripture does not give all the information one might wish, it shows the Resurrection of Christ to be objective, corporeal and glorious and consequently teaches that our Resurrection will be an actual or objective state of corporeal existence, changed or glorified for the harmonious control thereof by the Holy Spirit.

A. The Resurrection of Jesus was an objective fact. It may not be dismissed as a hallucination, a series of visions or other subjective experiences of His disciples.

---

33. Vos, PTR, xxvii, p. 206.
34. Cf. Althaus, *D.L.D.*, v.a.128.

From the fact that Jesus did not appear to all the people but to witnesses chosen before (Acts x.41) it has been inferred that He appeared only unto believers. Something similiar has been found in Enoch's reference to the Son of Man who was formerly hidden, kept in the presence of the Highest and revealed to the elect (62.6-7). The danger in this inference is that many treat faith as "the foe of fact," "the enemy of history," asserting that "where we believe and honor, we no longer see objectively." Thus, from the notion that Jesus only appeared to believers, it is only a step to the view that an unbeliever could not have seen Him, then to the conception that His was only "a 'spiritual' resurrection in a 'spiritual' body transformed and incorruptible and perceivable only in vision." [35] From these alleged "visionary appearances" the story is shaded off into visions, hallucinations and spiritual values.

However, Acts does not describe these chosen witnesses as believers. The Greek participle means chosen before, predestinated, designated in advance. God chose His elect before the foundation of the world, but He only called them to faith in the day of salvation. These witnesses chosen before were not already believers. Faith was not a pre-condition for seeing the risen Christ so that faith was first and the appearances second. Whatever faith the disciples had was so shaken or shattered by the Crucifixion that it took the appearance of the Risen Christ to awaken faith, so that the appearances were first and the faith second. Christ did not appear to all but to those whom God had foreordained to faith, to whom His appearances and the work of the Holy Spirit would produce faith. Faith was the fruit and result of Christ's appearances, not the necessary condition for His appearing.

There is a certain amount of ambiguity in the statement that Jesus appeared only to believers. Believers in whom? Believers in what? As in so many logical slips, it is a case of undistributed middle. The word "believer" is first used of one who is a disciple of Jesus, and then it is transferred to one who believes in

---

35. Grant, F. C., *The Gospel of the Kingdom*, p. 80.

His Resurrection. It is only in the latter sense that it properly comes into our discussion, and Jesus appeared largely to those who disbelieved in His Resurrection. Indeed it seems that only John was led to this faith before he saw Jesus, and that by an objective fact, by an examination of the emptied tomb (Jn. xx.8). It is clearly implied that not even the empty tomb wrought this faith in Peter but only the actual appearance of the risen Christ (I Cor. xv.5; Lk. xxiv.34). Nor did Christ limit His appearances to believers. Appearing to doubting Thomas, He said, "Be not faithless, but believing," "Because thou hast seen me, thou hast believed." (Jn. xx.27, 29). He appeared to his brother James who had previously been an unbeliever (I Cor. xv.7). He appeared to Paul who reiterates that his persecuting activity was done ignorantly *in unbelief* (I Tim. i.13; Acts xxvi.9; I Cor. xv.9).

The Risen Christ faced the objective fact of unbelief in His Resurrection and with difficulty overcame this stone wall of unbelief (Lk. xxiv.41; Jn. xx.24-29; Mt. xxviii.17; Mk. xvi. 14; Acts i.13) by appearances, by conversation, by eating with the disciples, by rebuking them, and by many infallible proofs over a period of forty days. By the force of circumstances external to themselves a group of dejected, discouraged, prosaic men were driven around the corner from unbelief to belief. They were aroused from disappointment over the apparent failure of their movement and from the lethargy in which it left them by the objective fact of His Resurrection. This transformation was a corporate change of the whole community and hence could not have been a hallucination. Hallucination is an individual and non-communicable experience. The disciples were changed from cowardice to courage, from unbelief to faith, from despair to exultation by objective evidence.

This evidence included the empty tomb which is attested in each of the four Gospels, implied in the "oral gospel" (Acts ii.24-32) and indicated by the Greek verbs *thapto* and *sunthapto* which Paul uses in I Cor. xv.4 and Rom. vi.4.[36] In the light of

---

36. Oepke, A., in Kittel's *Theologisches Worterbuch,* II.334.

the explicit identification of the grave, the placing of a watch over it, and the devotion attaching to the final resting place of a loved one the effort to account for the empty tomb as a case of finding the wrong tomb is too conjectural and improbable to carry conviction.[37] The quadruple tradition represents Joseph of Arimathea receiving the body and burying it in his own new tomb. The triple tradition represents the women following and identifying the tomb. John shows Nicodemus sharing in the burial; Matthew shows the officers placing a watch. The four gospels represent the women going, on Easter morning, to this tomb they had so carefully identified when the body was laid away and shows them followed by responsible leaders of the Disciples. The circumstances were such that if the body could have been produced it would have been produced by Roman or Jewish leaders.

The objectivity of the Resurrection of Jesus is further shown by His notable teachings during the forty days after the Resurrection. The indoctrination of this period is needed to form the *vinculum* between the pre-resurrection life of Jesus and the Apostolic teachings. Certain central convictions of the primitive Church finds insufficient basis in the earlier teachings of Jesus. The disciples were too "foolish and slow of heart to believe" other teachings earlier enunciated by Jesus and soon to be the primary dicta of their preaching. After the shock of the Crucifixion the disciples needed a repetition, elaboration and confirmation of old teachings and an addition of new teachings to overcome their doubts and establish their hearts for the task before them. Their hearts must be made to burn within them if their wills are to be set for the great task of establishing Christianity in the world.

This chapter of God's revelation is necessary to account for such characteristic elements [38] in the most primitive apostolic preaching as: (1) the conviction of the heavenly power, glory and Lordship, or the Divine essence of Christ. (2) The neces-

37. Duncan, G. S., *The Historical Value of the Gospels in The Christian Faith.* p. 132.
38. Seeberg, R., *Evangelium quadaginta dierum.*

sity of Christ's death and the connection between His death and resurrection. The two discourses recorded in Luke xxiv.26 and 46 and the "oral gospel" have led A. D. Heffern to the conclusion that primitive preaching included a collection of Old Testament passages relating to the death of the Messiah which comes from the Gospel Jesus taught in these forty days.[39] (3) The triadic formula, which overtly and covertly peeps through the apostolic literature, is everywhere presupposed, without any authorization except in this period (Mt. xxviii.18-20; Lk. xxiv.49; Acts i.4-5; 7-8; Jn. xx.21-22; cf. Didache vii.i, 3). (4) The fact of baptism, which is connected with the name of Christ or of the Trinity and valued as a means of salvation, lacks adequate authorization apart from this period. (5) The representation of the Spirit not merely as a Divine gift, but as the Subject and Giver of Divine gifts. (6) The common conviction of the world-wide mission of Christianity and the fact that the disciples remained for a definite period in the environs of Jerusalem and then went on this mission to the Gentiles. (7) A structure of fixed representations valued as "the traditions," "the Word," "the teachings," "the Gospel" or "the command" of Christ including elements of doctrinal belief, conduct, church praxis and Christian hope to which Alfred Seeberg has given the name, The Catechism of Primitive Christianity. Since the writer has elsewhere [40] elaborated this Gospel of the Forty Days, it is in order here only to stress the fact that both in content and elevation it is an objective entity that requires the Resurrection as its presupposition, the risen Christ as its author.

The Great Commission is in every respect worthy of all that has gone before and of the risen Lord Jesus Christ. If the story of the Resurrection had been only "the passion of a hallucinated woman," then the fishermen would have been left to their own resources, and the inventions of the poor publican would have marked a swift descent to Jewish narrowness, provincialism and bigotry, as is indicated in the question, "Lord, wilt Thou at this

39. Heffern, A. D., *Apology and Polemic in the New Testament*, p. 54.
40. Robinson, W. C., *The Gospel of the Forty Days in Our Lord*.

time restore the kingdom to Israel?" "Is there, then, such a swift descent? Are not the reported words of the Risen Lord . . . as noble, as impressive, as divine as any that have been preserved to us from the years of His life in the flesh? Search through this Gospel, and say if there can be found anywhere an utterance that has more of the King in it, that is more absolutely free from all Jewish narrowness and from all human feebleness, than this Great Commission which forms its magnificent close. It is very plain that these simple artists have their subject still before them. Manifestly they are not drawing from their imagination, but telling what they heard and saw." [41]

The four *alls* in the Great Commission suggest some of its unapproachable majesty. The Speaker asserts for Himself *all* authority in heaven and on earth; on that authority He commissions His followers to disciple *all* nations, teaching them to observe *all* of His commands, as though His words will never need revision; and He promises them His abiding presence in *all* times and places to the consummation of the age. In His name repentance and remission of sins are to be preached to all the nations (Lk. xxiv. 47). In the Lukan records He gathers together His own working and the working of the Spirit in the same manner as the working of the Father (Lk. xxiv.47-49; Acts i.4-8), as in the Matthean ending Jesus states the homogeneousness of the Father and of the Son and of the Holy Spirit by combining them into the one name of God. This "authoritative announcement of the Trinity as the God of Christianity by its Founder in one of the most solemn of His recorded declarations" [42] is necessary to account for the historical fact that "the Trinitarian creed is the distinctive mark of the Christian Faith." [43] The substance and the form of the truth revealed in the forty days is an objective intellectual confirmation of the fact of the Resurrection of Jesus.

---

41. Gibson, J. M., *The Gospel of Matthew*, 1900, p. 443.
42. Warfield, B. B., article *Trinity* in I.S.B.E.
43. Brunner, E., *The Word and the World*, *p.* 59; cf. Oxford *Essays on the Trinity and the Incarnation;* Caird, John, *Fundamental Ideas of Christianity;* Webb, C.J.C., *God and Personality.*

"His resurrection reaffirms, establishes and crowns all other forms of witness." [44]

B. The New Testament account of Christ's Resurrection reveals the corporeal nature of the Resurrection. We have noticed the repeated evidence that the tomb was emptied of the body of Jesus. Matthew narrates the meeting of the two women with Jesus at which time they "took hold of His feet" (XXVIII. 9) ; His forbidding Mary Magdalene to continue to keep hold of Him implies that He was tangible [45] (John xx.17). The account of Jesus having table fellowship with His Disciples after His Resurrection has received the scorn of Harnack's circle, but it is attested not only by Acts (x. 41), but also repeatedly in Luke (xxiv.30, 35, 41, 42) as well as John (xxi.1-14), and the present ending of Mark (xvi.14). In two of these accounts the risen Saviour is described as eating and in one as also drinking.

In Luke and John Jesus is represented as telling and showing them that He was not a mere spirit. "See my hands and my feet, that it is I myself : handle me, and see ; for a spirit hath not flesh and bones, as ye behold me having. And when He had said this he showed them his hands and his feet." (Lk. xxiv.39-40). Jesus "shewed unto them his hands and his side." But when it was reported to Thomas he said, "Except I shall see in his hands the print of the nails, and put my fiinger into the print of the nails and put my hand into his side, I will not believe." Jesus cometh again and saith to Thomas, "Reach hither thy finger, and see my hands ; and reach hither thy hand, and put it into my side : and be not faithless, but believing." Thomas answered and said unto Him, "My Lord and my God !" Jesus saith unto him, "Because thou hast seen me, thou hast believed !" (John xx.20, 25, 27-28). The account does not state that Thomas actually put his hand into the wound in the Saviour's side ; but those who accept the account and the truthfulness of the Lord agree that

---

44. Heffern, A. D., *Apology and Polemic in the New Testament.* p. 55.
45. Nicklin, T., *The Expository Times*, Li.10, 478 ; Westcott, B. F., *The Bible Commentary*, II:292.

Thomas certainly could have put his finger into the print of the nails and his hand into the side of the risen Jesus.

With this record agrees an old testimony which Ignatius, one of the apostolic fathers, has preserved presumably from *the Preaching of Peter*. Here the risen Lord tells the disciples, "lay hold, handle me and see that I am not an incorporeal spirit (demon)." (Smyr. iii.2). And with evident reference to the account of Thomas' conversion, the first epistle of John begins with the testimony that the Apostles had heard, seen with their eyes, examined, handled with their hands the Word of Life, and knew that they bore first-hand witness of what they had seen and heard concerning that Eternal Life which was with the Father and was manifested unto them. In this sevenfold reference to their sense perceptions of sight, touch and hearing the primitive Christians attest the adequacy of Jesus' manifestation of His bodily Resurrection.

In the "oral gospel" the testimony of the Resurrection means that "his flesh did not see corruption" (Acts ii.26, 27, 31). As the first Christian martyr dies, he sees Jesus, the Son of Man, standing at the right hand of God (Acts vii.56). The bodily character indicated by the table fellowship is so unmistakable that naturalistic scholars stumble at it. (Acts x.41). Thus, by many infallible proofs the risen Lord gave His disciples convincing evidence of the reality of His having risen. "Men were at liberty to apply every appropriate test, such as His conversing with them, His eating in their presence, the marks of the nails in His hands and feet, and of the spear in His side. Thus there was given by Him such a bodily identification in His personal appearance with what it was before His Crucifixion, as put the matter of the reality of His Resurrection beyond the possibility of doubt on the part of the many witnesses who saw Him." [46]

We may begin our study of Paul's testimony by observing that he was *a Hebrew of the Hebrews; as touching the law a Pharisee* (Phil. iii.5 ; II Cor. xi.22 cf. Rom. xi.1) and that "the

---

46. Cameron, J. K., *op. cit.*, p. 165.
47. Moore, G. F., *Judaism*, II :379.

primary eschatological doctrine of Judaism is the resurrection, the revivification of the dead." [47] Moreover, Paul is represented in Acts as repeatedly appealing to the hope of the resurrection of the dead (xxiii.6-8; xxvi.4-8). When Paul was brought before the Jewish council he aligned himself with the Pharisees who believed in the resurrection of the dead and was defended by them for this stand. And when the Apostle stood at Mars Hill he set forth the resurrection of the dead, a doctrine so different from the Platonic conception of the immortality of the soul that the Athenian philosophers mocked him as a babbler, a setter forth of strange gods (Acts xvii.18-32). According to Acts, the keenest minds of his day — the scribes of Judaism and the philosophers of Athens — decided that Paul's Gospel set forth the doctrine of the Pharisees, the resurrection of the dead, not the doctrine of the Platonists, the natural immortality of the soul. At this point he was acceptable to the Pharisees and incomprehensible to the philosophers. Paul Althaus brings out this distinction by contrasting Plato's understanding of death with that which Paul gives in II Cor. v.1ff: "The value-judgment concerning the nakedness of the soul is exactly opposite in the case of the Greeks and of Paul.' "The Greeks see the soul's separation from the body, its establishment in the condition of nakedness as a freedom, which one longs after with passionate desire; the nakedness of the soul signifies a higher, purer condition. On the other hand, Paul is afraid of becoming naked. The separation from the body brings not freedom for true living, but exactly the opposite damage to life. True, full life is not possible in a bodiless condition, but only in the body. Behind this whole opposing valuation of the nakedness of the soul stands the deep distinction between the Hellenistic and the Biblical thought in reference to the valuation of the soul." [48] Paul's doctrine of the body and of the future life is the doctrine of Hebraism, not of Hellenism.

The Apostle Paul certainly makes a difference between the body that is sown and the body that is raised (I Cor. xv.42);

48. Althaus, P., *DLD*,4.88, 123.

between the present body and the eschatological body; between the body of our humiliation and the body of His glory (Phil. iii.21); between the natural or animal and the Spiritual body (I Cor. xv.44). But it is evident that in making these distinctions the Apostle is not rejecting the bodily character of the Resurrection; for, "This corporeality is the object of the change, of the glorification through Christ." [49] (Rom. viii.11; Phil. iii.21). A large section of the fifteenth chapter of First Corinthians is devoted to showing that our inability to define the nature or manner of the future body is not a valid ground for rejecting the resurrection of the body. God who has at His disposal bodies that differ specifically and bodies that differ generically will give it a body even as it pleaseth Him (vss. 35-41). "Bodily the resurrection certainly is, and every attempt to dephysicize it, so often inspired by a dislike of the supernatural on its material side, amounts to an exegetical *tour de force,* so flagrant as to be not worth losing many words over." [50]

Some people have been deceived by failing to notice that the adjective *natural* defining the body which is buried is not *physical,* but *psychical* (I Cor. xv.44). Nor is this a casual term as though the Apostle might have really meant *physical,* since the terms and the contrast are repeated in verse forty-four and carried over into the distinction between the two Adams in verse forty-five. Thus, three times Paul contrasts the *psychical* body with the *Spiritual* body. Paul does not teach that the body which comes by generation from the first Adam and which is finally buried is composed of *psyche.* He is not setting forth Christian Science or Spiritualism. But the present body is controlled by the soul and is the fit organ and instrument for the expression of the soul. Accordingly, the word is properly translated a natural or an animal body. And, as the Apostle elsewhere teaches, this living soul was corrupted by sin, so that the *natural body* became a body dominated and controlled by a depraved, sinful psychology. Conversely, then, the other adjective *Spiritual* does not define

49. Althaus, P., *DLD*, 4.p.165.
50. Vos, G., *PTR*, xxvii, p. 19.

"the substance" of which the future body is composed, but the dominating principle controlling that body. "This adjective *Pneumatikon* expresses the quality of the body in the eschatological state. Every thought of immaterialness, or etherealness or absence of physical denseness ought to be carefully removed from the term. . . . In order to keep far such misunderstandings the capitalizing of the word ought to have been carefully guarded both in translation and otherwise: *pneumatikon* almost certainly leads on the wrong tract, whereas *Pneumatikon* not only sounds a note of warning, but in addition points in the right direction. Paul means to characterize the resurrection-state as the state in which the Pneuma rules." [51] The same two Greek adjectives are used in the second chapter of this epistle to distinguish between the *natural* man to whom the things of the Spirit are foolishness, and the *Spiritual* man who discerns these things (I Cor. ii.14-15). Now no one assumes that becoming a regenerated or *Spiritual* man makes one a ghost. And so this eschatological body has the characteristics which the Spirit gives it, and of which the Spirit's work in regeneration was a true foretaste. In place of a natural body, which historically has issued in a sinful flesh and blood, corruption, dishonor and weakness, the proper organ and instrument for the Spirit is a body either changed or else raised in power, glory, incorruption and immorality (1 Cor. xv.44-54) so that there shall be "full harmony of the Temple and of the Holy Spirit."

Barth has pointed the corporeal nature of the resurrection body by suggesting that *if* anything drops out in this discussion (vss. 42-46) it is *soul* rather than *body*. The figure of seed and plant, of sowing and germinating, indicates a real continuity between that which is sown and that which is raised; and the fact that what is sown is naked, dies, and is sown in corruption, dishonor and weakness precludes the Spirit as the subject of the process.

The statement in verse 50 that *flesh and blood cannot inherit the kingdom of God* is not a contrast in which *flesh and blood*

---

51. Vos, G., *PTR*, xxvii, p. 31.

are synonymous with *body*. For in verse 50 this statement parallels a contrast between *corruption* and *incorruption* and in verses 42-44 that which is raised in *incorruption* is the Spiritual *body*.

In another connection the Apostle knows how to distinguish the appetite for food and the sexual desire, as perhaps the most characteristic expressions of the "flesh," from the essence of the body. As the Saviour, in defending the Resurrection against the Sadducees, declared that the sons of the Resurrection neither marry nor are given in marriage (Lk. xx.34-36; Mk. xii.25; Mt. xxii.30); so in condemning fornication and gluttony, the Apostle asserts that the body is "for the Lord and the Lord for the body and God both raised the Lord, and will raise up us through his power" (I Cor. vi.14). Yea, he asserts that our bodies are members of Christ and temples of the Holy Spirit so that being joined in one Spirit with the Lord and having been bought with a price, we ought to glorify God in our bodies (vss.15-20).

The present body looks back to the first Adam; the eschatological body looks upward and forward to the last Adam. The first became a living soul, the natural parent of the human race. At His Resurrection, the final Adam became a life-giving Spirit, calling His people into fellowship with Himself by giving them of the Holy Spirit, a foretaste of that age in which they shall have a corporeality fitted for and wholly dominated, not by Adam's psychology, but by Christ's Holy Spirit.

Paul thinks of that risen Christ who appeared to Him on the road to Damascus as existing in heaven in "the body of His glory" (Phil. iii.21) and as such "the first born of every creature" (Col. i.15). "It is in Him as such also that it is said that, 'in Him dwells all the fullness of Godhead bodily' (Col. ii.9). All that God is is here said to have in Him a bodily *somatikos* dwelling place." [52] The Apostle's reference to the Parousia as an Appearing, an Epiphany (Tit. ii.13), accords with the Gospel prophecy that every eye shall behold Him, and the testimony at the Ascension that He shall so come in like manner as the Galileans saw Him ascend (Acts. i.11).

52. Cameron, J. K., *op. cit.*, p. 164.

There are certain more general considerations that confirm the exegetical interpretation of the Resurrection as corporeal. The Scripture assigns a dignity to the body that ought not to be overlooked. The world and like view of the Bible is not that of Hellenism. According to the former, God created the earth as well as the heavens, the body as well as the soul of man; according to the latter, matter is an eternally existing anti-God stuff. It is the intrusion into Christianity of Hellenism, as well as of naturalism, which has so limited the acceptance of the bodily character of Resurrection. The whole man was included among the works which the Creator declared to be good. "On him, as constituted of soul and body, the Divine image was impressed. On the body also, under the Jewish economy was imprinted the sign of the Covenant in circumcision; and under the Gospel dispensation the body receives the sign and seal of the Covenant in Baptism; while even in the outward part of the Sacrament of the Supper the body participates." [53] Paul concludes his chapter on the Resurrection by calling the disciples to abound in labors in the Lord, works that could only be wrought with the body (I Cor. xv.58), even as the Saviour called us to let men *see* our good works (Matt. v.16), that they might glorify our Father in heaven.

Consequently, the survival of the soul or a kingdom of mere spirits may suit a Platonist or a modern personalist, but it is not the victory which the Bible sees for God. If Christ did not rise in the body, then death and Satan have the last word in the things of the body; if He did not manifest Himself in the visible world, then God will never conquer the visible things, but Satan will ever wield the instrument of powerful and pernicious propaganda. The Bible sees no such capitulation for God. The visible bodily Resurrection of Christ is the sign of a victory that shall never cease until the age of sight replaces the age of faith and we shall visibly live and reign with Christ in risen bodies occupying a new earth under a new heaven. [54] The whole philosophy of

---

53. Cameron, J. K., *ibid*, p. 164.

the Bible testifies that "the future state is one of corporeal existence." [55]

In God's revealing activities He has not dealt with us in the bodilessness of a mystical experience or in occult phenomena but through the oral proclamation of the Word and the visible administration of the Sacraments. The content of this Gospel is the Word made flesh. With a bodily voice Christ called Lazarus from the grave and healed the leper. "Jesus' saving acts upon the body are the signs of the breaking in of the Kingdom in which also the body shall be made free from the sovereignty of death." [56] The Resurrection of Christ seals the fact that He and His works possessed body. Further, the Gospel calls the whole man, body and soul, to responsible decision. With the heart man believeth unto righteousness, but with the lips he makes confession unto salvation. At the judgment seat of Christ each man shall give account of the deeds done in the body. The rejection of Apollinarianism is the definitive assertion that Christ assumed the whole man and redeemed not a truncated, but the complete man.

The essential corporealities of our lives "receive their validity first *a posteriori* on the ground of the bodily Resurrection of Jesus." [57] Through His corporeal dealings with us God shows that body is an essential element-of man's constitution, a constituent part of his being. The I-consciousness is given in one's life and experience as a unity of the corporeal and the spiritual existence. "The will is a spiritual reality, and it belongs at the same time in the connection of the spatial-corporeal event, from which effects go out into the spatial-corporeal world" (Stange). All our activity in the world and our intercourse with one another is through our corporeality and is impossible without it. In speech, the word is physical and spiritual reality in one. "The speech is not a supplemental configuration of thinking, but speech is the *Gestalt* of thinking." Nor is there fellowship without the

54. Cf. Heim, K., *Jesus der Weltvollender*, pp. 178, 179, 199.
55. Cameron, J. K., *op. cit.*, p. 157.
56. Althaus, P., *D.L.D.* v.a., 116-121.
57. Kunneth, W., *Th.d.A.*, 1933, 224.

corporeality of the Word. Even the silent rhapsody of love pre-supposes the conversation that it comes out of and goes back into. Singing expresses the sentiment of the heart, but in this *expression* the emotion of the heart first comes to realization. "We are also present for one another only in the body." "I cannot represent to myself the soul of the other, except I think of his eyes, his face, the expression of his hand, his bearing." Thus the body is not only an expression or an instrument, or a dwelling or a clothing, but "the essential form of our inner being," "We are also body." [58]

From its early days the Church has reasoned that no one "can be so mad as to think that he will rise otherwise than as He rose who opened the door of the Resurrection." [59] Thus Calvin understands, "We shall rise again with the same bodies (flesh) as we have now, as to the substance, but that the quality will be different; just as the very body (flesh) which has been offered as a sacrifice was raised again, but with such new and superior qualities (added dignity and excellence) as though it had been altogether different." [60] Since Christ rose as man, He rose visibly and corporeally, and the Christian hope of immortality is not a mere persistence of the soul after the dissolution of the body. It is the resurrection and renanimation of the body itself that has been adopted in the credal affirmation of the resurrection of the flesh.[61] This phrase is the resurrection of the flesh in the Greek, the Latin and the French versions of the Apostles' Creed, the resurrection of the body in the English and the German forms.

In the Christian faith the body is never, as in Hellenic thought, the prison of the soul, the flesh is not the lower hull of an exalted kernel. "The body is not essentially either worse or better than the soul. Both are fallen away to the Evil One without Christ, both are redeemed and saved through Christ." [62] The Church of

58. Althaus, P., *D.L.D.* v.a.118-120.
59. Rufinus, *Apology*, 1.6,7,8; *Commentary on Apostles' Creed*, 45-47.
60. *Institutes* III.xxv.8.61.
61. Barth, *The Knowledge of God and the Service of God*, pp. 87; Taylor, *The Christian Hope of Immortality*, p. 13.
62. Althaus, P., *op. cit.*, p. 127.

Aquileia introduced the pronoun *this* into the Creed and taught the believer to make the sign of the Cross upon his own forehead as he said "the resurrection of *this* flesh" in testimony that he would receive his own and not a foreign body.[63] From Calvin's Chair in St. Pierre, Pastor Jean de Saussure writes, "As a Christian I believe not only the resurrection of the spirit, but I believe the resurrection of the flesh, that is to say of all our terrestrial being, of all our natural faculties, of our fleshly body, of our fleshly soul, and also of our fleshly thought and of our fleshly conscience, or if one prefers, natural." [64] The late C. W. Hodge, Jr., stressing the "indisputable" [65] fact that I Cor. xv.50 refers to the body of man's sinful estate, held that the resurrection body would be flesh and bones.

These scholars are perpetuating the distinction which Rufinus made between the sinful flesh which is given over to corruption with its frailties, its appetites and its lusts inflamed and the flesh of Christ which did not see corruption (Lk. xxiv.39; Acts ii.31). "For the faith of the Church . . . does not deny the reality of the natural flesh and body when it rises from the dead, but neither does it assert in contradiction to the Apostles' words, that in the Kingdom which is to come corruption will inherit incorruption. We therefore do not assert that the flesh or body will rise, as you put it, with one of its members lost or amputated, but that the body will be whole or complete, having laid aside nothing but its corruption and dishonour and frailty and having also amputated all the imperfections of mortality; nothing of its own nature will be lacking to that spiritual body which shall rise from the dead except this corruption."

Vos insists on the connection between the body which is sown and that which is raised as involved in the analogy of sowing and germinating. However, he understands the Resurrection as "the stripping off the flesh and the endowment of the believer with a Pneumatic *soma*." "The resurrection body will differ greatly

---

63. Rufinus, *Apology*, I.5.
64. Calvinistic Congress, 1938, p. 211.
65. Vos, G., *PTR*, xxvii, p. 204; cf. Bryden, W. W., *op. cit.*, pp. 133-134.

from the kind of body we now possess in its eradiation of glory," but "bodily the Resurrection certainly is." [66]

Whether one confess the Christian faith in English as the Resurrection of the body or in French as the Resurrection of the flesh, he is guarding the salvation of the complete humanity from the mere Platonic immortality of a part of the personality. The body which is buried is determined by the natural and sinful psychological life of man, by the sphere of the flesh which is evil, not by creation, but by the fall, by the world order which begins with Adam's sin. The body which is raised is part of the world order dominated by the Holy Spirit and consequently is the proper form for that human life which is controlled by the Spirit. As Christ's human life is now determined by the Holy Spirit, so will the resurrection life of the Christian be detemined. Christ's Resurrection is "the breaking in of the full corporeality of which all former corporeality was but the shadowy stage." [67]

C. Finally, the Resurrection means not only the objective reality of the risen body but also the fashioning anew of that body, a change as mighty as the miracle of the Resurrection. "If there be a somatic Resurrection, we cannot otherwise conceive of it than as a somatic transformation. There is not a simple return of what was lost in death; the organism is returned endowed and equipped with new powers; it is richer, even apart from the removal of its sin-caused defects. The normal, to be sure, is restored, but to it there are added faculties and qualities which should be regarded supernormal from the standpoint of the present state of existence." [66] "According to I Cor. xv.45-49, believers shall bear after Christ the image He Himself obtained in His own Resurrection." And of His Resurrection it has been well said, "the body which was buried was raised, but in a transfigured form. There was both identity and dissimilarity. The resurrection body was transformed and adapted to new spiritual conditions." [69]

66. Vos, G., *PTR*, xxvii, pp. 19, 198, 203, 224.
67. Heim, K., *Jesus der Weltvollender*, pp. 178, 179, 199.
68. Vos, G., *PTR*, xxvii.19.
69. *Evangelical Belief*, I.V.F. pp. 19-20.

Such a change is indicated in the accounts of our Lord's Resurrection. According to these accounts He was not always immediately recognized. In the case of Mary Magdalene that was partly because she was weeping and not turned directly toward Him (Jno. xx.14). On the way to Emmaus the eyes of the disciples were holden so that they did not recognize Him until, as He broke the bread, their eyes were opened to know Him and He vanished from their sight (Lk. xxiv.16, 30, 31). At the Sea of Tiberias the distance and the imperfect light of dawn contributed to their nescience (Jn. xxi.4). At the appearance in Galilee some doubted (Matt. xxviii.17). He told Mary not to cling to Him for He had not yet ascended (Jn. xx.17).

John records two appearances of Jesus to the disciples when the door was shut, without any explanation as to how He entered (Jn. xx.19-26). In view of the limitations of our knowledge of the power of the Resurrection, of the relation of His risen body to the present conditions of our material existence, and of the sovereignty of the Lord of all times, space, dimensions and matter, speculation about the mode of his entrance is likely to be vain and unprofitable. A line of commentators in the Reformed tradition, extending from Calvin through Gernler and Battier to Matthew Henry,[70] holds that Christ, by His almighty power, caused the doors to be opened, as the stone was rolled from the sepulchre and as the iron gate opened for Peter and the angel (Acts xii.10), passed through and stood in the midst. Many commentators hold that the doors remained fastened; and from this inference some draw conclusions of a ubiquity, others of a spirituality of Christ's risen existence. A group of wise commentators including Lange, Ryle and Westcott leave the how of His entrance unsolved.

In view of what He said and did during these two appearances (especially if, as seems probable, Luke xxiv.36-43 and I John i.1-3 refer to the same appearance) the comment of Bishop Ryle is appropriate: "When he rose from the dead, He rose with a

70. *Calvin on the New Testament*, III.363-364. Biblia edited by F. Battier and T. Gernler, approved by theological faculty of Basel, 1736. N.T. p. 118. "Nachdeme er die porten durch seine allmacht eroffnet hatte." Henry, Matthew, *Comprehensive Commentary*, Matthew-John, p. 826.

body of a far more spiritual kind than He had before, but a body for all that which was a real human body, and not a mere seeming and shadowy body, like that of a ghost or a spirit . . . a body that could be touched, and felt and seen and handled, yet a supernatural and peculiar body." [71] The present conclusion of Mark, which is frequently regarded as late, states that He appeared to two others in another, or *different form (en hetera morphe)* as they walked into the country (Mk. xvi.12).

Some scholars hold that Christ's body was raised as flesh and bones (Lk. xxiv.36-43) and later, at the ascension, changed into a body of glory, a Spiritual body. This apparently means that our resurrection does not entirely parallel His; that by the one resurrection change our bodies are to be conformed to what His body is as a result of the two changes. While this hypothesis is not impossible it runs counter to the Apostle's parallelism in First Corinthians fifteen. The clear implication of that chapter is that for Christ the first-fruits, as for His people, the body is sown in dishonour and raised in glory; sown a natural body, raised a Spiritual body. "The whole tenor of the argument . . . compels us to think of the Resurrection as the moment at which *Pneumatikon entered*. Christ appeared then and there in the form of *Pneumatikon* and as such inaugurated the eschatological era." [72] And, if this be the valid exegesis, the accounts of the body of the risen Christ in the Gospels and Acts forbid our denying the corporeality of the Resurrection in an effort to do justice to the glory, power and Spirit which characterize the risen life. Particularly, in dealing with a realm that is so far beyond our present experiences, it is far better to acknowledge paradoxes we cannot now solve than to erase a part of the New Testament testimony in order to harmonize the picture with our inferences based upon another part of that testimony.

Raised in Glory. The Apostle Paul distinctly teaches a change from our present to the eschatological body whether we died and are raised or remain unto the coming of the Lord and are changed

---

71. *Ryle, J. C., Expository Thoughts on the Gospels,* John iii.392, 391.
72. Vos, G., *PTR,* xxvii.33.

by being "clothed upon with our habitation which is from heaven" (I Cor. xv:51-54; II Cor. v.2). In both cases the contrast between the two bodies is marked and accords with the further statement that we look for the Parousia of the Lord Jesus Christ who shall *fashion anew* the body of our humiliation that it may be conformed to the body of His glory (Phil. iii.21). Again, referring primarily to inward, spiritual and moral change, Paul testifies that by looking to the Lord we are *transformed* into the same image from glory to glory, as from the Lord the Spirit (II Cor. iii.18). This glorification is to be externally consummated in the resurrection when we shall bear the image of the heavenly Adam (I Cor. xv.45-49). For, *the glory of the celestial is one and the glory of the terrestrial another (hetera)* (I Cor. xv.40). The fundamental distinction with Paul, then, is glory. "The resurrection body will differ greatly from the kind of body we now possess in its eradiation of glory." [73] And this glory is the image of the risen Christ, the body of His glory.

The great thing in the life of Paul was that he had seen Jesus, our Lord, that the risen Christ appeared also to him (I Cor. ix.i; xv.8). When it pleased God to reveal His Son to Paul, suddenly there shone a great light out of heaven around about him and his companions. Speaking from that uncreated light, the Lord Jehovah identified Himself as Jesus. For the glory of that light Paul could not see (Acts ix; xxii; xxvi), and the memory of the glory of Christ never faded. Even when the Apostle thought of the depths of Christ's humiliation, the shameful death on the Cross, he insisted that the princes of the world had crucified the Lord of glory (I Cor. ii.8).

Another account of the glory of the risen Christ is given in the testimony of Stephen. Beginning his speech with the God of glory who appeared unto Abraham, the martyr closed with a vision of the heavens opened for him to behold the glory of God and Jesus standing on the right hand of God (Acts vii. 2, 55.56). Then, the risen One appeared to James (I Cor. xv.7), and James speaks of the Lord Jesus Christ as *the glory* (Jas. ii.1). The New

---

73. Vos, G., *PTR*, xxvii.p.203.

Jerusalem hath no need of a Temple, for the Lord God Almighty and the Lamb are the temple thereof, no need of the sun or the moon, for the glory of God lightens it and the Lamb is the lamp thereof (Rev. xxi.22-23). "The Lamb is all the glory of Immanuel's land."

There is still another manifestation of His glory which may well be suggestive of the change which the living shall undergo at His Parousia. Peter says, "We were eyewitnesses of His majesty. For He received from God the Father honor and glory, when there was born such a voice to Him by the Majestic Glory, This is my beloved Son, in whom I am well pleased." (II Peter i.16-18). In the holy mount He was transfigured, or *transformed* (metamorphosed) before them, the appearance of His countenance was altered, became generically different *(heteros),* and His garments became dazzling, white as light, exceeding white as no fuller on earth can whiten them. Moses and Elijah appeared with Him in glory and talked with Him. And when the disciples were fully awake they saw His glory. Then, a bright cloud of the Divine glory overshadowed them, and a voice came out of the cloud, "This is my beloved Son: hear ye Him" (Matt. xvii. 1-13; Mk. ix.2-13; Lk. ix.28-36). It is interesting to notice that the term which Luke uses to express the alteration of the appearance of His face, *heteros,* is the same term Paul uses to distinguish between the glory of the earthly and the heavenly bodies (Lk. ix.28; I Cor. xv.40); that the term which in Matthew and Mark is translated transfigured (more literally *transformed* or *metamorphosed)* is the same Paul uses in II Cor. iii.18 to describe our transformation into Christ's image; and is about the equivalent of the two terms he uses for the change in Phil. iii.21, *fashion anew and conform with.*

Vos describes a variegation in *glory* as a difference in quality and manifestation. In Paul's discussion of the specific differences between the flesh of men, beasts and birds, and the generic differences between the terrestrial and the celestial bodies, or again the specific differences between the glories of the several heavenly bodies "the reasoning revolves not about the substantial make-up of these bodies, but about their kind, their quality, their appearance. This follows further from the fact that the close of vs. 38 links on closely to vss. 39-41, and there . . . the reference to plant-clothing in foliage and flowering is unmistakable." This connects with the fact that the word *glory* which Paul chooses to express the aspect in regard to which the variety exists is primarily a term of outward manifestation.[74] Through the fifteenth chapter of First Corinthians there run two Greek words both of which are translated *another,* one expressive of difference in species, and the other of a more fundamental difference in general. The argument issues in the thought that the heavenly bodies are not merely specifically different, but generically different from the earthly bodies ,(vs. 40). "It will be a case of *heteros* not merely of *allos." And as we have borne the image of the earthly we shall also bear the image of the heavenly* (vs. 49).

No one was ever subjected to such depths of shame and degradation as our Lord — arrested, tried, mocked, scourged, ridiculed, spit upon, jeered, crucified with thieves, buried in a borrowed tomb. And from that humiliation no one has ever been so exalted. *Wherefore also God highly exalted him and gave unto him the Name which is above every name; that at the Name of Jesus every knee should bow . . . and every tongue should confess that Jesus Christ is Lord to the glory of God the Father.* (Phil. ii.9-11). Thus Paul directs the gaze of faith not merely retrospectively to the Cross, but likewise upward to the glorified existence of Christ in heaven, where the merit of the Cross is laid up and made available forever, where the Lord is the life-giving Spirit, where His glorious body is the pledge of our glorification. To the end of his ministry, the Apostle labored in the Gospel of Jesus Christ, risen from the dead, that the elect might obtain the salvation which is in Christ Jesus with eternal glory (II Tim. ii.6-10).

Following in his Master's train the Apostle knew what it was to be smitten by his own race, of *the Jews five times received*

74. Vos, G., *PTR*, xxvii.2.

forty stripes save one (Acts xxiii.2; II Cor. xi.24). He was beaten publicly and condemned by the Romans despite his imperial citizenship (Acts xvi.37). He was pressed on every side, perplexed, smitten down (II Cor. iv.8, 9), poor, dishonored (vi. 8, 10), abased (xi. 7), hungry, thirsty, naked, cold (xi.27-28), persecuted, distressed, (xii.10). He was cumbered with a despicable infirmity (Gal. iv.12-13). He faced bonds, imprisonment and death for Christ's sake. The Christians of that day were surrounded by tribulation, anguish, persecution, famine, nakedness, peril and sword, for the Lord's sake they were killed all the day long, yea, accounted as sheep for the slaughter (Rom. viii.35-36).

It is against this background of the Cross and the sufferings of early Christians that we must read the promise. *It is sown in dishonor, it is raised in glory.* What a joy it was to know that bearing reproach for the name of Christ was evidence that the Spirit of glory, the Spirit of God rested upon them, that inasmuch as they were partakers of Christ's sufferings they should rejoice with exceeding joy at the revelation of His glory (I Peter iv.13-14). With what fondness must these followers of Him who endured the Cross, depising the shame, have treasured every vision of His enthronement (Hebrews xii.2), every promise of the epiphany of His glory (Tit. ii.12) and of their reigning with Him in glory (II Tim. ii.12).

Over the night of human hate, beyond the pit of sin's pollution, above the pain of wrenched frames and the shame of death's corruption the light of the knowledge of the glory of God shines in the face of Jesus Christ and the promise that we shall be like Him beckons onward. The glorified body of the risen Christ is the pledge of our glorification.

"The handsomest specimens of physical face and form, whether molded by the mystic forces of life, or framed in descriptive words by poet's imagination, or fashioned in stone and color by artist's skill, are at best like the remains of some hundred-gated Thebes lying amid its own ruins and proclaiming its own

departed magnificence. In splendid contrast, the future body
will be indescribably glorious — an object of admiration for God
and angels and men and women, a paragon of perfect beauty,
surpassing the color of all flowers, the plumage of all birds, the
garniture of starry skies, and possessing the symmetry and proportion of the balanced universe. Every true lover of beauty —
everyone whose soul cries out within him for the thought and
image, the word and phrase, the rhythm and rhetoric, which can
touch the fringe of Jehovah's garment — every musician whose
aspiring spirit would civilize wild noises into sweeter tunes, and
would wander on through the halls and galleries of sound in quest
of the sweet harmonies which unfallen angels make in the sanctuary of God — every artist who spreads colors and makes pictures and then sits down and weeps because the masterpiece falls
so far short of the ideal which begged and struggled to come
upon the canvas — every woman who longs to incarnate in her
person the poetry of form, the sweetness of music, the color of
life — every man who would like to be helmeted with that physical dignity which would enable him to stand in full consciousness
at the zenith of things — every being not infatuated with the ugly
and deformed, ought to commend his drainless soul to this Christian Hope of a Glorified Body." [75]

Raised in Incorruption. The adjectives which the Apostle uses
to characterize this contrast seem to have been carefully chosen,
since they are each repeated either in this or in other contexts.
The body is sown in corruption, in dishonor, in weakness, sown a
natural body; it is raised in incorruption, in glory, in power, raised
a Spiritual body (vss. 42-44. The Apostle returns to the thought
of corruption in the end of the chapter declaring: *the dead shall be
raised incorruptible, and we shall be changed. For this corruptible
must put on incorruption, and this mortal must put on immortality. But when this corruptible shall have put on incorruption,
and this mortal shall have put on immortality, then shall come to
pass the saying that is written, Death is swallowed up in victory.*

---

75. Webb, R. A., *The Christian Hope*, pp. 148-49.

Again, in his last epistle, Paul speaks of the grace that hath been *manifested by the epiphany of our Saviour Christ Jesus who abolished death and brought life and incorruption to light through the Gospel.* Since the same epistle defines the Gospel as *Jesus Christ risen from the dead, of the seed of David,* it is evident that His Resurrection abolished death and brought incorruption to life (II Tim. i.10; ii.8). Though the word immortality does not occur in this passage as the English translation implies, it recurs in II Cor. v.4 in the wish that the mortal may be swallowed up of life.

In the history of this world of decay and rust, disease and corruption there was one who tabernacled in hope (Acts ii.26). By the Resurrection, Christ *was not left unto Hades, neither did His flesh see corruption* (Acts ii.31). While from the standpoint of past history this is an exception, from the truer standpoint of eschatology and God's purpose it is the firstfruits of them that sleep. Herein is the assurance that death shall be swallowed up of life. The mighty Conqueror of death, the Lord Jesus Christ, shall raise up those that are His in incorruption. His victory over the curse of the law, over death, over mortality, corruption and the grave is the evidence that He shall one day preach the funeral of death itself. In anticipation of that victorious hour His disciples even now sing,

> *O death, where is thy sting?*
> *O grave where is thy victory?*

The grave is not the terminus, but only a tunnel through which we go to share the glory of His Resurrection.

The *death* that *works in us* (II Cor. iv.12, 16) bringing decay in this life, and corruption thereafter, is not the end. Beyond death there is Christ the Conqueror of death, the Lord of life — Christ whose flesh did not see corruption, Christ who will raise up those that are His in incorruptible immortality. With Polycarp let us drink whatever cup Christ gives us looking "unto the eternal resurrection of the soul and the body in the incorruption of the Holy Spirit."

Risen in Power. Perhaps the most conspicous thing about the Christian movement, as the world viewed it, was its weakness. The Apostle Paul, in a way, concurred in this judgment. Those who carry the Christian message are but earthen vessels (II Cor. iv.7), of themselves "incompetent to produce the effects which flow from their ministrations." [76] The churches are only small, weak, faction-torn groups of all too inconsistent Christians. The thing that pressed upon Paul for repeated utterance as he was writing Second Corinthians was his own weakness (iv.9-13; xi. 29, 30; xii.5, 9, 10; xii.4). But the very frailty of weak, suffering, perishing ministers testified that the wonderful efficiency of the Gospel was from God (iv.7, 20). Paul was able even to glory in the thorn which God placed in his flesh, since God said,

> *My grace is sufficient for thee*
> *For my power is made perfect in weakness.*

Thus, the Apostle writes of taking pleasure in weaknesses, *"for when I am weak, then I am strong."*

Now here again, the revelation of this paradox is to be found in Christ. *He was crucified through weakness, yet he lived through the power of God.* The *via dolorosa* is the great revelation of human weakness. Weak with loss of sleep and blood, in agony and pain, the Saviour staggers and stumbles beneath the weight of the Cross. No hands are so powerless as those that have been affixed to the Cross! No cause is so hopeless as the cause of the now Crucified! No heart was ever so broken as was His, no Head more mangled and weary, no throat more parched, no side more torn in death. No corpse was more hopeless, rigid and weak than the body of Jesus which was removed from the Cross and buried in the Tomb of Joseph of Arimathea. Verily, Paul was thinking of Christ when he wrote, *It is sown in weakness.* He was also thinking of Christ when he added, *It is raised in power.* And, at least according to one interpretation of Paul's great statement of the Gospel in Rom. i.1-4, Christ was

---

76. Hodge, *Second Epistle to the Corinthians,* p. 92.

installed in the full possession and exercise of the Spirit of holiness by the might of the Resurrection from the dead. This thought the Apostle certainly presents in describing Christ as constituted a life-giving Spirit by the Resurrection (I Cor. xv.45). In the power of His Resurrection Christ entered upon a broader and more effectual operation of His Lordship and Mesiahship, as the center of the new eschatological order of things.

Similarly, the "oral gospel" represents God exalting the Crucified Jesus to His own right hand as Lord and Christ by the Resurrection (Acts ii.23-36). In the hour of His weakness Herod and Pilate and Israel gathered together against, crucified and slew God's holy Child Jesus; but God hath made Him a Prince and a Saviour to grant repentance and remission of sins (Acts ii.24; iv.27; v.31), so that there is salvation in none other (iv.12). When Paul tries to describe the great change which has bridged the tremendous gap between the weakness of Christ's body as it lay dead in the tomb and the greatness of its power as He was raised from the dead and made to sit at God's right hand above every authority, power, dominion and name, he exhausts the vocabulary of power (Eph. i.19-22). And best of all he applies this Divine barrage of power not only to Christ, but to us. His prayer is that we may know, *the exceeding greatness of His power to usward who believe according to that working of the strength of His might which He wrought in Christ when He raised Him from the dead.*

The vision of the power of His Resurrection empowered a weak and faltering Church. Or rather that might which raised Christ from the dead poured forth from the Head into the body through every joint of supply, so that the resurrection power of Christ carried onward His Church while empires rose and fell. But even so, only a foretaste of this power has been given. It is not written of Him only but also of His, *It is sown in weakness, it is raised in power.* How feeble is our candle here, how weak our testimony, how fragmentary our knowledge, how inconsistent our lives, how broken, dead and helpless are we laid away. Nevertheless, the Resurrection for believers, even as for their

Head, is "the entering upon a new phase of sonship characterized by the possession and exercise of unique supernatural power." When we shall see Him we shall be like Him. His servants shall serve Him as they "the power of His resurrection share."

Risen a Spiritual Body. It is sown a natural body, it is raised a Spiritual body. Thus, the glorified body is a Spiritual body. When the Lord comes in His glory He shall have the likeness of His Resurrection (Rom. vi.5). And since at His Resurrection He became a life-giving Spirit, we shall be raised Spiritual bodies. By giving us of the Spirit, the last Adam hath given us a foretaste of the age to come, in which we shall have a corporeality fitted for and wholly dominated, not by Adam's psychology, but by Christ's Holy Spirit. Because it is to be raised a Spiritual body, therefore it shall be raised in *incorruption, power, glory* and *immortality*. The present work of the Spirit foreshadows these glories. By His power we are raised from the death of sin to the life of Christ. In the midst of this present mortality, we have, in Christ, life everlasting. But we have these things now only in principle, in Christ, and, alas, in contradiction to our present sinful existence.

In the wonder of His grace our Lord took the likeness of our sinful flesh to save us from the condemnation of the law that comes on account of the weakness of our flesh (Rom. viii.3). He will bring in the age to come by showering a kindness upon us that will make our bodies like unto His (Phil. iii.21). Specifically, this means that the sexual desire and relation will be done away. The sons of the Resurrection neither marry nor are given in marriage (Lk. xx.34-36; Mt. xxii.22.30; Mk. xii.25 I Cor. vi.13). The last reference apparently indicates that the need for meats will as well be transcended, a suggestion that raises the question as to the eschatological meaning of the Saviour's words, "Man shall not live by bread alone, but by every word that proceedeth out of the mouth of God." "I will drink no more of the fruit of the vine until I drink it new with you in the Kingdom of God." Fellowship with the Father transfigures

Christ on the mount; Resurrection made Him a life-giving Spirit. Resurrection shall lift His people into a closeness with God, an atmosphere of the Spirit in which there shall be no place for the lusts and passions of the flesh.

In the New Testament, however, the flesh is not confined to these more physical appetites; it refers to the old Adam, the heart out of which proceed evil thoughts as well as evil deeds. Now this Adamic nature lusteth against the Spirit; then all these sundry evil works shall be done away: fornication, uncleanness, lasciviousness, idolatry, sorcery, enmities, strife, jealousies, wraths, factions, division, heresies, envyings, drunkenness and revellings. And in that body which shall be given to the race of the last Adam there shall gloriously flourish the fruits of the Spirit: love, joy, peace, longsuffering, kindness, goodness, faithfulness, meekness, self-control. The sowing is a stripping off of the Old Adamic nature, which expresses itself in these works of the flesh, and the putting on of the nature of the last Adam, which expresses itself in the fruits of the Spirit.

"The resurrection of the flesh of which the *Symbol* speaks is the abolition of this position which is ours amid that contradiction between the grace and the gracelessness of our own existence as such. Resurrection of the flesh does not mean that man ceases to be a man in order to become a god or angel, but that he may, according to I Cor. xv.42f., be a man in *incorruption, power and honor, redeemed* from that contradiction and so *redeemed* from the separation of body and soul by which this contradiction is sealed, and so in the totality of his human existence *awakened* from the dead. Resurrection of the flesh means very simply that the man will be in himself what he already is in Christ, a new creation (II Cor. v.17); that the garment of unrighteousness drops away from him and the garment of righteousness which he has for long been wearing secretly becomes visible." [77]

Over against our sinful natural body there is set the Spiritual, supernatural body; over against the earthly, the promise of the

77. Barth, K., *Credo*, p. 169.

heavenly; over against the Old Adam, the New Christ. In place of our fallen, sordid history there shall succeed the new life of the completely renewed man; instead of an earth and sea over which the wrath of Satan rages, there shall be the holy city New Jerusalem coming down out of heaven. In place of nations rising against against nations, and kingdoms against kingdoms, and wars and rumors of wars, there shall be the one eternal Kingdom of glory, of Spiritual bodies in the new Spiritual order. In place of the wickedness, the weakness, the wretchedness, the shame and the corruption there shall be a new heaven and a new earth in which dwelleth righteousness.

With the march of civilization in South Africa a syringa grove was cleared for cultivation. In so doing the workers came upon the grave of a missionary buried there almost a century earlier. With the body was a soapstone tablet bearing this inscription:

"Beneath this lies interred Ja . . . wife of ye Revd. A. E. Wilson, M.D., Missy. of ye Am.Bd. to ye Metabili. Her spirit was called away to join ye assembly of ye just in heaven, soon after she commenced her toils in this land. Her flesh sleeps till ye resurrection when it will rise to testify ye benevolent desires of her husband and those connected with him to impart ye blessing of ye Gospel to ye natives of Afrika. Xtian reader remember thy time like hers may be short, work while thou hast life, for Christ. Ob. Sep 1836." [78]

That stone marks the grave of Mary Jane Smithey Wilson, a twenty-two-year-old mother from the First Presbyterian Church of Richmond, who was the first white woman to give her life that the Gospel might be carried to the Transvaal. In the Resurrection her body will testify to the spirit which carried our pioneer missionaries, J. Leighton Wilson from South Carolina, Caroline Elizabeth Bayard Wilson from Georgia, Henry I. Venable and his wife from Kentucky, Alexander Erwin Wilson and Daniel Lindley from North Carolina and their wives, Mary Jane

---

78. Kaigh-Eustace, Edyth, *The Tragedy of Masega*, pp. 21-22.

Smithey Wilson and Lucy Allen Lindley from Richmond, to Africa over a century ago.

On that day what witness will our bodies bear? That we have gone or given for the evangelization of the world? That we have lived and served and borne opprobrium for the Christian faith or that we have surrendered the bastions of the Gospel to appease a rampant naturalism and gain for our bodies posts of pleasure, places of plenty, and popular plaudits?

CHAPTER VI.

THE PAROUSIA OF THE SON OF MAN

MATT. xxiv.27.

● *"O Jesu, mach ein Ende*
Und fuhr' uns aus dem Streit,
Wir heben Haupt und Hande
Nach der Erlosungzeit."

Unser Bekenntnis zu Jesus Christus,
ZURICH, 1938, p. 85.

Mk. xiv.62 ; Acts i.11 ; Tit. ii.13 ; Rev. xxii.20.

I. A LOOK BACKWARD IN THE HISTORY OF THOUGHT.

The eschatological school a development out of the history of religions school. Weiss. Wrede. Schweitzer.

The documents represent Jesus as teaching His Parousia.

Jesus described Himself as the Danielic Son of Man.

The Parousia expectation in the Early Church, in the Creeds.

The Parousia an element in the Christian revelation that is integral to the rule of faith.

II. A LOOK UPWARD IN REALIZED ESCHATOLOGY.

The collapse of evolution and the apocalyptic character of history drove men to eschatology.

194

Time and Eternity.
The last days.
God revealed in Christ.
The living Word present in the preached Word.
In the heavenlies in Christ.

III. A Look Forward in Hope.

The eschatological hope of things that will occur.
History interpreted by means of Christ, not "the things of Jesus" subordinated to an alien concept of history.
The Parousia an event. The Day of the Lord.

IV. The Precursors of His Parousia.

Wars. Earthquakes. False Messiahs.
The Gospel of the Kingdom preached to all Nations.
The Conversion of Israel.
The Conversion of Israel.
Anti-christ.
The Great Tribulation.
The Rapture and the Resurrection.

In one of his earliest epistles, Paul describes the early Christians as those who serve the living and true God and wait for His Son from heaven, even Jesus whom He raised from the dead and who delivereth us from the wrath to come. In the Apostles' Creed the coming again is the final article in the Christological section of the rule of faith, and as such is immediately connected with Christ's revelation, incarnation, expiation, resurrection and ascension to God's right hand.

Thus for primitive Christian thinking the Parousia is the point of expectancy and the event that sets the stage for everything else. And the question concerning the Parousia is the prominent thing that is driving twentieth century scholarship toward the acceptance of eschatology as future or end-history.[1] This is the key to the eschatology of the Bible and the drive of those scholars who are demanding the acceptance of eschatology as events that will occur as, or at, the end of history. The main line of the twentieth century understanding of Christian eschatology may, therefore, be unfolded by noting how it has progressively apprehended the great meanings of this blessed hope.

The critical lives of Jesus written fifty years ago rejected eschatology and insisted that Jesus desired to found a kingdom only in the inward, spiritual sense. For these critics Jesus was only an ethical or "spiritual" deliverer, who could not have delivered the apocalyptical discourses the Synoptists represent Him as delivering, who could not have held theocratic ideas or have pictured Himself coming in super-human glory. That He predicted a Second Coming was brushed aside as absolutely impossible. The only admissible coming of Jesus was the coming of the Holy Spirit. The Son of Man was interpreted as simply man, an ideal human, a purely mundane figure, whose whole purpose was to establish a community of believers and commit to them the bringing in of a kingdom of repentance. By reading between the lines a host of things that are not specifically there this "liberal" school presented a Jesus whose spiritual, religious consciousness overmastered the eschatological elements of Judaism.

Eschatology, rejected by the nineteenth and progressively accepted by the twentieth century, is the most significant difference between the New Testament criticism of these two centuries. For the former the Son of Man is mundane and humanistic, for the latter heavenly and apocolyptic; for the former Jesus is ethical, for the latter eschatological; for the former the Lord is to come only in principle, in spirit, for the latter He is to come personally, catastrophically on the clouds of Divine glory; for the former the Kingdom is wholly present and largely Providential, for the latter it is primarily future and sharply Christological. Today in war-torn Europe, "Christian minds are much more open to an

1. Holmstrom, F., *op. cit.*, p. 373.

apocalyptic or eschatological interpretation of the Bible, and from it learn that the nations must pass through God's judgment, must fight with principalities and powers in faith with repentance, and wait for the coming of the Lord who is the only way of salvation for mankind." [2]

The progressive acceptance of eschatology in this century divides into three periods, each of which was a step in re-validating the Christian hope. The first studied the eschatological hope as ancient history, the second transmuted it into super-history, the third recognized it as end history.

From the turn of the century until the first World War eschatology was presented by J. Weiss, W. Wrede and A. Schweitzer as an interesting phenomenon in the history of ideas, a matter of antiquarian interest. Yet this study showed that the Christian movement issued from an eschatological matrix, and that the primitive Christians lived in anticipation of the glorious Appearing of Christ. From the first World War until late in the twenties the dialectic theology demanded an actual eschatology with the meaning and pressure of eternity upon the here and now. As a vertical straight from above the eternal impinges upon every moment, the Parousia cries for present decision. While the writer is not willing to change the distinction between the present and the future into a here and there, or to metamorphose the eschatological consummation into a metaphysical value, he recognizes in this theology a needed distinction between Divine judgment and human sin, Divine righteousness and human depravity, and a call to receive the blessedness of Christian hope into our present lives. In the last decade and a half, the Biblicists have been insisting that the eschatological look is primarily forward, rather than either backward or upward. The Bible directs the Christian hope to an end of history in the future. The backward look at eschatology as past teaching establishes the eschatological character of that thinking which history has called Christian; the upward look establishes the heart in the living, reigning Christ who gathers

---

2. Adolph Keller in *The Philadelphia Presbyterian*, 1/25/40, p. 8. cf. *Christian Europe Today*.

up in Himself the grace of His first and the glory of His second coming; the forward look anchors our hope in the victory which He shall accomplish in spite of the world, the flesh and the Devil.

I. A LOOK BACKWARD IN THE HISTORY OF THOUGHT.

The eschatological school of New Testament criticism appeared as a group within the school of comparative religions. In the name of historical truth this school sought a realistic understanding of the genuine individuality and distinctive characteristics of primitive Christianity. By presenting the thought world of late Jewish apocalyptic, the eschatologists succeeded in showing its impress upon early Christianity. Johannes Weiss distinguished between the thinking of his day and the eschatological world view of Jesus, and protested against reading the leading ideas of one's own times into such historical authorities as Jesus or Luther.

This broke the dominant Ritschlian systematics built on the idealistic model of the nineteenth century with its harmless little chapter at the end of dogmatics, which denied the conceivability of the contents and excluded a doctrine of the last things.[3] From the Ritschlian school came this confession: "Ritschl's thought of the Kingdom of God and the idea in the preaching of Jesus which goes by the same name are two very different things. . . . Further studies have convinced me that the proper roots of Ritschl's ideas lie in Kant and the Enlightenment." [4]

Wilhelm Wrede charges "the modern historical view" with foisting upon the text a host of things of which Mark knows nothing and of making these the foundation of the "modern" view. An evolutionary development of the Messianic consciousness of Jesus is unknown to the oldest Gospel. Psychological explanations which are used to connect the several pericopes do not exist save in the *a priori* of the theologian. Each pericope must be studied separately, the "solder" material will not stand. The modern student has supplied the rationale for this scheme

3. Barth, K., *Der Romerbrief*, 1922, p. 484; M. Kahler in re. Kaftan.
4. Schmollers, O., *Die Lehre vom Reiche Gottes in den Scriften des Neuen Testaments*, cited Holmstrom, *op. cit.* p. 62.

from his own presuppositions which are not those of the record. The idea of a "historical kernel" must be given up until it is shown that the kernel can be separated from the husks. The kernel method detaches a logion from its own context, places it in an alien frame and so transforms it into something different. For this school of eschatology, "the Jesus of Nazareth who stepped forward as the Messiah, who preached the ethical nature of the Kingdom of God, founded the Kingdom of Heaven upon earth and died to consecrate His work, never existed. He is a form that was designed by rationalism, animated by 'liberalism' and clothed by modern theology with historical scholarship." [5]

Indeed, this school swung the pendulum for the concepts of both the self-consciousness of Jesus and the Kingdom of God to the opposite extreme from nineteenth century "liberalism." Weiss held that the Kingdom of God was a purely future and super-worldly magnitude, a catastrophic removal of the present world-order breaking in from above, and that the messianic consciousness of Jesus during His whole earthly life was only a claim upon the future in which He would come again in glory as the apocalyptic Son of Man. "If the Kingdom were future, so also were the Messiah." Holding that the messianic glory must be construed in an entirely apocalyptical manner, Wrede denied that Jesus could have made a public messianic claim or even have held that He would appear as the Son of Man of the apocalypses. For him, the messianic secret was unhistorical and the dogma of Jesus' messiahship was a secondary product of church theology.

Even this radically negative criticism is not, however, without some positive testimony. Wrede admitted that the Gospels as we have them do represent Jesus' identification of Himself with the Son of Man as the Messianic secret. The volumes on *The Beginnings of Christianity* find the Son of Man in the Similitudes of Enoch closely connected with the great day of judgment at the end of the Age and with the Resurrection which opens the door

---

5. Schweitzer, A., *The Quest of the Historical Jesus*, pp. 331, 396,

of life to those who are worthy of the age to come. "That Son of Man of Enoch ushers in the End and the Age to come." The writers of the Gospels regarded Jesus as the Son of Man who would come in the clouds of heaven, and these references to His Pourousia are wholly intelligible in the light of Jewish thought. In Mark and in Q, "There is a series of passages in which the Son of Man is used in connection with the Parousia. He is to come unexpectedly on the clouds of heaven, seated at the right hand of power." Further, Acts vii.56 is an obvious reference to the words of Jesus before the Sanhedrin as given in Luke xii.69. "The opinion of the writers of the Gospels is thus clear that Jesus used the phrase, and used it of Himself." [6] Similarly, Professor F. C. Grant holds that "Mark aimed to set forth in his Gospel the outward career of Jesus and his 'mighty works' as evidence that Jesus was Messias or 'son of Man' — even during his earthly life and hence long preceding his resurrection and glorification, not to say his final Parousia." [7] Accordingly, even for radical criticism, "There can be no doubt that an unbroken tradition going back to his actual hearers identified Jesus with the Son of Man of whose coming he had spoken and whose functions are accurately indicated in such passages as Acts x.42; xvii.31."

Further, the more completely this term is placed in its documentary, linguistic, contextual and messianic configuration, the more clearly does it fit the sundry factors of Christian life and development into an orderly picture. And this fixation of the Son of Man into the Gospel picture sustains the intrinsic probability that the Evangelists rather than the school of Wrede have correctly interpreted Jesus' use of the term.

As far as the records go, the Son of Man is almost exclusively Jesus' self-designation. The Gospels and the predicated sources of the Gospels show that Jesus identified Himself with the Son of Man in contexts which speak of the humiliation and passion He was immediately facing (Mk. viii.31; ix.9, 12, 31; x.33, 45;

6. *The Beginnings of Christianity*, I:373, 374, 376, 378; IV.129.
7. Grant, *The Gospel of the Kingdom*, p. 122.

xiii.41; Matt. xxvi.45; Jn. xii.34) as well as in His explicit claim to the heavenly and eschatological glory of the Son of Man given in His answer to the High Priest (Mk. xiv.61-62; Matt. xxvi.63-66; Lk. xxii.69). The Gospels place the phrase eighty times on the lips of Jesus and nowhere on the lips of others, save one repetition of His usage (Jn. xii.34). Thereafter there are allusions to the Greater Confession which Jesus made to the High Priest (Mk. xiv. 61-62) on the lips of Stephen in his martyr ecstasy (Acts vii.56), and a smiliar one in Hegesippus' account of James' testimony which led to his martyrdom.[8] According to Johannes Weiss, *the Man from Heaven* (I Cor. xv.47) is a translation of this primitive Aramaic title, a part of the tradition which Paul received from the first disciples. Ross sees in this *Second Man* a reference to *the Seed of the Woman* which occurs in Genesis after mention of the first man and before his son Cain appears.[9] Then the title underlies John's vision of *one like unto a son of man,* who reappears on the cloud with angels for the final judgment (Rev. i.13; xiv.14). Accordingly, the New Testament places the Son of Man almost exclusively on Jesus' lips, and on the lips of others only as reflecting His usage, or as describing a vision of Him in Heaven.

The linguistic background of the term has been carefully studied and presented by Gustaf Dalman and K. L. Schmidt.[10] The incident of Jesus reading the prophetic portion of the synagogue lesson (Lk. iv.16) shows that He knew Hebrew, the language of His Bible. "The Biblical Aramaic does not differ from the usage in Hebrew" and in Daniel vii.13 the Aramaic phrase *"bar enosh* is simply the translation of the Hebrew *ben adham."* Anyone hearing Jesus' Aramaic use of the Son-of-Man would have recourse to Scripture for an explanation of the strange erm. "And Scripture offered the like Aramaic expression only in Dan. vii.13, *kebar enosh."* While the term in Daniel stands as a representative of the Kingdom of the saints of the Most

---

8. Eusebius, *Church History,* II.xxiii.13.
9. Ross, A., *The Evangelical Quarterly,* 6.1.46-47.
10. Dalman, G., *The Words of Jesus,* pp. 248, 245, 238, 240, 256; *Jesus-Jeshua,* p. 37; Schmidt, K. L., Ekklesia in Kittel's *Theologisches Worterbuch,* III:528.

High (vii.18, 22, 27), even there the Son of Man denotes a definite personality which was sometimes understood to denote the Messiah, for example, by Akiba and in Enoch. The greatest teacher that the world has ever known was certainly able to make clear to His disciples that He was the Danielic Messiah by the use of the same term and its context, by explanatory remarks, intonations, gestures, questions, etc. Thus, Dibelius admits that Jesus may have spoken of the Son of Man as in Luke xvii.24 and Mark viii.38, and in spite of the reserve and mystery of His speech and the ambiguity of the Aramic expression, the reference would have been clear to those who shared this eschatological expectation.[11]

Moreover, the significant context in which the Son of Man occurs in Daniel is taken over by Jesus in His description of the Parousia of the Son of Man on *the clouds of heaven.* The clouds are the symbol of a Theophany. Hence, "the scene in Daniel means to describe the introduction of a superhuman, heavenly Being into the lower world, and that after a theophanic fashion." [12] In Daniel and Enoch, the Son of Man is the title that expresses most clearly that the Messiah comes from Heaven, from the other side, from God. "In seeing in that designation the title of soveregnty *par excellence,* G. Kittel has only reproduced the general opinion, one that in this case is well established." [13] Further, by using this title which stresses the sole agency of God in shattering hostile sovereignty and in establishing this messianic glory (Dan. ii.34, 35; vii.13, 27), Jesus directed the eyes of His hearers away from schemes of political deliverance and appropriation of the Messiah's sovereignty by human force. The Son of Man waits for God to bestow upon Him universal dominion, and as He waits upon God, He accepts as indispensable whatever the Divine will ordains. His meat is to do the will of Him that sent Him.

In Enoch lxii.6; lxix.26-29 "the existence of the Son of Man was twofold: on the one hand he will exist in the future *with*

11. Dibelius, M., *Jesus,* pp. 75f, 83f; *Gospel Criticism and Christology,* pp. 47f.
12. Vos, G., *The Self-Disclosure of Jesus,* p. 241.
13. Schmidt, K. L., *Jesus Messie et Fils de l'Homme, Revue D' Histoire et De Philosophie Religieuses,* 1938:1:44, 51-52, citing Jean Hering and G. Kittel.

power, and on the other hand, he has not yet come *with power,* but is still hidden with God *before his power."* In the Gospels the Most High reveals the Son of Man to the elect before His power (Matt. xvi.13-17; xi.25; Lk. x.22; cf. Acts x.41), but the coming of the Son of Man on the clouds of heaven with power and great glory shall be as lightning that is seen from the East to the West (Matt. xxiv.27-30; xvi.27). Thus, "He was from the outset the Elect One of whom the Book of Enoch continually speaks, and thereby actually was already the Son of Man *before His power."* And when Jesus solemnly designated Himself as the Son of Man with associations of the judgment, the coming world, the right hand of God, the throne, the coming with the clouds of heaven it meant to His disciples the King in the coming world.[14]

Apocalyptical writers in later Judaism put together in an exterior way the Servant of Jehovah and the Messiah, or the Servant of Jehovah and the Son of Man, but in so doing removed every trace of the suffering Messiah.[15] But the Voice at His baptism directed Jesus to the Isaianic Servant of Jehovah, and this figure is the suffering Servant. Hence, as soon as the disciples had confessed His Messiahship, Jesus showed them that even though He is the Son of Man, He has come not to be ministered unto, but to minister and to give His life "as a *lutron,* a means of atonement" instead of many (Mk. x.45; Mt. xx.28). This verse, Mk. ix.12 (cf. Isa. liii.3) and the words of the Last Supper show that Jesus had synthesized the Son of Man and the suffering Servant of Jehovah. As Jesus represents Him the Son of Man is the Man of Sorrows who was to be despised and rejected of men (cf. Lk. xxii.37). Even the transcendent glory which belongs of right to the Son of Man cannot exempt Him from the experience of humiliation and death. "In the message of the New Testament the unheard-of paradox of the Messiah Son of Man who suffers constitutes the full revelation of the love of

14. Otto, R., *op. cit.* pp. 186, 192, etc.
15. Schmidt, K. L., *supra,* pp. 41, 43, 49, citing Syriac Baruch, IV Esdras and the Targum on Isaiah lii.13-liii.12.

God for men who have fallen under the thralldom of sin." [16]
"This marvelous term, the Son of Man . . . embraces the heavenly
glory and the earthly humiliation of the Son of God. The glory
is concealed, till under the canditions of the Resurrection and
Ascension and Advent it is manifested; and yet the glory is there,
operating under the conditions of earthly humiliation." [17]

By putting together the Son of Man and the Servant of the
Lord, Jesus mightily changed the Messianic conception and presented the Kingdom of God as at hand as He cast out demons,
as actually come when He ascends the Throne of David, without
ceasing to be the eschatological magnitude that shall be realized
at the Parousia of the Son of Man. With such paradoxical
thoughts as suffering and reigning, the Son of Man was a title
of revelation to those who received it and an enigma of mystery
to those who refused the messianic secret. Upon this mystery
element Wrede, Schweitzer, Jean Hering and Karl Barth have
fixed. Before appearing at the end of time as the Messiah of
the Kingdom of Glory, Jesus has already appeared in time as a
Messiah more or less hidden, walking the path of suffering designated for Him when God's Voice identified Him with the Servant of the Lord. Having first appeared as the Son of Man in a
paradoxical role, He testified to the High Priest that He would
enter upon the appropriate glory of the Son of Man at His
Ascension to the Throne, His session at the right-hand of Glory
and His Parousia on the clouds of Heaven.

This conception of the Son of Man and His Kingdom has led
to the rehabilitation of the direct connection between Jesus and
the Church and has thereby given a new insight into the whole
of Christian history. In Daniel the Son of Man is both a Messianic figure and the representative of the saints of the Most
High.[18] "The Messiah is the divinely appointed Head of the
people of God and the bearer of His Kingdom to the whole

---

16. Staerk, Willy, cited by Schmidt, *supra*, p 42. Similarly, G. Vos, N. B. Stonehouse,
R. Otto, A. Ross.
17. Hebert, A. G., *The Throne of David*, p. 135.
18. Duncan, D. S., in *The Christian Faith*, p. 127.

world." [19] Our Lord concentrated the Son of Man figure in Himself as the central and for the time the sole representative of that people. As the one perfect Citizen of the Kingdom of Heaven, the Messiah is the pledge of a society in which the will of God shall be done on earth as it is in Heaven, and the gracious ground on which God makes Himself our Father and leads us on toward that perfect order. As the Shepherd presupposes the Flock, as the Servant of Jehovah stands for the Remnant of Israel, as the Son of Man gathers the people of the saints of the Most High,[20] so the Messiah builds His Church This Messianic conception carries with it the implication that the self-revelation of God in the person, words and works of Jesus is the foundation of the Church (Mt. xvi.17).

"Both as to its form and as to its meaning, the term *Messiah, Anointed* is absolutely unique in the history of religions. In fact, it finds itself established today only in the Biblical world, in Judaism and in Christianity. It designates the King who will come *at the end of the days.*" [21] This fundamental conception of the Messiah as the Coming One is accentuated in the Son-of-Man title. That is, our Lord used as His favorite self-designation that Messianic term which would not, by his historic ministry, exhaust and destroy the hope of His future Appearing, but would rather serve to accentuate that hope. The Son of Man shall come on the clouds of heaven (Matt. xxvi.64; xxiv.30); come with power and great glory (Matt. xvi.27; xxiv.30); come with His angels (Matt. xxv.31; xvi.27; xiii.41); come in His Kingdom (Matt. xvi.28); come for the final judgment (Matt. xxv.31).

Indeed, the future coming of Christ is the *Parousia,* the coming spoken of both in the Gospels and in the later books of the New Testament (Matt. xxiv.27, 37, 39; I Thess. ii.19; iii.13; iv.15; v.23; II Thess. ii.1, 8; I Cor. xv.23; Acts i.11; James v.7-8; II Peter iii.3-4, 12; I John ii.28). The word *parousia* describes the formal, public state coming of a ruler; and accordingly is

19. Dodd, C. H., *History and the Gospel,* p. 67.
20. So F. Kattenbusch, R. N. Flew, *Jesus and His Church,* K. L. Schmidt, Ekklesia in Th.W-b. iii:522-530.
21. Schmidt, K. L., *Jesus Messie et Fils de l'Homme,* p. 39.

used in the New Testament as parallel with *epiphany* or public manifestation (Heb. ix.28; I Tim. vi.14; II Tim. 1.10; Titus ii. 13), with the revelation of Jesus Christ (Luke xvii.29-30; I Cor. i.7; II Thess. i.7-8), and with the day of the Lord Jesus (I Cor. i.7-8; Matt. vii.22-23; II Peter iii.11-12; Matt. xxiv.3 -37; Luke xvii.24; xxi.34; x.12; Acts ii.20; Rom. xiii.12; I Cor. iii.13; II Cor. i.14; Phil. i.6; ii.16; I Thess. v.2, 4; II Thess. ii.1-2; II Tim. i.12, 18; iv.8; Heb. x.25; II Peter iii.10).

From our look backward, therefore, we conclude that the New Testament looks for the coming of the Messiah as distinctly as does the Old Testament. Indeed, the New Testament testifies that He has Himself appeared in the flesh and given repeated assurances that He will manifest Himself a second time apart from sin unto salvation. "If evidence can establish anything, that Christ Himself stated He would reappear as Judge of all mankind, is beyond doubt." [22] Jesus' own teachings as definitely center on this glorious coming as do the life and teachings of the primitive Church. The Old Testament, later Jewish apocalyptic writings, John the Baptist, Jesus, the Acts, the Epistles, Revelation and, the Apostolic Fathers agree in holding out the promise of the Messiah's coming from heaven. As we integrate ourselves into our own heritage, we look for the blessed hope, even the epiphany of the glory of our great God and Saviour, Jesus Christ (Titus ii.13).

"This hope of the Second Coming dominated the life, thought and prayer of the Early Church down to the time of Tertullian, at least." [23] "Jesus shall so come in like manner as He went into heaven" (Acts i.11). For heaven has received Him until the times of the restoration of all things (Acts iii.20-21). The Resurrection is God's declaration that this Man is ordained to judge the world (Acts xvii.31). Timothy is charged in the sight of God and of Christ Jesus who will judge the living and the dead, and by His appearing and His kingdom (II Tim. iv.1). Polycarp writes of Him "who comes the Judge of the living and

---

22. Davies, D. R., *The Two Humanities*, p. 223.
23. Davies, D. R., *The Two Humanities*, p. 223.

the dead" (Philippians ii). Irenaeus includes in *the received faith*, "His future manifestation from heaven in the glory of the Father;" "who will come in glory, the Saviour of those who are saved, and the Judge of those who are judged." And again, "He will come in the glory of the Father for the resurrection of all flesh and the manifestation of salvation and to show the rule of judgment to all who are placed under Himself." *(Against Heresies,* i.10.1; iii.4.122; iii.16.6). Hippolytus writes that He cometh to judge the living and the dead *(Against Noetus).* According to *the Didascalia* (vi. 23, 80) He "cometh with glory to judge living and dead." [24] *Second Clement* quotes the Lord as speaking of coming to gather all nations, that is, of the day of His own appearing. *The Didache* (xvi) inculcates watching since we "know not the hour in which our Lord cometh" and gives a number of pre-cursors of His coming. *Barnabus* exhorts, "set your hope on Him who is about to be manifested to you in the flesh, even Jesus." *Hermas* thinks of the end as coming when the building of the tower shall be finished and when the elect, spotless and pure, go to dwell in the coming age.[25]

In the New Testament the Second Advent is the Coming, the Parousia, the term being used only once of His former Advent and that in connection with the Glory of the Transfiguration which was more characteristic of His return than of the days of His humiliation. In the second century, however, the fathers began to distinguish the first and second comings and so the expression the *Second Coming* took form. Thus, Justin Martyr writes,

> "For the prophets have proclaimed two advents of His: the one, that which is already past, when He came as a dishonored and suffering man; but the second, when, according to prophecy, He shall come from heaven with glory, accompanied by His angelic host, when also He shall raise

---
24. Lietzmann, H., *Symbolstudium* in *Zeitschrift fur die neutestament. Wissenschaft*, 1923.
25. Pieters, A., *Chiliasm in the Writings of the Apostolic Fathers, The Calvin Forum*, August and September, 1938.

the bodies of all men who have lived and shall clothe those of the worthy with immortality, and shall send those of the wicked, endued with eternal sensibility, into everlasting fire with the wicked devils." *(The First Apology, III)*.

The Epistle to Diognetus sets forth,
"He sent Him as calling not as pursuing, He sent Him as loving not as judging. For He will send Him as Judge, and who shall endure His Parousia?" (vii.5, 6).

Tertullian holds that *the rule of faith* was taught by Christ and concludes it with the affirmation that Jesus Christ "will come with glory to take the saints to the enjoyment of everlasting life and of the heavenly promises, and to condemn the wicked to everlasting fire after the resurrection of both these classes shall have happened, together with the restoration of their flesh." [26]

Thus, the most primitive form of the rule of truth included the Parousia of Christ, whence it has continued to be an integral part of the Apostles', of the Eumenical and of Athanasian Creeds, as of the doctrinal statements of the various denominations. "This doctrine of the second advent has been held always, everywhere, and by all, in all churches, ancient and modern, oriental and western, primitive, mediaeval and protestant, as one of the fundamental doctrines of the Christian Church, one of the first principles of the oracles of God, concerning which there ought not to be, and never has been any doubt." [27] The 1939 General Assembly of the Presbyterian Church in the United States declared that the acceptance of Christ's coming again to judge the world was involved in the ordination vows to which we subscribe.

The look backward has shown that the Parousia of Christ is an article of the Christian faith. To those who say it is merely

---

26. Tertullian, *Against Heresies*, xiii; Cf.*On the Veiling of Virgins*, III.1. Ante-Nicene Fathers III.248; iv.27.
27. Smyth, Thomas, *Works*, IX.367.

a piece of Christian ideology, we reply it is a genuine piece, integral to the whole picture. It is not a detached segment, it is a true sector of the circle, an important bastion in the line. Accordingly, the rejection of the Parousia is the rejection of Christian revelation. And Jesus Christ is God's Yea and Amen to the Christian faith.

"Speaking historically, it is hardly too much to say that the belief in Christ's first coming has not been more general, more firmly held, more a part of the consciously or unconsciously held doctrinal possessions of the Church from the apostolic times until now, than the belief in his second coming." [28]

II. A Look Upward in Realized Eschatology.

So long as political and economic prosperity encouraged "the belief that man is capable of creating a just and perfect society," the Kingdom of God was treated as a perfection that man him- self would inevitably achieve in this world [29] and the eschatolog- ical thinking of the New Testament was treated as a chapter in the history of ancient ideology. But the first World War and its failure to end wars "took the lid off that human nature of sup- posed fundamental goodness" and the humanistic "myth of inevitable, unchecked progress." The fallacy of adapting and subordinating New Testament Christianity to secular philosophies began to appear. With the realization that there was no answer to the yearning for the Golden Age in a self-contained historical process, men looked for the fulfillment of the hopes and dreams and promises of history in some kind of super-history. In the days following the Great War history itself took on for that generation an apocalyptic character. An eschatological period calls forth theological eschatology.[30]

Time and Eternity. However, a clean break with the philoso- phical misinterpretation of Christianity did not occur. Troelsch's

28. Foulkner, J. A., *Crises in the Early Church,* p. 98.
29. Davies, D. R., *On to Orthodoxy,* 1939, pp. 10, 16, 25, 106, 114.
30. Althaus, P., *Die Letzten Dinge,* 1922, cited F. H., *op.cit.,* p. 177.

effort to found an eschatology in a timeless metaphysics according to which "the last things have above all nothing to do with time" carried onward the erroneous Kantian distinction between time as a necessary subjective form of human consciousness and the timeless reality of the thing-in-itself. The super-historical world of eternal values and holy norms issued in axiological eschatology with the eternal judging the historical and temporal, and teleological eschatology with this judgment pointing the believer upward to higher living. In this period, Althaus held that "eschatology has to do neither with end-history nor with the end of history, but with that which is beyond history. It is not apolcalyptic." [31] Brunner accepted Plato and Kant as "pacemakers for the evangelical understanding of the Word," as schoolmasters to Christ.[32] Barth, professing "the importance" of Plato and Kant, declared that the New Testament End was "no temporal event, no legendary destruction of the world," no "coarse and brutal spectacle." "It has nothing to do with any historical or 'telluric' castastrophe." [33] In Dodd's "realized eschatology," "the myth of the Last Judgment" was actually attained in the death and resurrection of Jesus Christ.[34] Thus, Tillich and the dialectic theology "changed the primitive cosmological eschatology into a theory of knowledge." [35]

Barth has, however, corrected his earlier views by accepting the Parousia, the Resurrection, the Judgment, the New Heavens and the New Earth as events that will occur. He presents eschatology not as mere apocalyptic, but as a dialectic between a present transcendence and an end consummation. He also distinguishes four "times." In *created time* God's grace was an actuality. As a result of the Fall there is *our time* or *sinful time*

31. Althaus, P., *DvD*, 1922, cited F. H., *op. cit.* p. 177.
32. Brunner, E., *Die Mystik und das Wort*, 1924, p. 105, cited F. H., *op. cit.*, p. 202.
33. Barth, K., *The Epistle to the Romans*, pp. 4, 500.
34. Dodd, C. H., *History and the Gospel*, p. 170.
35. Koehler, W., *Dogmengeschichte*, p. 32; Tillich, P., *The Kingdom of God and History*, pp. 120-121.
36. Cited, Schilder, K., *Zur Begriffsgeschichte des "Paradoxen,"* Kampen.

in which the Most High — Jesus Christ — is rejected and finds
no home. Though in "our" time, *Revelation time* is not of it and
cannot be interpreted in terms of our chronology else Revelation
would be, at least in part, discovery and not Revelation. When
"our" chronology shall be no more (Rev. x.3) the final or fulfilled or *Redemption time* shall make actual what is only anticipated in hope today. It has been suggested that when Barth
speaks of the contemporaneity of *chosen before the foundation
of the world* with that which took place at Bethlehem and Calvary he is referring to *Revelation time* in a dialectic which recognizes their historical sequence in *our time*.[39]

The classical Calvinist can also think of Eternity overarching
time somewhat as heaven overaches earth and of God's act flash-
ing down vertically into the horizontal plane of our human life.
"For us also the difference between time and eternity is quali-
tative and infinite, and eternity is not merely an infinite lineal
extension backward and forward of our time."[40] "When we say
that God is eternal we mean that there never was or shall be any
possibility of relationship in sequence independent of God." [41]
For of Him and through Him and unto Him are all things (Rom.
xi.36). However, we do not agree that the birth of Christ or
our own regeneration are in eternity in the same sense that God's
election is. God has created the earth as well as the heavens.
God has decreed time, establishing its beginning, its objective
chronological measurements (Gen. i.14) and determined its end.
"History is the creation of the Creator and therefore, it is also
a whole to which God has set the Beginning and the Ending." [42]
The eternal God, who is master of time and space, is also the one
who governs through time and space, and can use it as a medium
of His revelation. "In God and for God there is neither before

39. *The Knowledge of God and the Service of God*, p. 78.
40. Kromminga, D., in *The Sovereignty of God*, p. 75.
41. Buswell, J. O., *What is God?* pp. 25-28.
42. Gogarten, F., *Ich Glaube an den Dreieinigen Gott*, pp. 17-39.

nor after." [43]   But God has acted in temporal reality, and in dealing with us has used the terms *pre* and *fore* to indicate the point
of view in time at which He has placed us and at which He
wishes us to place ourselves. In accommodating His eternal
truth to our finite comprehension, God has spoken in the terms
He has ordained distinguishing between election before the foundation of the world, or before the beginning of time, and the
decree that went out from Caesar Augustus in time. The Incarnation is the acme of accommodation, and the Incarnate Word
foretold the treachery of Judas and the repentance of Peter. We
do not get closer to Biblical realism by substituting for this
Biblical terminology one derived from idealistic philosophy. Since
the Most High has graciously taken our nature and spoken our
language, why should we not be content to speak the only language we can understand?

The "naive" imagery that compares time and eternity with a
bounded and an infinite line is not made less anthropocentric by
being exchanged for a "philosophically purified" concept of time
and eternity. Rather the "naive" concept ought to be qualified by
Biblical, that is, by theocentric and soteriological thinking.
Accordingly, the meaning of history and the importance of any
event in history are determined by the decrees of God which both
transcend and become history. The Divine Act of Redemption
which occurred in Christ is the foundation on which God has
granted the fallen creation a history and enrolled the names of
His elect from the foundation of the world in the Lamb's book of
life. "When the Christian speaks of the fulfillment of time with
eternity, he can properly mean the fulfillment of revelation in
the Incarnation period of saving-history, also the execution of
personal decision in the subjective time of grace for the individual, and still further the conclusion of universal history in end-
history." [44]

43. Lecerf A., in *De L'Election Eternelle de Dieu.* Cf. Hodge, A. A., *Commentary on the Conf. of Faith.* p. 76; Berghof, *Summary of Christian Doctrine,* p. 35.
44. Holmstrom, F., *op. cit.* p. 329.

"The Christian dwells not in the cosmical, but in a thoroughly redemptive heaven. It in principle beatifies and beckons believers onward to its final consummation. Heaven, so to speak, has received time and history into itself, no less than time has received unchangeableness into itself. Herein lies the significance of the repatriation of Christ into heaven carrying thither with Himself all the historical time-matured fruit of His earthly stage of work, and now from there guiding with impartial solicitude the two lines of terrestrial and celestial development of His Church." [45]

The Last Days. There is a place in the Biblical frame of time for the upward as well as the forward look, and the great eschatological events of the Bible, in distinction from mere apocalyptic, are important for our present life. According to the Bible, the last things began with the coming of the Messiah who placed the verticals of the Father's eye (Mt. vi.4, 6, 18), the Father's care (vi.8, 22), the Father's example (v.45-48), the Father's glory (v.16) over all life.

In the Old Testament, the Messianic times were spoken of as the "last days" or "the latter days" (Gen. xl.i, 10; Num. xxiv. 14, 17, 20; Isa. ii.2; Mic. iv.2). The New Testament Christians understood that these "last days" or the end of the times had begun with the first appearance of Jesus (I Peter i.20; Hebr. i.2). Since the end of the ages has come unto them (I Cor. x.11), their own present is also the last time. Peter introduces this phrase in his Pentecostal account of the outpouring of the Spirit (Acts ii.17) and the epistles use it in describing the approaching evil of the times (II Tim. iii.1; James v.3; II Peter iii.3; I John ii.18). Calvin understands that the whole New Testament era from the Incarnation to the Judgment is designated as "the last time," "the last times," "the last days." [46] Ignatius writes that these are "the last times" (Ephesians).

Realizing that the latter days have already begun, the disciples look for the last day and the last plague; they anticipate over-

45. Vos, G., *P.T.R.*, xxvii:443.
46. *Institutes*, IV.viii.7.

coming the last enemy; they listen for the sound of the last
trumpet (Rev. xv.1; xxi.9; I Cor. xv.26, 53; John vi. 39ff).[47]
They heard things which prophets and wise men had desired to
hear, and saw things which they had vainly desired to see (Matt.
xiii.17). "The Christian message from the beginning was dominated by the conviction that the New Israel was already being
constituted because the new era had already dawned."[48] That
which the Old Testament had lumped together as the last days
of the Messianic times was now outspread, so as to include the
immediate past in which Christ had been manifest, the urgent
present in which they were living, the immediate future, as well
as the final day of the Lord and the endless forever in which
God's people will walk in the Name of the Lord (Mic. iv.5).

Since the realization of eschatology has already begun in the
Resurrection of Christ, God now commandeth men everywhere
to repent. Now is the accepted time. Today is the day of salvation! Today, if ye will hear His voice, harden not your hearts!
The axe lieth at the roots! Be not high-minded but fear. For
if God spared not the natural branches neither will He spare
thee. Knowing therefore the fear of the Lord, we persuade
men! Be ye reconciled to God! Receive not the grace of God
in vain!

God revealed in Christ. The driving impact of this appeal is
just the whole saving revelation of God in Jesus Christ our
Lord. The heart and life of the Christian message is, "that Jesus
Christ is very God and very man, God manifest in the flesh, the
one only power unto salvation from sin and endless death by
atoning expiatory sacrifice, through faith alone." "Not bare
sovereignty, arbitrary will, naked power, but a personal God of
grace, the God revealed in Christ is the God of Calvinism."[49]
While Calvinism maintains that God is absolute, responsible only
to His own character,[50] it also insists that the character of our
God is revealed in the Lord Jesus Christ.

---

47. Cf. Kittel, G. *Th.W.* II.695.
48. Flew, R. N., *Jesus and His Church*, pp. 143-144.
49. Smith, E. W., *The Creed of Presbyterians*, 1901, pp. 44, 200.
50. McGiffert, A. C., *The Rise of Modern Religious Ideas*, p. 245.

Mindful of Staupitz' advice to Luther to find himself in the wounds of Christ ere he contemplated predestination, Calvin tells us not to contemplate our election in ourselves or even in the Father apart from the Son. "Christ, therefore, is the mirror in which it behooves us to contemplate our election, and here we may do it with safety." What he said of this much discussed doctrine is typical of Calvin's intent in all doctrines. He recognized in *the analogy of the faith* "an invariable standard by which all interpretations of Scripture ought to be tried." [51]

Among more recent theologians, Dr. T. C. Johnson has been quoted as frequently answering the objections of students with the remarks that they were seeing only a part of the whole, only an arc in the circle of Divine truth. Barth's students object to the voluminousness of his dogmatics, but the professor says that he has to sketch the whole circle of revelation before taking up any one doctrine lest he fail to apprehend a particular doctrine in the light of the central truth of the Word. This means that in discussing God one ought always to remember that He is the Triune God, in His unity, His plentitude, and His distinctions, in His Lordship and His glory, in His love and His freedom as revealed in Christ. It means that Providence is not apart from Christ, for the world was created as a theatre for the glory of God manifest in the flesh. It means that one never knows man in contradiction until he finds man in grace. It means that the Christological doctrine — Christ as true God and true man — is the organizing principle for Christian theology and an analogy by which to test other doctrines. Thus, is Christ both the electing God and the elected man, the sanctifying God and at the same time the sanctified man.

Through the ages the rule of faith has kept something of the total revelation of God in Christ in the minds of both theologians and everyday Christians. In the early church, the Bible was regarded as the expanded rule of truth, the baptismal creed as the same rule of faith in its compressed form. The catechisms of the Reformation, the outline of the Institutes, the liturgies of

---

51. *Institutes,* III.xxiv.5; III.ii.35; Dedication.

Calvin, Knox and Cranmer show that the Creed held as important a place in the Protestant age of faith as it held in the early church. As expounded in the Heidelberg Catechism, the Apostles' Creed unfolds "a panorama of the facts of redemption, as they move from the purpose of the Father in the untrodden past to the everlasting life which awaits His sons and daughters in the untrackable future." [52]

The use of the Creed places the worshipper in the theocentric realism of the Bible rather than in an alien world and life view. This view recognizes the primacy and might of God in His threefold activities as Creator, Redeemer and Regenerator. Indeed the Creed throws such an exclusive emphasis upon the acts of God for our salvation that it implicitly teaches justification solely by faith in these acts. And history approached in the credal way is not a descent into an alien gorge. "Providence is God in operation as the Maker of History." [53] Born of the Virgin Mary, suffered under Pontius Pilate, rose again on the third day are not myths, but events in which God the Father Almighty, miraculously acted in history. The Creed is anchored in the factual, once-for-allness of the Incarnation, Crucifixion and Resurrection. And the path of a vigorous and a victorious Christianity will never be marked by the surrender of these bastions of the faith in order to appease the naturalism of the Enlightenment or the secularism of the world.

Since these actual events are final, "Everywhere in the New Testament the Christ is, even as to His humanity, an eternalized figure whose redemptive significance is not subject to eclipse." [54] The Creed immediately associates with the historic data, Christ's living presence in the plentitude of Divine omnipotence, and His coming again to judge the quick and the dead. In the Christian rule of faith Jesus Christ, our Lord is God's own Son, who became incarnate by being born of the Holy Spirit and the Virgin Mary, who was crucified for our offenses and raised for our

52. Smellie, A., *The Reformation in its Literature.* p. 132.
53. Davies, D. R., *The Two Humanities,* p 60.
54. Vos, G., *The Self-Disclosure of Jesus,* p. 18.

justification, who is at the right hand of God, the Father Almighty, who will come again to judge the world. The Symbol which led the hosts of primitive Christianity to victory over ancient paganism kept the past, the present and the future work of Christ in close conjunction so that the believer could not think of one without the other. Christ in the plentitude of His saving activities ever faces one in the Symbol. Perhaps, our putting asunder that which God hath joined together is the weakness of modern Christianity. The Word who calls us is the God who became incarnate for us men and for our salvation, the Christ who died and rose again, the reigning King and the returning Judge. By the grace of His Word and Spirit, and out of the future, the Lord is here and now present, and His coming Kingdom of glory determines man in the present. "He shall come again with glory to judge both the quick and the dead; whose Kingdom shall have no end."

In the stained glass window in the Church at Mansfeld, Luther gazed at a picture of Christ seated on a rainbow, coming to judgment. The Christ of judgment sent Luther on a quest for righteousness which only ended when he found forgiveness in the Christ of Calvary. Faith keeps the two together: "In all miseries and persecutions, I left up my Head and wait for Him, who did before stand in my stead before God's Judgment-seat, and did take away my curse from me, to come from Heaven as a Judge, to throw all His and mine enemies into everlasting pains, and to receive me with all the elect unto Himself, into heavenly joys and everlasting glory." [55]

> "When I soar to world unknown,
> See Thee on Thy judgment Throne,
> Rock of Ages, cleft for me!
> Let me hide myself in Thee."

"For Jesus Christ really comes from heaven as He who sits at the right hand of God, therefore as the Risen One, therefore as the Revealer of the reconciliation accomplished in Him, therefore as He who accomplished this reconciliation, and therefore

---

55. *The Palatinate Catechism, authorized* in Scotland, 1591.

in fact as the Judge who has anticipated the judgment for us and through whose punishment we are righteous." [56]

The new age, the Messianic times, began with our Lord's work, and, while our old man still lives in the age of Adam and of Pontius Pilate, our new man, by revelation participates in the new age of Christ. His present glory is a prophecy and a pledge of our eschatological glorification (Phil. iii.21; I John iii.2). By beholding His glory we are transformed into the same image, for to that end the living Lord puts forth the Spirit. (II Cor. iii.18). Christ at the right-hand of God, the Father Almighty, is the assurance that the Father's heart is watching over and the Father's hand is guiding every step of our way. Since the Father hath given Him for us all, and He is at the right-hand of Power, His yoke is easy and His burden is light, and in all the vicissitudes of life He gives rest to our souls. As we look to Him, as we live by faith in the Son of God who loved us and gave Himself for us, as Christ in us is the hope of glory, we have a present appropriation of all His saving activities, whether they be past, present or future in the chronology of the world.

In the mind of God, the Lamb was slain before the foundation of the world, so that His atonement is the theodicy which justifies God in giving sinful man a history and in forgiving believers before Calvary. Further, whereas in the Old Testament the way into the holy of holies was opened only to the High Priest and that once a year when he entered to apply the expiatory blood upon the mercy-seat; in the New Testament God hath openly set Christ forth as the perpetual mercy-seat so that the efficacy of His propitiation is as great today, and every day of grace, as it was the day He first offered it in the Tabernacle which God pitched. (Rom. iii.25; Hebrews). "I feel as if Jesus had died only yesterday," said Luther. And as Christ ever liveth to make intercession on the basis of His one sacrifice, made once for all, His blood is daily cleansing, or justifying us from every sin

---

56. Barth, K., *Credo*, pp. 123-124; cf. Barth, P., *Unser Bekenntnis zu Jesus Christ*, pp. 83-84.

(Hebrews; John i.7). Hence, Christianity is the religion of the common man who lives daily by the sacrifice of Christ.[57]

As the benefits of the atonement were enjoyed even before Christ came, as the efficacy and actuality of the Cross is carried into every present moment, making each day a day of grace, there is every reason why *mutatis mutandis* the Resurrection, Ascension, Session and Return ought to be carried into every day of our Christian lives. Paul charges the young pastor in the sight of God and of Jesus Christ who will judge the living and the dead and by His appearing and His kingdom, to preach the Word (II Tim. iv.1-2). As the Living One, the One who was dead and is alive, who has the keys of death and of Hades, who cometh with the clouds, Christ appeared to John (Rev. i.7, 10, 17, 18)

Since the Parousia of Christ means the age when He will be directly and visibly present, the age to come of which the present age of grace is a foretaste, and since at the right hand of God He is now invisibly exercising the powers of the age to come, perhaps one ought to be able to actualize the Coming of the Lord more readily than even the ministry of His humiliation. "What is and remains future for the Christians, on which they wait, is in Jesus Christ, solely in Him, a Today" (Cf. Lk. iv.21).[58] The living Christ who calls us in the day of salvation is the Man of sorrows, the Lord of glory, the Judge of the quick and the dead, and fellowship with Him is fellowship with the whole Christ.

> "Thou are the King of glory: O Christ.
> Thou are the everlasting Son of the Father.
> When Thou tookest upon Thee to deliver man;
>   Thou didst humble Thyself to be born of a Virgin.
> When Thou hadst overcome the sharpness of death;
>   Thou didst open the Kingdom of Heaven to all believers.
> Thou sittest at the right hand of God in the glory of the Father
>   We believe that Thou shalt come; to be our Judge."[59]

In preaching the Word concerning the Son of God who has come and will come again the Church presents the witness to

---

57. Forsyth, P. T., *The Place of Jesus Christ in Modern Christianity.*
58. Schmidt, K. L., *Die Polis in Kirche und Welt*, p. 39.
59. *Te Deum Laudamus.*

Jesus Christ with which she is commissioned in the face of everything that opposes this testimony. Therein she does not forsake her God-appointed task and rush about Don Quixote fashion, seeking to make out of some contemporary problem, related to the faith, a giant against which she is to tilt. Anchored in the Christian faith she confesses Christ as Prophet, as Priest and as King with a conviction that does not hesitate to oppose so mighty a foe as National Socialism when that impinges on her loyalty to Jesus Christ.[60] Preaching the Word of God supports the prayer that Christ may everywhere reign supreme, governing His people by the sceptre of His Word and the power of His Spirit, and by the strength of His truth and righteousness crushing all the attempts of His enemies.[61]

The living Word present in the preached Word. Christ is present in the institutions and instruments of His own ordering. One of the most hopeful signs of the present is the reviving recognition that Jesus founded, or re-founded the Church on the basis of God's self-revelation of which Christ is the central content. (Matt. xvi.13-20).[62] The living Christ is present in the Church which He hath built as the Church faithfully administers His gifts, the Word and the Sacraments. As His Word is truly presented, the living Word is Himself present, as when Mary sat at His feet and heard His Word. "Where two or three are gathered together in my name, there am I in the midst" (Matt. xviii. 20), and "he that heareth you, heareth me" (Lk. x.16). *Christus presens* who appeared to His disciples during the space of forty days is now with His own as they teach the things which He has commanded them (Matt. xxviii.18-20).

As Mary treasured the words of the angel in her heart, so the ancient Church treasured the words of the Lord and recited them in her worship, until it was said, "Where the Church speaks, there the Lord is." (Didache iv.1). Since "holy men have spoken as moved by the Holy Ghost" (II Pet. i.21), "all scripture is

---

60. Barth, K., *The Church and the Political Problems of our Day.*
61. Cf. *Calvin's Tracts,* II.104.
62. *Ekklesia* in *Theologisches Worterbuch;* Flew, *Jesus and His Church;* Wahlstrom et.al. in *World Conference on Faith and Order,* No. 92.

God-breathed" (II Tim. iii.16). "The inspired Scriptures are the mouth of the Lord" (Clement of Alexandria, *Protrept* 77.1), and the law was given "by the Logos through Moses as the servant of the Logos" (Paed. i.7). For Ignatius, "Jesus Christ is the Old (Books); His Cross and Death and Resurrection, and the faith which is by Him (are) the undefiled Old (Books), by which I wish, by your prayers, to be justified." *(Philad. 6)* Accordingly, "What is accepted as Revelation can be expressed in one word: Christ." [63] For in Him are hidden all the treasures of wisdom and knowledge and He is the revelation of the mystery of God (Col. ii.2-3).

While Zwingli severed the work of the Holy Spirit from the means of grace and so listed notable heathen in his roll of saints, Calvin stressed "an inviolable union" and "a mutual connection" between the Word and the Spirit. The Scripture is the mouth of the Lord, the sceptre of Christ. "The departure of the Lord signifies the removal of His Word." [64] The proper administration of the sacraments and especially the true preaching of the Word are the pledges or seals that the living Word is present in the sovereign saving power of the Holy Spirit, enabling sinners to do what they otherwise could not do, that is, believe on the Lord Jesus Christ to the salvation of their souls. The Westminster Confession teaches that, since God's former ways of revealing His will have ceased, the Word is His present and perpetual mode of revealing Himself. Accordingly, the acceptance of Christ on the authority of Scripture is accepting Him on His own authority, faith "being in fact the living flesh of identification between the Word as written and the living voice of Him whose Word it is." [65]

Through the preaching of His Word the living Christ speaks grace and peace to His people. "Son, be of good cheer, thy sins be forgiven thee." "Daughter, thy faith hath saved thee, go in peace." "Fear not, only believe." "Lo, I am with you always." "I will never leave thee nor forsake thee." "Let not your heart

---

63. Koehler, W., *Dogmengeschichte*, p. 65.
64. *Institutes*, I.ix.i, 3; II.v.13; Dedication.
65. Martin, Hugh, *The Westminster Doctrine of the Inspiration of Scripture*, p. 18.

be troubled, neither let it be afraid." "Follow me." "Take My yoke upon you and learn of me." "Love your enemies, do good to them that hate you, bless them that curse you." "Be ye merciful even as your Father is merciful." "Judge not." "I am the Resurrection and the Life." "Come unto Me, all ye that labour and are heavy laden." "My peace I give unto you." "Thou art Mine; when thou goest through the waters, I will be with thee."

In the Heavenlies in Christ. The early Christian expectation of the coming of Christ was a matter of affection for Him, zeal for His glory and absorption in the things of Christ rather than a mere date in the temporal succession. *He sitteth at the right hand of God, the Father Almighty,* the next thing in the faith is *from whence He shall come to judge the quick and the dead.* The last days have begun and He is enthroned in power to bring in the next great redemptive event, the glorious consummation. Though they had been warned that the day of Christ was not just at hand (II Thess. ii.1-2), "they were eager for it with all their hearts. Time just faded away, and they saw Jesus only." [66] Finding the focus of Christian living, not in this age, but in the things of Christ, they looked for the blessed hope with eager expectancy.

When the life is hid with Christ in God, the mind is set on the things above. The new age which dawned in the Resurrection of Christ is established in heaven by His session at the right hand of God. Hence, our citizenship is in heaven, whence also we look for a Saviour, the Lord Jesus Christ (Phil. iii.20-21). When Christ, our life, is manifested, we also shall be manifested with Him in glory (Col. iii.1-4). Indeed, in Ephesians the Apostle is so conscious of being raised up with and made to sit in the heavenly places in Christ Jesus (i.3; ii.6) that the time perspective is momentarily forgotten and a perpendicular rather than a horizontal relation emerges. However, a fuller study of the epistle shows that this vertical realization of the age to come does not destroy the Apostle's forward look to God's complete redemption in the day of Christ (Eph. i.14; iv.30; ii.12; iv.4);

66. Freeman, David, *op. cit.,* p. 43.

nor to an age following this one in which the enthroned Christ is still King (i.21; ii.7).[67]

The Greek words express somewhat more clearly than our translations the heart interest of the Christians in Christ's return. The word usually translated Coming, is Parousia, Advent, Being Near, Presence or Arrival. As such, it is "expressive of the most ardent hopes of a St. Paul." [68] Is there a Christian heart that does not look for and hasten unto the manifest Presence of the Lord? The eyes of our hearts are turned to Him as certainly as the compass needle points to the magnetic North. Since He is the center of our affection, the theme of our Gospel, the author and object of our faith, His Parousia is the guiding star of our hope.

Again, His return is described as His revelation, appearing or manifestation. The more faith appreciates and appropriates the true nature or glory of Christ, the more the riches of His grace constrain our feeble affection, the more earnestly we yearn for the visible manifestation of that glory, and the more surely we love His Epiphany. Oh! that the world which crucified Him might behold His glory. Forcing other considerations aside, the Christian heart leaps forward in hope to the day of His vindication. Within the soul of Christ's bride, "there is a great longing for the hour, when all the shadows will flee before 'the flaming of His Advent feet'." [69] We who have tasted His graciousness (I Peter ii.3), who have beheld the glory of the only begotten of the Father, full of grace and truth (John i.14), who know that the Princes of this world crucified none other than the Lord of glory (I Cor. ii.8) are awaiting the day when,

> "this Lord Jesus
> Shall return again,
> With His Father's glory
> With His angel train;
> For all wreaths of empire
> Meet upon His brow,
> And our hearts confess Him
> King of glory now."

67. Vos, G., *Pauline Eschatology.*
68. Deissman, A., *Light from the Ancient East*, p. 368.

Moreover, the Bible specifically relates this upward look of the eschatological hope to our present stability and growth in grace. In guiding the early Christians in the narrow way between the Sylla of antinomianism on the one side, and the Charybdis of perfectionism on the other, John used the eschatological hope as the guiding star. "We know that when He shall be manifest, we shall be like Him; for we shall see Him even as He is. And everyone that hath this hope in Him purifieth Himself, even as He is pure" (I John iii.2-3). And in the hour of adversity, tribulation and persecution, *hope* maketh not ashamed (Rom. v.5). Though put to grief in manifold trials, we cherish a living hope that our faith, after it has been proved by fire, will be found unto praise and honor and glory at the revelation of Jesus Christ (I Peter i.3-7). *For our light affliction, which is for the moment, worketh for us more and more exceedingly an eternal weight of glory* (II Cor. iv.17). Thus the Christian hope is the sure and steadfast anchor of the soul. Christ hath begotten us unto hope by His resurrection (I Peter i.3), established us therein by His entering within the veil of the heavenly tabernacle (Hebr. vi.19-20), and confirms our hearts and steadies our hands in laying hold of the hope that is set before us by His present appearing before the face of God to make continual intercession for us (Hebr. vi.18; iii.6; vii.25; ix.24).

Our comfort concerning our departed loved ones is that those who are alive at the Parousia of the Lord shall in no wise precede them that are fallen asleep. But when the Lord shall descend from heaven, they shall rise first and be caught up together with the living to meet the Lord in the air, ever to remain with HIM (I Thess. iv.13-18). In other words the Parousia means the coming of the Lord with ten thousand of His saints (Jude 14), and all the tendrils of our affection are moved with rapture for this moment. As we contemplate that occasion we hear those gentle voices calling, and look for our gathering together with our Lord and with those whom we have "long loved and lost awhile."

The Bible actualizes the eschatological hope into a call for fidelity to our daily tasks. A flight from the world may suit the hermit, but our Lord proclaimed His glorious coming as an appeal to visit the sick and the imprisoned, and to minister to the needy (Matt. xxv.31-46). The Montanist may forsake his work to gather at Pepuza, and the Irvingite be rapt in such upward gaze that he forgets the daily occupation; but Paul's grip on the blessed hope made him work night and day that he might not impose on others (II Thess. iii.8). His safeguard against disorder and indolence in view of the day of the Lord is, "if any will not work, neither let him eat." The Lord has directed that the servants whom He has set over His household watch for His coming by giving those households their food in due season (Matt. xxiv.45-46). The Apostle directs the Church to withdraw from anyone who, misconceiving that Coming, walks disorderly and not according to the apostolic word (II Thess. iii.6, 14). Formally expressed, "eschatology presupposes the theistic conception of history, and when it is not isolated from theism it does not foster an anti-worldly conception of religion. If God is the God of all history, He who will make the new world of glory must demand that His creatures in the present world, which is also His, recognize and seek to advance the recognition of His sovereignty in all the world." [70]

"Faith is not purely prospective; it enables one to anticipate; it draws down the imperishable substance of eternity into its vessel of time and feeds on it. The believer knows even now there is in him that which has been freed from the law of change, a treasure that moth and rust cannot corrupt, true riches enshrined in his heart as in a treasury of God." "We must learn again to carry a heaven-fed and heaven-centered spirit into our walk and work below. The grand teaching of the Epistle (to the Hebrews) that through Christ and the New Covenant the heavenly projects into the earthly, as the headlands of a continent project into the ocean, should be made fruitful for the whole tone and temper of our Christian service. Every task should be at the same time a means of grace and an incentive to work for heaven." "A religion that has ceased to set its face towards the celestial city, is bound sooner or later to discard its supernatural resources in its endeavor to transform this present world." [71]

The Coming of Christ is related to every moment of our daily life. For one thing, we know not which moment may be the immediate precursor of His Coming. Even the Son knew not the day or the hour of that Coming, and His word to us is "in the day that ye think not, the Son of Man cometh." Then we shall all appear before the judgment seat of Christ to give account of the deeds done in the flesh, and thus the light of His Coming, which will one day illumine every act, stands behind each day's task. Accordingly, "whether the end be chronologically near or far, it is essentially quite near to every hour." [02]

III. A LOOK FORWARD IN HOPE.

The Christian hope does have and must have a present, actual meaning calling men to faith, repentance and loyal testimony to Christ, our Saviour and our Judge ; but this hope has its present urgency and infinite importance only because it is gathered around an event that will occur. The New Testament religion is a thoroughly eschatological religion because it sees the goal and end for history realized in the consummation of the Kingdom which cannot be shaken in the new heavens and the new earth. Yes, and because in the mission, death and resurrection of Christ, and in His gracious reign at the right hand of God it has an earnest of that ultimate redemption, a foretaste of the age to come.

Without this actual fulfillment of the Kingdom which is to be wrought by God's own hand and direct interposition in the Parousia of Christ, we are left with merely human, self-contained philosophies of history. And these generally present a periodicity of endless cycles except where, as in Marxian socialism, they

---

71. Vos, G., *Grace and Glory*, pp. 149, 150, 151.
72. Althaus, *DLD*, 1933. p. 265.

have borrowed from the Christian-Chiliastic course of thought.[73] "History *by itself and in itself* is the realm of death, of disintegration and futility." [74] "The meaning of history has its ground not in history, but in Christ. Therefore, it is the fundamentally eschatological direction of the life of history which gives depth to its meaning." [75] "We do not interpret revelation by means of historical existence, but *historical existence by means of revelation*," [76] in the light of Jesus Christ, the Word made flesh. Without the Second Coming of Christ and the final judgment, "a Christian philisophy of history is ineffective and fragmentary" and History, including the Incarnation, the Cross and the Resurrection, loses its meaning.[77]

In the Word, the Reconciliation, the Resurrection, the Reign, the Return and the complete Redemption of the world hang together. The Resurrection of Christ is the dawn of a new dimension of reality, *the age to come* has already reached into the present. But detach the Resurrection from the Return and a catastrophic renewal of all things, place it in the pagan mould which conceives the flux of history as mere illustrations of eternal ideas, subordinate it to general truths drawn from man's fallen reason, and as an isolated, unrelated phenomenon it ceases to carry meaning or conviction. The result is a "high-handed mutilation" of the Creed which, omitting the Conception, the Crucifixion, the Resurrection, the Ascension and the Return, consigns Jesus to a "private closet" in order to attain a "world faith." [78]

In other words, the look upward gets its efficacy from the fact that the look forward is true. "If there is any truth in the Christian philosophy of history, then the Last Judgment and Christ's Second Coming are more than humanly certain — they are super-humanly certain." These are not only integral to the Christian philosophy of history, they are part and parcel of the

73. Gerlich, Fr., *Der Communismus als Lehre com tausend jahrigen Reich,* 1920.
74. Davies, D. R., *The Two Humanities,* p. 140.
75. Kunneth, W., *Theologie der Auferstehung,* 1933, p. 242.
76. Wendland, H. D., *op. cit.,* p. 191; Barth, K., *Kirchliche Dogmatik,* 1.2.64.
77. Davies, D. R., *On to Orthodoxy,* pp. 196, 197, 153.
78. Hocking, W. E., *Living Religions and a World Faith,* pp. 159, 10, 22.

Gospel of the grace of God. "The Biblical thought of grace can not be preserved in its purity, when it has not a living thought of judgment as its necessary background. And the unconditioned seriousness of the thought of judgment is dissolved as soon as the Christian revelation is loosed from its firm anchorage in a temporal, really historical, process. The chief interest which the eschatological has to preserve, according to our conviction, is the proclamation of the Gospel by the call of God in a limited time of grace. Were this not considered then would the central doctrine of the Gospel-justification by faith — which Althaus has, in such a notable way, made the center of eschatology be distorted in its deepest contents." [79]

Accordingly, we rejoice that, for the last two decades, Continental eschatological thought has moved in the direction of the acceptance of the Biblical eschatology as an integral part of the Christian faith rather than as a piece of Jewish mythology. This has meant the progressive acceptance of the Biblical configuration in place of Platonic and Kantian idealism. In the timeless speculation of Plato the world of eternal ideas is far exalted above the flux of time and history, which latter is partly the product of an eternal matter and hence never completely at the command of God. For Kant time was a condition supplied by the human mind. With the new realization of the fallen nature of man, it became easy for Kantians to assume that space and time were forms of sin in which God could only manifest Himself in a hidden way. According to the Bible, God created all things visible as well as invisible, and ordained time, space and causality (Gen. i). "The eternal God, who is master of space and time is also the one who governs through space and time" and therefore can use it as a medium for His revelation.[80] "The writers of the New Testament as well as their readers had been taught by the Old Testament that history is the medium of God's saving activity." [81]

79. Holmstrom, F., *op. cit.*, p. 416.
80. Hoffman, G., *Das Problem der letzten Dinge in der neueren Theologie*, 1929, p. 58, cited F. H., *op. cit.* p. 393.
81. Piper, O. A., *USR*, liii.4.283.

In sharp criticism of the merely super-historical view, Rudolph Otto points out that the eschatological preaching of the Kingdom includes the temporal opposition between the *now* and the *then*. The eschatological order is not a Platonic story above the order of time calling for decision. On the contrary the eschatological order *comes,* as something that breaks in upon the final generation universally. While the categorical imperative calls for decision, the eschatological order calls for repentance, for hungering and thirsting after righteousness, and for preaching the Kingdom of God. The coming of the Kingdom points man to the blind abyss before which he stands and in which he will lose not indeed his existence but rather his salvation. "And all this not allegorically, but because salvation or damnation really comes, because it will have an actual, temporal, real advent and parousia, and because man actually and in an actual future will have salvation or damnation." [82] For Holmstrom, "The line between time and eternity is fixed by God, depending upon how long it pleases Him to let the invitation of grace seek man in his wayward paths." At a definite limit unknowable to us *regnum gratiae* becomes *regnum gloriae* and God's judgment stands fixed as eternal life and eternal death.[83]

Incarnation, Revelation and Inspiration all testify that God can accommodate His eternal truth to our temporal apprehension. In Christ, God has graciously, tenderly spoken to us, as a mother to her babbling babe. He has put His Word nigh us, in our mouths and in our hearts, His Word unveiled to us in the Incarnation of His only Begotten, and recorded for us by men whom He Himself formed, called, sanctified and inspired.

God who has revealed Himself in a medium of His own ordaining can be understood when He repeatedly uses temporal terms to describe the Parousia. To be understood here, the Bible requires neither paradoxes, nor bifurcations of knowledge, nor Platonic Philosophy. Even H. Maldwyn Hughes admits that "the thought of the *Parousia* as a definite historical event ending

82. Otto, R., *The Kingdom of God and the Son of Man,* pp. 51-53.
83. Holmstrom, F., cited Ferre, *Swedish Contributions to Modern Theology,* pp. 170-171.

the present age and inaugurating the age to come is undoubtedly
a prominent element in the teaching of our Lord as recorded
in the synoptic Gospels.[84] There are time and seasons which
the Father hath set within His own authority (Acts i.7); there
is a day and an hour of the Parousia known to the Father (Mk.
xiii.32). The time and the place of the Ascension are recorded
together with the promise that, in like manner as He went, so
shall He come again (Acts i.3-12). "The Second Coming is
not a process — but will be an EVENT. No one will seriously
argue that the birth of Christ in Palestine was a process. It is
agreed that it happened in time and space. Equally so will be
the Second Coming, which by means of the Last Judgment, will
bring History to its conclusion. It will be an even in History —
the last event."[85] Indeed, in and by this event Davies sees the
Kingdom of God shattering time, as the chrysalis bursts its
enfolding skin, and passing beyond time into "a new transcendent
duration."[86]

The word Parousia means coming, arrival, appearing, advent,
or presence. Its New Testament usage in other connections than
those of the return of Christ indicate at least two definite
thoughts. The Apostle Paul uses Parousia to distinguish his own
bodily presence with a Church from his absence. In these cases
it means a formal apostolic visitation, the Apostle's authoritative
presence with a view to effective action, II Cor. x.10; Phil. ii.12;
cf. i.26. Again, when the Apostle was in want and dispirited,
he was refreshed and made to rejoice at the Parousia of Steph-
anus, Fortunatus and Achaicus with the supplies they brought
and the exhilaration of their company (I Cor. xvi.17-18). And
when he was bowed low with bodily afflictions, fightings and
fears, "God who comforteth the lowly comforted us by the
Parousia of Titus" (II Cor. vii.5-7). Then Parousia is used
both of the Coming of Christ the first time (II Peter i.16-18)
and of the Coming of the lawless One (the Anti-Christ) (II
Thess. ii.3-10), in connections that indicate the power and glory

84. Hughes, *Our Basis Belief*, 1929, Abingdon, p. 201.
85. Davies, *On to Orthodoxy*, p. 155.
86. Davies, *The Two Humanities*, p. 223.

of the term. That event in the Saviour's ministry which is described as the Parousia is His Transfiguration, at which His disciples witnessed the majesty and power of His Parousia. For He received from God the Father honor and glory, when, on the holy mount, the Voice of the Divine Majesty proclaimed "This is my beloved Son, in whom I am well pleased." Similarly the Lawless One's Parousia is according to the working of Satan with all power and signs and lying wonders so that he exalteth himself against God and setteth himself forth in the temple of God as God. Christ's Parousia was in the Power and Majesty of God; Anti-Christ's will be in the power and glory Satan gives him. In each case Parousia refers to a personal manifestation in might and glory.

This Biblical usage of Parousia is amply supported by Deissman's researches in the papyri.[87] "From the Ptolemaic period down to the second century we are able to trace the word in the East as a technical expression for the arrival or the visit of the King or the Emperor." In the Flinder Petri Papyrus II, 39e of the third century B.C. contributions are noted for a crown of gold to be presented to the King at his parousia. This brings to mind "the crown of glory" or "the crown of righteousness" the Apostle will receive at the Lord's Parousia. A requisition of corn is made for the parousia of the Saviour King Ptolemy about 113 B.C. There is a reference to the Parousia of Asclepius to cure a sick devotee in a temple dedicated to this god. At Tegea there is an inscription "in the year 69 of the first Parousia of the God Hadrian in Greece." These formal official advents, marked by the pomp and splendor of the Emperor, were occasions for dating new eras, for coins and for monuments.

In the light of this linguistic usage we see that the description of the future Coming of Christ as a Parousia means His own bodily Advent, the manifested brightness of His Presence (cf. II Thess. ii.8), the Epiphany of His Parousia, the revelation of the Son of Man (Lk. xvii.29-30) in His Divine Majesty, glory and power. Deissman finds its best interpretation in the

---

87. Deissman, G. A., *Light from the Ancient East*, pp. 368-373.

prophecy, "Behold thy *King* cometh unto thee" (Zech. ix.9., cf. Mt. xxi.5). A. T. Robertson discerns in the "shout" of I Thess. iv.16 a military command. "Christ will come as the Conqueror with a cry of command ringing forth like that of the general of a great army." The mere manifestation of His Parousia will bring to naught the Adversary, whom the Lord Jesus shall slay with the breath of His mouth (II Thess. ii.8). The Parousia in the New Testament is primarily and explicitly the Advent of the King to sit upon the Throne of His glory (Matt. xxv.31-46), to be worshipped by every knee and confessed by every tongue (Phil. ii.9-11), to divide between the nations, welcoming His elect into the Kingdom of the Father and assigning others to the lake of fire. At the Parousia, "Jesus is represented as a victorious King, giving the word of command to the hosts of heaven in his train for the last onslaught, at His final triumph over sin, death and Satan." And the Coming of the King of Kings and the Lord of Lords means the truly new era, the inauguration of the Coming Age, the setting up of the Kingdom of Glory in a new heaven and a new earth.

In II Peter iii.3,12, the conflagration of the heavens and the introduction of the new heavens and earth synchronize with the Parousia of Christ.[88] "Everywhere in the Gospels it refers to the triumphant Advent of our Lord at the close of the present world-period." [89]

The distinct character of the Advent as an event is further brought out by the early Christian description of it "the day of the Lord," "the day of Christ," "the day of Judgment" or as par-excellence "the day." (Acts ii.20, Phil. ii.16; I John iv.17; Mt. vii.22; John vi.40, 44, 54, xi.24; I Cor. v.5; Phil. i.10; I Thess. v.2; Heb. x.25; II Peter iii.12, 18; I John iv.17; Rev. vi. 17). "Now the world has its day; 'this is your hour' said Jesus to the Jewish officers, 'and the power of darkness' (Luke xxii.53); then comes the Lord's Day, when He will be vindicated in salvation and in Judgment. At a later date the weekly date of Christ's

88. Cf. Bromall, W., *The Issacharian, Winter* 1940, p. 3.
89. Reese, A., *The Approaching Advent of Christ*, p. 140.

Resurrection received this name (Rev. i.10) ; this also is a day of divine vindication and anticipation of the great Day." [90]

IV. THE PRECURSORS OF HIS PAROUSIA.

As an event that will occur there are signs preparatory to the Coming of Christ. However, the most significant of these signs are so wisely given by the Lord that they have both a meaning and a task for our present lives and also a specific historical fulfillment. This is true of the preaching of the Gospel of the Kingdom to all nations, the conversion of the Jews and the rise of Anti-Christ and Anti-christs.

Before developing this thesis in detail it may be well to point out that while Jesus concurred with His Jewish contemporaries in accepting the eschatological drama of a cosmic catastrophe with definite events and did not take up the wishful thinking of a political Messiah, but awaited the coming of the Son of Man on the clouds of heaven (Dan. vii.13) ; nevertheless He remained definitely and consciously behind His contemporaries in portraying these last things and in reckoning the preparatory signs thereof.[91]

In the eschatological discourse in the Synoptics, Jesus presented in one prophecy of the future two things that history shows to be widely separated in time, namely, the destruction of Jerusalem and the end of the world. This is to be expected in prophecy which in its nature does not distinguish stages and intervals, but sees future events together somewhat as spatially widely separated stars appears together in the sky above us. Yet in this very discourse the Saviour emphatically asserts that no one knows the day or the hour of the coming of the Son of man, that even He, the Son, knows it not (Mt. xxiv.36-37 ; Mk. xiii.32). And as He leaves them the Lord admonishes the Disciples that it is not for them to know the times and seasons that the Father has

90. Findlay, G. G., *The Epistles of St. Paul and Apostle to the Thessalonians*, p.|109.
91. Cf. Schmidt, K. L., Th.W., I.586-587. Edersheim, A., *Life and Times of Jesus the Messiah*, II.vi.432. "In the pseudepigraphic writings, which expressed the apocalyptic expectancies of the Jews before the time of Christ, there is a marked difference from the New Testament."

put in His own authority (Acts i.7). Further, Jesus sees a succession of events before His Coming, such as wars and rumours of wars with nation rising against nation and kingdom against kingdom (Mk. xiii.7-8), earthquakes and famines (vs.8), false Christs (Mk. xiii.6, 21, 22), the preaching of the Gospel of the Kingdom in the whole world for a testimony unto all nations (Matt. xxiv.14; Mk. xiii.10). And Paul writes Second Thessalonians to instruct that Church that the coming of our Lord Jesus Christ is not just at hand, but that a succession of things must intervene including the falling away, the removal of the one that restraineth, and the revelation of the son of perdition (II Thess. ii.1-12).

It is immediately evident that some of these signs are of constant recurrence and should teach constant readiness. For example "from the year 1496 B.C. to A.D. 1862, a period of 3,358 years, there were only 228 years of peace. Within the last 300 years there have been 286 wars in Europe." [92] Between 1496 B.C. and 1932 A.D. "91.7 per cent of all the years included were characterized by war." [93] And each great war is more intense and destructive than the last, and occurs after a shorter interval. Between the Napoleonic Wars and the Franco-Prussian War was a period of fifty-five years; from the Franco-Prussian to the World War was forty-three years; from the World War to this Greater War only twenty-one years.[94] At this writing there is war from one end of Eurasia to another, and its orbit has included not only Africa, but America as well. Notable earthquakes have recently occurred in Turkey, Rumania and Japan, with less serious shakes in New England; while a sermon on the signs of the times preached near the close of the nineteenth century chronicles the increased number of earthquakes reported in the first three-quarters of that century as 6,637.[95] Certainly no American needs to be reminded that new religious movements with their claims of new Messiahs and new methods of salvation

92. Minn, H. R., *The Evangelical Quarterly*, 12.1.80.
93. Bossard, Dr. J. H. S., A.P., Chicago, Dec. 29, 1940.
94. Davies, D. R., *The Two Humanities*, p. 34.
95. Girardeau, J. L., *Sermons*, p. 112 citing Canon Fausset in London *Theological Monthly*, 1889.

are constantly arising. Indeed, the Unitarian poet sings, "Some great cause, God's New Messiah."

The Gospel of the Kingdom to all Nations. Let us return, however, for special consideration to the three precursors of His coming already mentioned. There has been a notable increase of foreign mission interest in the last century and a half. Indeed, William Carey has been described as the father of modern missions, and the progress of world missions in the Orient, Africa, South America and the isles of the sea is comparable to that of the Gospel in the first century through the Mediterranean World. Dr. Emory Ross reported to the Foreign Missions Conference in March, 1940, that there were then 27,577 foreign missionaries, with a national staff of 72,215 other workers with 55,395 organized churches and 6,045,726 communicants.[96] Our own denomination is only one division in the King's great army; but the Southern Presbyterian fathers declared missions to be the mission of the Church. As a result there are more members of the Church in the foreign field today than in the whole church when we began our independent existence; more communicant members in Africa and more Sunday School members in Korea than in most of our home synods.

A century after Carey's beginning, the Bible was published in nearly 300 human dialects;[97] now, fifty years later, the Bible societies report that, in whole or in part, it is in over a thousand languages and dialects. The one hundred and twenty-fourth report of the American Bible Society estimated that nearly 26,-000,000 volumes were sent to the peoples of the world by Bible Societies in 1939. Since the first World War, world missions have so advanced that the newer churches receive an equal place and recognition with the older ones in the exchange of inspirational speakers and at the mission congresses. By this great missionary enterprise God has been building up a world-wide Christian fellowship, which even in its incompleteness and imperfec-

96. *The Foreign Missionaries*, May, 1940, Baltimore, Md.
97. Girardeau, *op. cit.*, p. 104.

tion stands as an earthly counterpart and an earnest of the coming of the City of God in its perfection.

Christ declared that the Gospel of the Kingdom should be preached in the whole inhabited earth for a testimony to all nations and then should the end be (Matt. xxiv.14). The volume prepared for the Madras Conference protests against identifying the Kingdom of God with the social, economic, political or cultural programs of our historic human life, and insists upon its transcendental, supra-historical order.[98] The City of God "in its perfection is of eternity and not of time; but, as the central doctrine of our faith assures us, it is God's will that the things of time should, as far as may be, represent to us the eternal realities." [99] The thought of the Kingdom as man's achievement has stirred many wills to intense activity. When the Biblical vision of the Kingdom as God's miracle of righteousness, plenty, peace and love is apprehended, it will the more mightily stir our lagging zeal. If the collapsing confidence in humanism be supplanted by a Christian faith in God who giveth us the victory through our Lord Jesus Christ, we may be steadfast, unmoveable, always abounding in the work of the Lord, forasmuch as we know that our labor is not in vain in the Lord (I Cor. xv.57-58). The Gospel charges every hearer to wait for God's Son from Heaven (I Thess. i.9) and every minister to be faithful in view of His Appearing and His Kingdom (II Tim. iv.1). If the push of faith and the constraint of love be reinforced by this blessed hope pulsing through Christians of every name, the next fifty years will be greater mission days than the last.

The Conversion of Israel. The existence of Israel scattered among the nations, somewhat as the Gulf Stream sweeps through the ocean without losing its identity, indicates that God has spared His ancient people for a future. If we would learn a parable from the fig tree, Jerusalem shall be trodden down of the Gentiles until the times of the Gentiles be fulfilled (Lk. xxi.24). A hardening in part has befallen Israel until the fullness of the

---

98. Kraemer, H., *The Christian Message in a Non-Christian World*, p. 93.
99. William Temple, Archbishop of Canterbury, at his enthronement.

Gentiles be gathered in; but if the casting away of them be the reconciling of the world, the receiving of them shall be life from the dead, that is, the Resurrection (Rom. xi.25, 15). So Israel shall be grafted into his own olive tree.

When Pilate presented Jesus to the Jews saying, *Behold your King,* they answered, *Crucify Him, We have no King but Caesar.* Thus Israel solemnly recanted her Messianic faith and accepted instead a military tyrant. Today, as the full weight of Caesar's heel impresses upon the Hebrew the fatality of his choice, one may pray for its speedy reversal. Nor is the present without signs that the answer to this prayer may be at hand. Radio preaching and Bible circulation make the facts of Christ easily and quietly known. Jewish scholars like Rabbi Klausner are studying Jesus of Nazareth. In the land of the Reformation the Confessional Church is suffering under the bludgeoning of the same Paganism that is decimating the Jews. And the Confessional Church is suffering just because she will not give up the Jewish elements in the Christian faith. This Church holds to Jehovah, the God of Israel, instead of the gods of race, blood and soil, to the ethics of Moses and Jesus in lieu of those of Nietsche and Rosenberg, to the Scriptures of the Old and New Testaments rather than to *Mein Kampf,* to Jesus of Nazareth as Lord and Leader rather than to Hitler. The Confessional Church offers the sacraments to non-Ayrans, for the Gospel is the power of God unto salvation to the Jew first. She maintains the Old Testament for the Gospels says that Jesus is the Messiah of the Old Testament. The Gestapo demanded that Niemoller preach on Luther as the Apostle of the German people. But the Vicar of Berlin-Dahlem defied the Gestapo and represented the Luther who put the Cross with the Saviour back in the centre of the Church. Realizing that Jesus, as to His flesh, was a Jew, Martin Niemoller cried, "Praise and glory to the man on the cross, to all eternity." And Leo Stein the Jew who suffers in the concentration camp with this Christian Pastor, comes out realizing that here is a friend of Israel, here is a man of God. Nor is the Hebrew likely to forget that his greatest champion and defender against Pagan persecution, the nation that has given him back Palestine, is that Empire which has been most influenced by Christianity — Great Britain.

The Jewish question is at bottom a religious question.[100] As *in the beginning God shows* the God of Israel to be the God of history, so *even so come Lord Jesus* shows that He hath committed the future to the Lord Jesus. "If the future belongs to Christ, so does Israel."[101] "Joseph knew his brethren when they did not know him. When the time came that he could refrain himself no longer he told them who he was. So his Antitype knows his kinsmen after the flesh while they know Him not; and when the times comes for disclosing the truth that is veiled from their eyes He will see to it that the promises shall be fulfilled." The Spirit of grace and supplication shall be given them that they may learn to call upon the Name of the Lord. They shall see that the Prophet like unto Moses has come. As they return to seek the Lord their God and David their King they shall show themselves to be Israel indeed. "And the Egypt of this world shall know that His brethren have returned to Joseph and that He has made Himself known to them."[102]

"More than ever, the mystical body of Christ needs the people of God. In the darkness of the present day, that moment seems invisibly to be in preparation."[103] Indeed, if the Hebrew Christians prove the same effective ambassadors of the Cross they were in the first century, it can easily be seen that the conversion of Israel will be life from the dead for the whole Christian world. A careful exegesis of Acts iii.19 by Thomas Peck suggests such an order, that is, (a) the conversion of the Jews, (b) times or seasons of refreshment, (c) the Coming of Jesus Christ, (d) the times of restitution of all things.[104]

Anti-Christ. The most explicit single sign of the coming of the Son of Man is the revelation of the man of sin. Anti-Christ

100. Piper, O., *God in History*, pp. 72-92.
101. Luthardt, C. E., *Saving Truths of Christianity*, 1886, p. 304.
102. Macleod, John, in *Free Church Pulpit*, pp. 137, 138, 140.
103. Maritain, J., *Ransoming the Time*, p. 179.
104. Peck, T. E., *Miscellanies*, III.81.

is not always limited in Scripture to a single individual, but in the Synoptic Apocalypse there are false prophets and false Christs (Mk. xiii.12), and in First John a group of false teachers are designated Antichrists. This manifoldness of the Biblical picture of the Anti-christ and the New Testament certainty that the last hour has already dawned call the Church to seek the Antichrist in her present and as a threatening possibility in her immediate future.

So, as Professor Paul Althaus puts it, "We recognize the Antichrist in the Demon of the *State,* which sets itself up as absolute, and claims for itself Divine majesty and authority; in the Demon of *Society,* which through its culture or its orders will bring salvation and redemption and be like God; in the Demon of *Religion,* which even if it call itself 'Christian,' forgets the fear of God and the Cross of Christ and becomes a means for the security and rebellious pride of man; in the Demon of the *Church,* which flees from the form of the Cross into the glory, from hiddenness into false visibility and arrogates to itself God's own authority over man, thus putting itself in the place of God. All this is Antichrist: the will to place oneself alongside of Christ, to crowd Him out, to supplant Him, opposition against Him in the form of likeness to Him, the 'Vicar of Christ.' Therefore, the last Demon, the demon of the Church, of 'the Grand Inquisitor' is antichrist in the narrowest and most fearful sense. Antichrist is the Messiahship, which Jesus in the temptation banished from Himself with the words, 'Get thee behind me, Satan,' the Church as world power and authority, the Evangel as social gospel, the ruling Church which forgets and betrays the Cross as the sign of the Kingdom of God on earth." [105]

Our appropriation of these timely warnings should, however, not blind us to the fact that the Antichrist does appear in Scripture in the singular, as a unique figure, "the man of lawlessness" (II Thess. ii.3) who sets himself up as God. We have no authority to say that John did not expect these antichristian forces to be concentrated in a personal adversary. Nor is there any ground

105. Althaus, P., *DvD.* 4:273-274.

for saying that the forces, as Althaus presents them, may not be summarized in one individual; indeed, there is ground for concern lest such a shaping up be now in progress. Each of the factors which Althaus names as well as another which he earlier mentions — "a heathen or pseudochristian, syncretistic world religion" — may conceivably be embodied in a single totalitarian world Conqueror.

According to Paul's account (II Thess. ii.1-12) *the son of perdition* must be revealed before the Parousia of Christ. In this account the man of sin stands as the adversary and counterpart of Christ, but hardly as a counterfeit Messiah since he lacks the messianic submission to God. He does not claim to be the Messiah, nor profess to be the fulfillment of prophecy; but he does the work of a false messiah in deceiving the people with miracles which accompany his system of lying. His coming is *according to the energizing of Satan,* that is, in such a supernaturalism of evil that men believe his lies, accept his counter gospel and receive his counter faith. As Christ is the source and embodiment of the righteousness of God, so the Antichrist is the source and embodiment of unrighteousness, of natural lawlessness, of might in lieu of right. The Man of Lawlessness setteth himself up in the temple of God against all that is called God or is worshipped, declaring that he is himself God. In this attitude of emancipation from God the Antichrist can scarcely be a Jewish figure; but is rather typified in such pagan rulers as Antiochus Epiphanes who "attempted for the first time the Totalitarian State," [106] Ptolemy IV who attempted to enter the Holy of Holies, and Caligula who planned a statue of himself in the Temple.

In the self-deification of the Roman Emperors, the Apocalypse apparently finds a type of the Antichrist. This emperor worship was not a complete monotheistic self-deification, but it was a principle working in that direction and hindered at Paul's writing by some restraining force, or person. The eleventh of Daniel and the twentieth chapters of Revelation suggest that the restraining force is an angelic person. Accordingly, the Apostle finds in

---

106. Montgomery, J. A., *Journal of Religious Literature,* June, 1940, p. 309.

the supernatural world a restraining power and personage who restrains the Lawless One from exercising his full force until shortly before the Parousia of Christ. With the removal of this restraining power there will be a tide of apostasy from the Christian faith; and the Lawless One, deceiving those who are being lost, will place himself at the head of and give new impetus to this movement. And even so he will be an instrument of punishment in God's hand; for God will send this working of error into those who love not the truth, but take pleasure in unrighteousness.[107]

It may be said, at this point, that one of the signs of the times calls for the conversion of the heathen, another for the salvation of the Jews and this last for a collective falling away from Christianity. How shall one reconcile revival and apostasy? Perhaps it is difficult to solve the paradox in a theoretical vacuum; but life shows that such diverse movements may take place at the same time. Since the first World War there has been notable missionary progress in Africa, China and India; and yet we have seen the startling fact of nominally Christian nations rejecting Christianity and substituting for it atheism or paganism. Accordingly the end may well be marked by the coming in of the fullness of the Gentiles from the heathen world, the conversion of the Jews, and alas, a collective falling away. Each of these things seem to be predicted in the eleventh of Romans. There the fullness of the Gentiles and the salvation of Israel are specifically mentioned, while the warning to the branches already grafted in from wild olives hints at such an apostasy. "Be not highminded, but fear: for if God spared not the natural branches neither will He spare thee."

While, perhaps, no scholar has grasped every detail of God's program with complete accuracy, there has been an interesting movement in the direction of just such a conclusion since Luthardt drew the lines of the following picture over a half century ago: Coincident with the conversion of the Jewish nation there

---

107. For this presentation of the Antichrist cf. Vos, G., *The Teaching of Paul*, class lectures, 1920-21.

will be a period of indifference and apostasy among the other nations and the approach of an age in which the hitherto Christian world will divide into two camps, the Christian and the non-Christian. Then there will be a determined opposition to the Christian as there was to Jesus and the Christians of the first century. Again Christians will, in vain, demand the right of liberty of conscience. It will be a time of persecution and sore temptation when public opinion and natural intellectual progress will be enlisted against the confession of Christ. This will occur in a time of tremendous efforts to unite different nations after a long period of separation. It will be an era of great monarchies reaching its goal in a great universal ruler who will call the earth his Kingdom, and like the Roman Emperor claim Divine honour. This will be the official religion of his Kingdom and all who refuse to conform will be esteemed enemies of the State. The persecution of believers will have reached such an intolerable height that a direct interposition will take place. Christ Himself will appear for the victory and recognition of His Church in the world.[108]

The Great Tribulation. One is forgetting the distinction between man's thoughts and God's thoughts when he is dogmatic about the detailed order of the events culminating in the Parousia, or is unwilling to alter his opinion, or expects exact agreement among believers. Nevertheless one can modestly offer his understanding of Scripture. Revelation suggests a gathering together of the Kings at Armagedon (xvi.12-16), a surrender of their power and authority to the beast for war against the Lamb (xvii.14), the spread of Gog and Magog over the breadth of the earth, and their compassing of the camp of the saints and the beloved city (xx.7-9). Such a situation befits the great tribulation that is to lead in the end-period (Dan. xii.1; Mk. xiii.19; Matt. xxiv.24, 29; Rev. vii.14; cf.iii.10). From the special promise in the Gospels that the Holy Spirit will speak for the Christian when he is delivered up to judgment (Mk. xiii.9-11; Mt.

108. Luthardt, C. E., *The Saving Truths of Christianity*, 1886, pp. 304-308.

x.19, 20; Lk. xxi.15, John xiv.16, 18), we understand that the Church will endure the horrors of the great tribulation, sustained by the Presence of her Lord until the consummation (Matt. xxviii.20).[109] "After that tribulation, the sun shall be darkened. and the moon shall not give her light, and the stars shall be falling from heaven, and the powers that are in the heavens shall be shaken. And then shall they see the Son of man coming in clouds with power and great glory" (Mk. xiii.24-26). We collate with this record in the Synoptic Apocalypse the account of the changes of the heavens and earth at the Coming of the Lord in Second Peter, chapter three, and of the fleeing of heaven and earth from the face of Him that sits on the throne in Revelation xx.1.

> "Jesus comes on clouds triumphant,
> When the heavens shall pass away;
> Jesus comes again in glory,
> Let us then our homage pay,
> Alleluia! Ever singing,
> Till the dawn of endless day."

The Rapture and the Resurrection. The Apostle Paul goes more fully into the order of the Parousia, the Rapture and the Resurrection in First Thessalonians (iii.13; iv.13-18) than elsewhere. In the former of these passages he prays that the Thessalonians may be established unblameable in holiness that they may form a worthy contingent of the universal host of the saints which Jesus will bring with Him at His Coming. In the longer passage Paul assures his readers that God will bring those, who through the mediation of Jesus sleep with the Lord, into the Kingdom of God, and that those living at the Parousia shall not enter ahead of those who sleep. "For the Lord Himself . . . shall descend from Heaven and the dead in Christ shall rise first; then we that are alive . . . shall together with them be caught up in the clouds to meet the Lord in the air: and so shall we ever be with the Lord." This implies that the Resurrection shall take place before Christ in His descent out of heaven reaches the

---

109. Bruce, F. F., *The End of the First Gospel, The Evangelical Quarterly,* 12.3.213.

earth. Both the raised and the changed saints shall be caught up to meet the Lord in the air in their embodied states to accompany Him in His final descent, so that our Lord Jesus Christ shall come with all His saints.[110]

Thus, the Rapture of the living so immediately follows the Resurrection of the just that they are caught up together to meet Christ in the air and to swell His glorious retinue in His descent to the earth. In our study of the Kingdom of Glory we shall see that this descent brings these who are so caught up to the great white throne, and then into the new heavens and the new earth in which dwelleth righteousness, into the everlasting habitations to be ever with the Lord.

The glorious union of the Parousia with the Resurrection is heralded and accompanied with the shout, with the voice of the archangel and with the trump of God (I Thess. iv.16; cf. I Cor. xv.52). Our Lord promised that the hour would come in which all that were in their tombs would hear the voice of the Son of God and come forth (John v.28-29). Here at His Coming, He gives the shout of tremendous command that awakens the dead. With this reverberating command sounds the voice of the archangel and the trumpets of dawn, suggesting the angelic hosts who swell the train of the Kingdom of Glory and the resurrection reveille at which the dead shall be raised incorruptible and the living changed into the likeness of the body of His glory (Matt xxiv.37; Rev. x.7; xi.15; I Cor. xv.52; Phil. iii.21).

As an indication that believers, differing in their understanding of the detailed order of eschatological events, unite in their love of the Lord's appearing, we find that five of Dr. John L. Girardeau's stanzas well express our Christian hope.

> "Thou who from Olive's brow did'st rise
> In glorious triumph to the skies,
> Before the rapt disciples' eyes,
> For thy appearance all things pray,
> All nature sighs at thy delay,
> Thy people cry, no longer stay,
> Lord Jesus, quickly come!

---

110. So Vos. G., *PTR*. xxvii.1.1-2.

Hear thou the whole creation's groan,
The burdened creature's plaintive moan,
The cry of deserts wild and lone;
See signals of distress unfurled,
By states on stormy billows hurled,
Thou pole-star of a shipwrecked world —
   Lord Jesus, quickly come!
     *   *   *   *

Flush the dark firmament afar,
And let thy flaming sign appear;
Shine forth, O lustrous Morning Star.
Break through the lowering clouds of night,
Put these sepulchral shades to flight,
Flash out, O Resurrection Light —
   Lord Jesus, quickly come!

Come with Thy beauteous diadem,
Come with embattled Cherubim,
Come with the shout of Seraphim;
Come on Thy seat of radiant cloud,
Come with the Archangel's trumpet loud,
Come, Saviour, let the heavens be bowed —
   Lord Jesus, quickly come!

And when the astonished heavens shall flee,
When power of earth and hell to Thee
Shall bend the reverential knee,
Be ours the happy lot to stand
Among the white-robed, ransomed band,
And hear Thee say, with outstretched hand,
   Ye blessed children, come."

CHAPTER VII.

THE JUDGMENT-SEAT OF CHRIST

II Cor. v. 10

● *"When I soar to worlds unknown,*

      See Thee on Thy judgment throne;
      Rock of Ages, cleft for me,
      Let me hide myself in Thee!"

II Cor. v. 10

I. The Revelation of the Righteous Judgment of God. (Rom. ii.5)

The Judgment a doctrine of Paul, of the OT, of the Gospels.

The wrath of God in the NT and in re. the justice of God. Confirmation of the Judgment found in:

A. The biblical plan of salvation. Not unconditional pardon, but expiation. God can do all His holy will.

B. The dictates of conscience and the consent of the people to the justice of God. Luther and the judgment. Kierkegaard's Protest. Holmstrom on the seriousness of decision.

C. The testimony of history. Traces of judgment here. If judgment begin at the house of God what will the end be of those that obey not the Gospel?

246

II. THE MANIFESTATION OF THE SERIOUSNESS OF LIFE.

Judgment enhances the importance of every moment.
Our ministerial duty. Our goodly heritage.
Christian as well as unbelievers before the judgment seat.
Distinction between justification and final judgment.
All generations meet at the judgment.
A call to repentance.

III. THE VINDICATION OF CHRIST.

Judgment committed to Christ.

A. Christ's session on the Judgment Throne the proper
reward of His humiliation, He who was shamed now
glorified.

B. Fitting that Christ execute judgment. No foreigner
to the human race. The faith He exercised in His
human life justified. Doom for His enemies, comfort
for His servants.

C. In the final judgment Christ completes the saving work
committted to Him. Redemption fully applied. The
Church perfected. Creation freed from bondage.

I. THE REVELATION OF THE RIGHTEOUS JUDGMENT OF GOD.
Rom. ii.5.

The Apostle Paul writes to the Corinthians that we must all
be made manifest before the judgment seat of Christ; that each
one may receive the things done in the body, according to what
he hath done, whether it be good or bad (II Cor. v.10). He
warns the Romans that the practice of evil is treasuring up for
oneself wrath in the day of wrath and revelation of the righteous judgment of God, who will render to every man according
to his works (Rom. ii.5-6). Similarly, he preached to the
Athenians that God had appointed a day in which He would
judge the world in righteousness (Acts xvii.31). When he stood
before Felix, Paul reasoned of judgment to come (Acts xxiv.25).

In preaching a future judgment Paul was speaking the language
of Judaism as well as of Christianity, of the Old Testament as
well as of the New.

God manifested His justice and judgment in the revelation He
made of Himself in Eden. "In the day that thou eatest thereof,
thou shalt surely die." Abraham knew that the Judge of the
whole earth would do right (Gen. xviii.25). The merciful manifestation of God in His forgiving grace, includes the warning
that God will by no means clear the guilty (Ex. xxxiv.7). The
precepts of God disturb the consciences of the impious with recollections of the judgment.[1] The Psalms begin with the assurance
that "the ungodly shall not stand in the judgment" (i.5) and,
resting in the conviction that justice and judgment are the habitation of God's throne (lxxxix.14), repeatedly prophesy the coming of the Lord to judge the earth (xcvi.13; xcviii.9). According
to Proverbs, "he that justifieth the wicked, and he that con-
demneth the just, even they both are abomination to the Lord"
(xvii.15). That the later prophets presented justice, righteousness and truth as fundamental attributes of God is so well recognized by all schools of interpretation as not to need citations.
Jehovah of Hosts is the Holy One of Israel, who setteth justice
to the plummet line.

When we open the Gospels we find the words *the day of judgment* (Mt. x.15, 22; xii.36; Mk. vi.11) and *the judgment* (Mt.
v.21, 22; xii.41-42; Lk. x.14; xi.31-32) continually on the lips
of the Saviour, as He sees one generation rise to be weighed
against another in the final assize of Judgment Day. In the first
chapter of the Sermon on the Mount the danger of the judgment
appears twice (Mt. v.21-22), and the sermon reaches its culmination and climax in the Judgment (vii.15-27). The preaching of Passion Week reached its peak in the magnicent portrayal
of the Son of Man sitting on the throne of His glory and separating the nations of the earth as a shepherd divideth the sheep
from the goats (Mt. xxv.31-48). Again the Sermon on the

---

1. *Institutes*, II.v.10.

Mount reiterates the solemn picture of hell as Gehenna, or as the Gehenna of fire three times (Mt. v.22, 29, 30). The implications of the Fourth Gospel are that Jesus insisted so much on righteous judgment that men questioned His right to speak on the subject, and that, instead of recanting, He answered their doubts with the assertion of His own authority to execute judgment (vii.24; v.22, 27, 30; viii.16).

This element in Jesus' teachings is recognized by scholars of widely different schools. For example, McGiffert finds that Jesus sharpened the law and preached judgment.[2] Windisch writes, "the Sermon on the Mount taken as a whole, is a proclamation which takes the expectation of the eschatological judgment and salvation as its foundation, as the guide-post for living and for conduct, for the attitude towards men in this life as for that towards God."[3] A. N. Wilder discovers this sanction present in every strata of Jesus' teaching as it was in the Baptist's.[4] Maldyn Hughes quotes with approval Leckie's summary:

"We cannot fail to note in the teaching of our Lord the continual prophecy of a decisive separation of the heirs of the Kingdom from the rest of humanity. The King is constantly depicted as closing the gates of the city against those who are without, being deaf to all appeals, all entreaties, all knocking at the door (Matt. xxv.1-12). This note of exclusion is so dominant as to suggest a most solemn thought in the mind of Jesus. It belongs to a minor strain which is heard in the voice of our Lord — a sadness of foreboding, a stern perception of ominous possibilities. There is a broad and easy way that leads to destruction (Matt. vii.13f); it profits a man nothing if he gain the whole world and lose his own life (Matt. xvi.26); it had been well for Judas if he had never been born; apostate disciples are as salt that has lost its virtue, and is hence-

2. McGiffert, A. C., *The God of the Early Christians*, pp. 4, 5, 12, 13.
3. Windisch, *Bergpredigt*, quoted Wilder, *op. cit.* p. 20.
4. Wilder, A. N., *op. cit.*, pp. 101, 64, 58, 70.

250   *Christ — The Hope of Glory*

forth good for nothing but to be cast out and trodden
under foot of men (Matt. v.13) ; there is an obscurity of
the soul, wherein the very light is as darkness (Matt. vi.
23) . . . there are offenders for whom it were better that
a millstone were hanged about the neck and they were
drowned in the depths of the sea (Matt. xviii.6). These
are all sayings that are weighted with a burden of prophetic **warning. They** compel us to recognize with an awe
of spirit which is the deeper the more humbly we acknowledge the authority of Jesus, that he believed in an immeasureable danger which threatened the souls of men ; a
horror of a great darkness from which they had to be delivered."⁵

Kuyper has counted four times in which Jesus is recorded as
repeating that at the end of the last judgment there *shall be
weeping and gnashing of teeth* (Mt. xiii.40-42; xxii.1-14; xxiv.
51; xxv.30; cf. Lk. xiii.28). Since only a part of what Jesus
said is recorded, the four-fold repetition indicates that "this
conclusive saying of Christ: There shall be weeping and gnashing of teeth," undoubtedly belongs to Christ's habitual manner
of speech. "It would seem as if Christ was always thinking of it,
How frequently he speaks of it, and never but with the deepest
solemnity." ⁶ And "this imposes the solemn obligation upon us
all in preaching, in catechetical or confirmation classes, continually to point to this incisive word of Jesus, and to inculcate it
on the rising generation and those who hear or read us. Our
Lord evidently intended that this hard saying, which cuts off
every way of escape, should deeply be impressed upon our mind,
and this not only justifies, but demands the attempt in every
way of placing salvation and reprobation antithetically over
against each other." This shows that in the days of His earthly
ministry Christ perceived the inclination to soften the absolute
antithesis and refuted the same with utmost positiveness of

5. Leckie, J. H., *The World to Come and Final Destiny*, p. 152f; Cited Hughes, H.M.,
Basic Beliefs, pp. 191-192.
6. Quoted by Plumer, N. S., *The Grace of Christ*, p. 393.

speech; and He insisted ever anew upon the inexorable and distinct drawing of the dividing line between those who are to be eternaly saved and those who are to be eternaly doomed.[7] Speaking of Jesus' use of the term, *everlasting fire,* Colonel Turton says, "the language certainly implies some form of endless misery" and "it would be difficult to exaggerate the strength of texts in favour of this." (e.g. Mt. xxv.46; Dan.xii.2).[8]

Among current Continental theologians, Karl Heim finds on one side of the Passion of Christ the Satanic hatred of God. "However, on the other side stands the wrath of God against the rebellion which is directed against God. Repeatedly, in the New Testament, the words, *'the Wrath of God'* come forward in this connection. Paul can summarize the fruit of the death of Christ in one sentence: 'We will be saved from wrath through Him' (Rom. v.9). Christ is the one 'who redeems us from the wrath to come' (I Thess. i.10). We are all 'by nature children of wrath' (Eph. ii.3). 'Whosoever believeth not on the Son, the wrath of God abideth on him' (John iii.36). As a cloud, in which the electrical energy is stored up for a great discharge, so hangs the wrath of God over the unreconciled Humanity. In the End, 'the golden bowls full of the wrath of God, which burneth for ever and ever,' will be poured out over the earth (Rev. xv.7)." "Logically, it would only ever follow from God's holiness and our guilt, that we were all lost. We have all deserved eternal damnation." [9] K. L. Schmidt observes that when one understands Christ's salvation as being a judgment in the present, he must see it as an eschatology in the present. "But that cannot destroy the picture of the future judgment as it is given in Revelation and in Luke xvi.19f and xxii.43." [10]

In Romans ii.6 there is this inspired definition of the justice God will reveal at the day of Judgment: "Who will render to every man according to his works." "There is no respect of persons with God" (vs.11). Thus, as R. L. Dabney puts it, "It is

7. Kuyper, A., *The Revelation of St. John,* p. 349.
8. Turton, W. H., *The Truth of Christianity,* 1925, p. 474.
9. Heim, K., *Jesus, der Weltjollender,* pp. 115, 228.
10. Schmidt, K. L., *Eschatology,* Lectures on NT Theology, Winter Semester, 1937-1938.

the divine equity and impartiality which cause these awards." [11]
The integrity of God's character, the rectitude of His being
requires the punishment of sin. "The divine impartiality, then,
must prompt God with an everlasting certainty to render to every
one according to his works." [11] As His will is the expression of
His own perfections, the unchangeable properties of His being,
"God can no more fail to punish sin justly than to reward holiness
faithfully." [12] "God does right . . . because such is His nature
that He cannot do wrong." [13] The manifestation of His glory
as a Being of eternal rectitude, the honor of His impartial justice
necessitates God's dealing with every moral act as it deserves.
Accordingly, there is "an intrinsic obligation to penalty in every
sin." [12] God can no more fail to punish sin than He can lie.[13]

Thornwell traces the blessedness of God to the moral perfections of His being, and shows that being social God must be
holy, since "social relations imperatively demand the exercise of
moral perfections in order to harmony, perpetuity and peace."
"The necessity of His nature determines the decisions of His
will, and as He Himself is holy, the law must be holy, just and
good." Penalty is the sanction necessary to uphold the obligation
of the law, to constitute it law rather than merely advice. Thus,
"the necessity of punishment is as inexorable as the necessity of
obedience." [13] and Divine justice is simply the triumph of Divine
holiness.

At the great judgment the glories of our God and King shall
be vindicated. "Sovereign grace, heavenly mercy, spotless holiness, insulted justice, unerring truth, resistless power, and consuming wrath, will all be present and preside at the solemnities
of the occasion." "There will be nothing lacking to clothe the
scene with the authority and sanction of the present Godhead.
Heaven will lend its glories and hell its horrors to emphasize the
proceedings of the day." [14]

11. Dabney, R. L., *Discussions*, I.468, 477, 474, 479.
12. Dabney, R. L., *op. cit.*, I.468, 477, 474, 479.
13. *Thornwell's Collected Writings*, I.406-424; II.227, 230, 235.
14. Girardeau, J. L., *Sermons*, p. 18.

> "That great Day of wrath and terror,
> That last day of woe and doom,
> Like a thief that comes at midnight,
> On the sons of men shall come;
> When the pride and pomp of ages
> All shall utterly have passed,
> And they stand in anguish, owning
> That the end is here at last;
> And the trumpet's pealing clangor,
> Through the earth's four quarters spread,
> Waxing loud and ever louder,
> Shall convoke the quick and dead;
> And the King of heavenly glory
> Shall assume His throne on high,
> And the cohorts of His angels
> Shall be near Him in the sky:
> And the sun shall turn to sackcloth,
> And the moon be red as blood,
> And the stars shall fall from heaven,
> Whelm'd beneath destruction's flood.
> Flame and fire, and desolation
> At the Judge's feet shall go:
> Earth and sea, and all abysses
> Shall His mighty sentence know."[15]

The Plan of Salvation. A true apprehension of the plan of salvation confirms the conception of the justice of God which is to be revealed at the great judgment. The Bible does not teach an unconditional pardon. From the day of the Fall to the Lamb of God, bloody sacrifice remains "the grand characteristic of the religion for sinners." "Forgiveness and expiation are bound together in the Scriptures, so that expiation alone opens the way for forgiveness" (Rom. iii; Heb. ix.22; Lev. iv.3).[17] In Galatians Paul categorically asserts, "If there had been a law given which could have given life, verily righteousness should have been by the law, but the Scripture hath concluded all under sin, that the promise by faith of Jesus Christ might be given to them that believe" (iii.21). These words carry the implication that no method could have been adopted which would have cleared the guilty apart from the righteousness which God demands. In His

---

15. *Dies Irae* translated by Neale.
16. Dabney, *op. cit.*, p. 466.
17. Bavinck, H., *Gereformeerde Dogmatiek*, III.348.

infinite wisdom God does not vindicate one of His attributes at the expense of another.

The Cross is the power of God and the wisdom of God because it offers a field, magnificent and ample, in which God displays the resources of His wisdom and unfolds the riches of His grace. Here God shows Himself a just God and a Saviour. His justice required the punishment of sin, His sovereignty transferred that curse to a substitute, His love gave His Son to be this propitiation for our sins. The Christian Creed teaches the forgiveness of sins only after and because it has first confessed Jesus Christ, God's only begotten Son, who was crucified, dead and buried, descended into Hell and rose again from the dead. Our sins are forgiven because He bore them in His own body on the Tree. The Gospel is the power of God unto salvation for therein Jehovah's strength brings salvation consistent with His own righteousness. Thus the Gospel is a mighty "memorial to all generations of those principles of rectitude which spring from His essence and regulate all the decisions of His will." [18] Since the wrath of God is revealed from heaven against all unrighteousness, "every sin will be adequately punished, but blessed be God not every sinner." [19] For,

> "The eternal Life His Life down laid
> Such was the wondrous plan;
> And God, the blessed God, was made
> A curse, for cursed man."

According to the Gospel plan of salvation, "A future day of judgment is as sure as the fact that God lives and that Jesus died to deliver His guilty people from the condemnation due to their sins. Only in the light of His vicarious obedience 'even unto death' can the doctrine of eternal death be seen in its true perspective. Hell is a lesser mystery than Calvary's cross. A sinner, convicted by the Holy Spirit, can understand more easily that God should punish him eternally, than that God in the person

---

18. Thornwell, *op. cit.*, II.209, 207, 233.
19. Stuart, M., *Recollections of Duncan*, p. 220.

of His Son should have obeyed and suffered in order to save his soul from eternal punishment. The language of his heart its:

> "Depth of mercy! can there be
> Mercy still reserved for me?
> Can my God His wrath forbear?
> Me, the chief of sinners, spare?"

"The work of Christ for the redemption of His people is clearly revealed throughout the Word of God, as involving their deliverance from eternal damnation, never from a mere temporal penalty." [20]

Conscience. Conscience is as a thousand witnesses, searching the secret motives and purposes of the heart. The dictates of conscience and the consent of the people confirm the Biblical teaching of the justice of God.[21] As the human soul has expressed itself in its systems of jurisprudence, in its great literature,[22] in its profounder philosophies, and in its nobler ethical codes it has always spoken of justice as a fundamental attribute of conscience. And conscience speaks as "the lower tribunal which God hath erected in the human soul."

Conscience seems to be the last point at which the human consciousness is separated from its Maker and the first point at which the energy of the Holy Spirit in re-awakening sinners becomes evident. "Eternal law has, in all ages, poured itself down through the human conscience, like a fountain through the channel it has worn for itself, and in this instance like hot lava down a mountain gorge." [23] Conscience derives its force from the fact that its decisions are not felt to be final, but premonitory and prospective of the sanctions of a higher tribunal.

"It derives all its authority from anticipations of the future. It brings before us the dread tribunal of eternal justice and almighty power; it summons us to the awful presence of God; it wields His thunder and wears His smiles. When a man of principle braves calumny, reproach and persecution, when he stands

---

20. Lloyd-Jones, M., in *Peace and Truth*, xxv.94, 28, 25.
21. Turretin, F., Locus III.Q.xix.S.13. cf. MacGregor, J., *A Vindication of Natural Philosophy*, Edinburgh, 1859.
22. Hutton, John, *Ancestral Voices*, pp. 130-238.
23. Shedd, W. G. T., *Discourses and Essays*, p. 300.

unshaken in the discharge of duty amid public opposition and
private treachery, when no machinations of malice or seductions
of flattery can cause him to bend from the path of integrity —
that must be a powerful support through which he can bid
defiance to the 'storms of fate.' He must feel that a strong arm
is underneath him; and though the eye of sense can perceive
nothing in his circumstances but terror, confusion and dismay, he
sees his mountain surrounded by 'chariots of fire and horses of
fire,' which sustain his soul in unbroken tranquility. In the appro-
bation of his conscience there is lifted up the light of the Divine
countenance upon him, and he feels the strongest assurance that
all things shall work together for his ultimate good. Conscience
anticipates the rewards of the just, and in the conviction which
it inspires of Divine protection lays the foundation of heroic
fortitude. When, on the contrary, the remembrance of some
fatal crime rankles in the breast, the sinner's dreams are dis-
turbed by invisible ministers of vengeance and the fall of a
leaf can strike him with horror; in every shadow he sees a
ghost, in every tread he hears an avenger of blood, and in every
sound the trump of doom. What is it that invests his conscience
with such terrible power of torment? Is there nothing here but
the natural operation of a simple and original instinct? Who
does not see that 'wickedness, condemned by her own witness,
and being pressed with conscience, always forecaseth grievous
things?' — that the alarm and agitation and fearful forebodings
of the sinner arise from the terrors of an offended Judge and
insulted Lawgiver? An approving conscience is the consciousness of right, of having done what was commanded, and of being
now entitled to the favour of the Judge. Remorse is the sense of
ill desert. The criminal does not feel that his present pangs are
his punishment; it is the future, the unknown and portentous
future, that fills him with consternation. He deserves ill, and
the dread of receiving it makes him tremble." [24] Conscience represents God in the human soul and testifies to His judgment
throne.

24. Thornwell, II.241-242; Cf. Girardeau, *Sermons*, p. 15; Dabney, *Discussions*, I.475.

It is well known that a picture of Christ coming on the clouds in judgment mightily stirred Luther's conscience. Terrified by a clap of thunder, Martin vowed to enter a monastery because he doubted whether he could do enough to win a gracious God except as a monk. Luther's doubt, before and after his breach with Rome, was not the philosopher's problem, *How can one know that God exists?* but the penitent's agonized cry, *How can I know that God is gracious to me?* Luther never doubted God's existence; he doubted Martin's ability to satisfy God's requirements. Whenever he turned to Paul the words of Romans stared him in the face: *For therein is revealed the justitia Dei . . . for the wrath of God is revealed from heaven against all unrighteousness and ungodliness of men.* Similarly, Calvin testifies, "When I trusted in ceremonies, I was far removed from any certain peace of conscience. For as often as I descended into myself or raised my heart to Thee such an extreme horror surprised me that neither purifications nor satisfactions could heal me . . . Being vehemently terrified and lost for the misery into which I had fallen and still more by the knowledge of eternal death which awaited me . . . I condemned with tears and groans the fashion of my past life and entrusted myself to Thee." Thus, in that mighty revival of Christianity which we call the Reformation God used the voice of conscience pointing to the judgment and the fearful retribution of eternal death.

A century ago a penetrating Danish thinker was startled with the thought, "It must be terrible at the Day of Judgment when all souls come to life again, to stand there entirely *alone,* solitary and unknown to all." Consequently, Soren Kiergegaard objected to the exchange of the doctrine of judgment for the question of immortality, to making out "of a task for action a question for thought." After being long ignored, his challenge, "Thou art immortal and thou shalt give account unto God how thou hast lived," bore fruit in the theology of crisis. Judgment again appeared as the necessary background of grace. The living God personally confronts man in His judgment and in His grace and calls for immediate decision. In the momentary *deed* of this event or decision was placed the whole existence of man. Responsibility and existential decision became the watchwords.

However, the decisive moment of the Biblical thought of final judgment was robbed of its unconditional seriousness by the introduction of a question concerning the final outcome. Paul Althaus affirmed as "equally true" two logically irreconcilable positions, namely, "all will be blessed" and "a part will be lost." Traub admitted that only one can be true; but added, "the decision which is true is outstanding for our thought until Eternity breaks." [25] These two positions, the paradoxical or the agnostic, are characteristic of many theologians of crisis. In so far as universalism is thereby countenanced the Gospel is changed from the unique way of salvation from eternal doom that necessitates present repentance into a pedagogical plan that will work either here or hereafter for everyone.

After presenting the case for the view that God's omnipotence in the service of His love must triumph in the salvation of all,[26] Karl Heim admits that Jesus' words point in the opposite direction (Mk. ix.42f; Mt. xii.32; xxvi.24; cf. Jn. iii.36; I Jn. v.16). And when "we question our conscience, it gives these words of Jesus an involuntary right. For so often as we stand before a decision for or against a sin, our conscience says to us quite definitely: By this decision for or against the command of God, everything stands at stake; there hangs not merely a temporal fate on this, whether I break with sin or surrender to it, Eternity hangs thereon. To everyone who has been apprehended by Christ and has experienced the power of His reconciliation it becomes clear, first after his salvation, in what a fearful danger he has been suspended." [27]

Folke Holmstrom is more stringent in his rejection of this softening of the seriousness of decision. The consciousness of being responsible is reflected in the possibility of eternal damna-

25. Althaus and Traub cited Holmstrom, *op. cit.*, p. 310.
26. Cf. Paterson, W. P., *The Rule of Faith*, pp. 312-313, 353; Kerr, H. T., *A God-centered Faith*, pp. 73-75.
27. Heim, K., *Jesus, der Weltvollender*, pp. 226-227.

tion, the consciousness of being elect in the hope of eternal happiness. "This dualistic end perspective of Hell and Heaven is the consequent expression for the Biblical proclamation of the sovereign God, who deals with the sinner in judgment and grace. Therefore the doctrine of restorationism is always a symptom of the curiosity of the natural man peering into the counsel of the hidden God instead of giving himself to tranquality in the simplicity of faith with the revealed Word." "Only the double outcome is truly laden with a dangerous enough tension to be the eschatological correlation to the paradox of justification, to the *simul justus et peccator*." To surrender this eschatological dualism would be to distort in its deepest import *justification by faith alone,* which "in such a notable way Althaus has made the center of eschatology," and to dissolve the seriousness of the call to accept the Gospel in a limited day of grace.[28] At a definitte limit, "God's judgments stand eternaly fixed as definite facts: 'eternal life' and 'eternal death'." [29]

In his return toward orthodoxy D. R. Davies has some inkling of the fact that "the dogma of hell is fundamental in Christianity." He holds that free spirits can go on rejecting God eternally, and *"that means eternal punishment."* It ought to be only a step from this to the truth that sin is naturally and certainly self-propagating, and hence that an everlasting series of sins is the just ground of everlasting punishments. Davies holds that hell can only be abolished at the price of freedom; what he fails to see is that man *dead in trespasses and sins* cannot come to Christ *except the Father draw him*. Except Christ effectually call man he will not come to repentance; and Christ has inaugurated this age of grace as the acceptable year of the Lord. The assumption of an *a priori* ground of improbability against endless punishments, goes beyond the depth of created reason,[30] and presents the case as though men had it in their power to undo this distressing fact.[31] "There has been *one Man* on earth who did

28. Holmstrom, F., *op. cit.,* pp. 310-311, 416. cf. Ferre, N.F.S.
29. Davies, D. R., *On to Orthodoxy,* pp. 150, 151.
30. Dabney, R. L., *Endless Punishment, Discussions,* I.134, 139, 140, 141, 142.

appear to frame his whole life and nerve his energies in accordance with this solemn and dreadful view of human destiny. He seemed to love, and strive, and preach, and die, just as a good man should do who really believed the sinner's ruin to be everlasting. And this was the *one Man* who knew by experience, because He came from the other world, and returned to it." [31]

History. History adds her testimony to the presuppositions of the Gospel and human conscience that there is to be a final judgment. God has begun the process of judgment in this world. God has chastised men, churches and nations in this life. To a limited extent, the history of the world is the judgment of the world. "World history is not the judgment, but is proceeding towards the judgment. God's judgment in history, in the downfall of peoples and empires, in the visitation of whole churches, in chastisement, foreshadows the last judgment." [32] Even here there are indications that "though the mills of the gods grind slow, they grind exceeding fine." From the leaves and branches that floated out to him Columbus knew he was approaching a new world. So all about us in life there are intimations of the final judgment. "The divine Judge has made incomplete and unequal inflictions upon men for their sins in this world." [33] Here too often the wicked prosper and the righteous suffer. One nation is crushed by a more wicked nation. The Assyrian becomes the rod in Jehovah's hand for the chastisement of His people. But knowing the justice of God, we look for the casting away of the rod and the preservation of Israel his son even through the affliction. If judgment begin at the house of God, what shall be the end of them that obey not the Gospel of God? (I Peter iv.17).

God has begun the work of judgment here, and considerations of His perfections and His omnipotent hand forbid the thought that He will rest until He has carried judgment to final and perfect adjustment. In Providence, in history and in human jurisprudence there are clear indications of the principle of

---

31. Kuyper, A., *The Revelation of St. John*, p. 346.
32. Wendland, H. D., *op. cit.*, p. 164.
33. Dabney, R. L., *Discussions*, I.477; Girardeau, J. L., *Sermons*, p. 16.

retribution. And with God all things are possible. His infinite wisdom, power and sovereignty assure us of the completion and consummate exhibition of this principle at the Great White Throne. A perfect God will at last exhibit a perfect government. "When God finally declares his judicial work complete, its equity will be, in all its multitudinous particulars, as absolute as the perfection of the Judge." [33]

Our Lord had this application in mind when He referred His hearers to the several exhibitions of Providential chastisement in His day. *Think ye that these Galileans were sinners above all the Galileans, because they have suffered these things? I tell you, Nay: but, except ye repent, ye shall all in like manner perish* (Lk. xiii.1-5). In a broader compass, the dealings of God with fallen creatures and their surety are reviewed in Second Peter, Jude and Romans. God spared not the angels that sinned, but cast them down to pits of darkness reserved unto judgment. God spared not the ancient world; but brought a flood upon the world of the ungodly. God spared not Sodom and Gomorrah. God spared not the natural branches, His ancient people Israel (Rom. xi.21). The deepest and most solemnizing judgment of God is that God spared not His own Son (Rom. viii.31). God's inflexible justice is seen in the punishment of sin reaching from the condemnation of the angels to the weight of Divine wrath that fell upon His own Son when He stood as our substitute and bore our sins in His own body on the tree. All these things are preludes and prophesies of the future judgment. Let the man who makes light of eternal doom consider the angels that fell and ponder these words of the Redeemer, "Then shall he say unto them on the left hand, Depart from me, ye cursed, into the eternal fire which is prepared for the Devil and His angels."

II. The Manifestation of the Seriousness of Life.

The judgment seat of Christ lends a seriousness to all life. The things we do are not trivial and unimportant, they shall be judged by God. "Each man's work shall be made manifest: the day shall declare it" (I Cor. iii.13). Our daily doings are not to be dismissed as mere deeds of the body; these are the very things that are to make us manifest before His judgment. In the risen body each one is to receive the things done in the body whether it be good or bad (II Cor. v.10). The idle talk and gossip in which we too easily indulge is not inconsequential. James warns us that the tongue is a world of iniquity, set on fire of hell. The thoughtless, spontaneous, unguarded word reveals the abundance of the heart, so that for every idle word that men speak they shall give account in the day of judgment (Mt. xii.35-36). The judgment seat of Christ enhances the meaning and importance of every thought, word and act. It is an impetus to all holy desires, all good counsels and all just works, and a deterrent from the lusts of the flesh, the pride of the eye and the pride of life. The judgment casts its shadow over death as the final event in one's day of grace. "As the tree falleth, so shall it lie." Accordingly, "we must learn to speak more seriously and severely of death. It is the wages of sin and the portal to judgment." [34]

Only as grace restores our vision of the Judgment shall we seriously seek to enter through the strait gate and to walk in the narrow way. Only the judgment can revive in our hearts a concern for either the weightier matters of justice, mercy and the love of God, or for the jots and tittles of His law. Only the realization that we must give account to God will deliver us from being time-servers and men-pleasers. Only the faith — that the LORD is our Judge, the LORD is our lawgiver, the LORD is our King (Isa. xxxiii.22) will bring us back to serious exegesis of God's Word that our social and individual conduct may be determined not by the opinions of the hour, but by the law of the Lord; that our confession of faith may be reformed not by the wish of the Church, but by the Word of our God; that our order of service may not be a will-worship, fashioned by human

---

34. Koberle, A., *The Quest of Holiness*, p. 167.

aesthetics or expediency, but that we may tread His courts in the ways warranted by His Word. We shall be more zealous, in our personal lives, to sanctify Christ as Lord in our hearts, and, in our official positions, to minister the gifts of His bounty as good stewards of the manifold grace of God, when we realize each shall give account to Him that is ready to judge the living and the dead (I Peter iv.5). When the Apostle Paul came to the end of his course and sought to lay on his successor the most solemn obligation to carry on, he wrote,

"I charge thee in the sight of God, and of Christ Jesus, who shall judge the living and the dead, and by His appearing and His kingdom: preach the Word."

A sense of responsibility to God, a realization that one must give account to God at His throne for every moment of his life, moved John Wesley to unceasing service and molded him in methodical piety. A conscience sensitized to the judgment-seat of Christ will quicken in each of us something of the zeal and urgency in our ministerial vocation which characterized Wesley, Asbury or "Brother" Bryan who died lamenting that there were so many people out of Christ.[35]

At the passing of our great Christian Warrior, B. M. Palmer tenderly said, "Whilst Dabney sleeps with the honored dead in the rural graveyard in Prince Edward, those who stood by his side, fighting for the truth of God in his generation, are standing at the edge of their own graves opening at their feet. Together with their departed brother they will awake in the triumphant resurrection morn. Will those who take their places be faithful to the trust, and hold the truth of God in this age of empiricism, in which human devices are substituted for the power of Divine truth, and artificial combinations usurp the functions of the Church of God?"[36] At Dabney's funeral, Moses D. Hoge affirmed, "No church on this continent has been more favored of heaven in having at its very organization three such men as

---

35. Rev. Dr. J. A. Bryan of Birmingham, Ala.
36. Palmer, B. M., *The Christian Warrior* in the *Southern Presbyterian*, January 20, 1898.

Thornwell, Palmer and Dabney." The judgment-seat of Christ calls us to build worthily on the heritage God has given us through them.

The Judgment Faces Christians. Some well-meaning people have robbed the judgment-seat of Christ of its Christian application by forcing Scripture to conform to their theological schemes. It is all too easy to set up our systems, over-simplify them and then force the fuller and richer truths of the Word into the petty grooves of our making. Thus, all too often the shadow of little man limits the fullness of God's revelation. The true process must ever be to reform our thinking, our systems, our preconceptions and assumptions by the fullness of God's Word.

In the text which has furnished the theme for this lecture, II Cor. v.10, some have said that the Greek word, translated judgment-seat, is used in classic Greek only for the bench used by the judges of a contest, such as the Isthmian games, who award prizes to the victors. From this alleged usage it has been affirmed that the Christians appear here only to receive their rewards. However, a study of the New Testament shows that this word, *bema,* is frequently used of the judgment-seat of an official who hears criminal cases, such as Pilate, Gallio, Festus and Caesar (Mt. xxvii.19; Jn. xix.13; Acts xviii.12, 16, 17; xxv.6, 17).[37]

In His Gospel teaching, our Lord declared, "The Son of man shall come in the glory of His Father with His angels; and then shall He render unto every man according to his deeds" (Mt. xvi.27). And speaking from heaven to the Church in Thyatira, "These things saith the Son of God, who hath his eyes like a flame of fire . . . I am he that searcheth the reins and the hearts: and I will give unto each one of you according to your works." (Rev. ii.18, 23).

No one stated the doctrine of salvation by free grace and justification by faith alone more vigorously than Paul or Luther. Yet Paul says, "He that judgeth me is the Lord. Wherefore

37. Pieters, A., *The Lamb, the Woman, and the Dragon,* pp. 341-342.
Thayer, J. H., *Greek-English Lexicon,* 1889, p. 101.

judge nothing before the time, until the Lord come" (I Cor. iv. 4-5) ; and "Every man shall receive his own reward according to his own labor" (I Cor. iii.8). He further states that we are stewards of the mysteries of God and "it is required in stewards that a man be found faithful." In commenting on Psalm vi, Luther writes, "So in a just man there must always be the fear of the judgment of God, because of the old man within." [38]

Among the evangelical theologians of today, Professor W. D. Wendland of Kiel recognizes that "the Christian church cannot anticipate this judgment, especially as it must itself appear before the judgment seat of Christ." [39]

On a re-study of the whole matter, Professor Koberle, a Lutheran theologian of Tubingen, states the case thus:

"It is impossible to restrict the statement of the New Testament concerning the final judgment to the ungodly or to self-righteous zealots for the Law, to say nothing of trying to explain them as remnants of Jewish ideas in the theology of St. Paul. The Son of Man will require a special reckoning from those who have been engaged in His service and have been endowed with His gifts. That the returning Judge would reward every man according to his work was told to the disciples. Every idle word spoken by man must be accounted for at the last day. St. Paul regards every earthly tribunal and every earthly self-judgment as unimportant, whether it be approval or disapproval, for that day shall declare it; the day in which the Lord will judge. Then will man's work first be revealed, of what sort it is. Each one will reap what he has sowed. All must appear before the judgment seat of Christ to receive the final judgment on this earthly life. Whoever in the earthly congregation continues to serve evil shall not inherit the

38. Cited by Koberle, *op. cit.* p. 169.
39. Wendland, H. D., *op. cit.,* p. 162.

Kingdom." [40] Accordingly, "at the end of days the judgment will actually be passed on the works of the sinner and of the righteous, and so the fear of displeasing God must accompany even the life of the believer as a holy fear and as an aid in overcoming temptation. Insincere life, an unbridled tongue or body, impure passions, implacable enmity which faith that possessed the Spirit might have restrained or turned aside, will go with us and accuse us before God. But when the idea of judgment on the entire attitude of one who is justified has been maintained, there will be no room for the ancient antinomian misunderstanding which has always accompanied Paulinism and Lutheranism like a dark shadow; the question of whether the Christian cannot continue in sin because of the working of grace would thus become so much more mightily evident Rom. vi.1 seq.). If even the justified sinner must face the judgment it is no longer a matter of indifference as to the degree in which he has allowed himself to be purified by the Spirit from the 'defilement and evil of the flesh'." [40]

The Judgment in re Justification. If our theology is to be conformed to the Word, we cannot allow even the great doctrine of grace to obliterate or remove the Judgment. And properly understood there is no reason why it should. Justification is an anticipation of the judgment, a piece of realized eschatology, a taste of the powers of the world to come. It presupposes the judgment it does not dispense with it. The Jew looked for the judgment at the last day; the New Testament sees Christ taking our curse, removing the handwriting in ordinances that was against us by nailing it to His Cross, and proclaims the justification, here and now, of everyone that believeth on Him. But this anticipation of the final judgment does not make that unnecessary or a mere duplication. There are several differences.

---

40. Koberle, A., *The Quest for Holiness*, pp. 165, 166. Citing St. Luke xix.11-26; St. Matt. xvi. 24-27; xxv. 32; xii. 36; I Cor. iv.3,iii.13 *seq.;* vi.9 *seq.;* Gal. vi.7 *seq.;* v.19-21; II Cor. v.10; II Thess. i.8-10; Rom. ii; I Peter iv.11. Cf. H. Braun, *Gerichtsgedanke und Rechtfertigungslehre bei Paulus*, Leipzig, 1930.

The soteric principle is foremost in justification; and its great truth is that *God is for us.* The ultimate principle in the judgment is theological, a vindication of God by showing that the justified have been *for God* in their faith, testimonies and lives. There is no disharmony between justification by faith alone and the manifestation of the believer's faith by His obedience and love and service in the final assize. There the whole process of redemption is seen in its outcome in such a way as to vindicate God's wisdom, power and grace in the method He has adopted, in His patience and long-suffering toward His fallen creatures. The Judgment manifests the glory of God, showing that His plan of salvation has been a success not a failure.

Again justification is a secret thing occurring in the forum of human conscience. It is a dealing between God and the soul, unseen by the world. The sinner *believeth on Him that justifieth the ungodly,* and is justified by faith not by sight. On the other hand the Last Judgment is a public acknowledgement of those who have put on Christ. Then each man and his work shall be manifest for the Day will declare it. When God judges the secrets of men, there will be nothing hidden that is not made manifest. Further, God the Father is the author of justification; while Christ presides at the great judgment (Jn. v.22; Acts xvii.31; Rom. ii.16; Mt. xxv.31f.).

In the present justification, the sinner's works are entirely out of consideration. We reckon that a man is justified by faith, apart from the works of the law (Rom. iii.28). We know that a man is not justified by the works of the law but through faith in Jesus Christ (Gal. ii.16). But in the future judgment his work done under the impulse of God's grace will enter into the judgment as a factor upon which the decision is made (I Cor. iii.15). However, there is a basic difference between the Judaistic principle that God gives a man a stipulated equivalent for his own works, and the Pauline principle that a man being justified by grace through faith alone is moved to express his gratitude to God who has saved him by doing the good works God before ordained. God works in us to will as well as to do these good works (Phil. ii.13) ; in Christ Jesus faith worketh by love (Gal. v.6). Being made new creatures, His Spirit works these good deeds as the expression and outcome of a living faith. Thus Paul sees an organic connection between faith and works. It is not as though good works, atomically considered, made a good man; but a man justified and sanctified by a saving fellowship with God does good works. And these works shine before men to the glory of God, and the vindication of His salvation. These good works are not the exact equivalent of the reward. The Apostle's figures, a race and a prize, sowing and reaping, sons and an inheritance, suggest a real connection between the antecedent and the consequent, but not an exact equivalent. The prize is more than exact wages, the harvest than the sowing, the inheritance of a son than the wages of a laborer. And even the Saviour's parable of the laborers employed at different hours in the vineyard represents full reward for those who have labored only briefly. Grace is resplendent in the glory of the Judgment, as it is in the act of justification.

Using the figure of two sets of books employed in Revelation (xx.11-15), Professor Albertus Pieters pictures the clerk of the heavenly court calling off a name. "One angel looks in his book to see what the works were of the one named. He finds, in the midst of a sad and shameful record of failures and offenses, as a precious jewel in the rubbish, this entry : 'He believed on Jesus Christ as his Saviour.' He looks further, and finds works on record in accordance with this faith. Then he turns to the angel with the Book of Life, and asks: 'Is his name written there?' —'It is'."

Thus, as Alford says, "we should say that those books and the Book of Life bore independent witness to the fact of men being or not being among the saved : the one, by inference from the works recorded : the other by inscription or non-inscription of the name in the list. So the 'books' would be as it were, the vouchers for the Book of Life." [41]

41. Pieters, A., *The Lamb, the Woman and the Dragon*, p. 337, citing Alford, Henry, *The Greek Testament*, IV.ii.733.

Works are an indication of the reality of our faith, a measure of the servant's fidelity; and hence, in the parable of the talents, an indication or scale of the honors he receives; but the ground of righteousness is here also all that which the Lord Jesus did for us. Our faith, our testimony, our service, our ministries to His brethren, the fruits of His Spirit in our lives testify that in our weak and imperfect ways we confessed Him here below; and in that awful day He will confess us before the Father and the holy angels.

The Two Processions. The difference between the true believers, and the hypocrites and unbelievers is not that the former shall not and the latter shall appear before the judgment seat of Christ; but rather that the believer shall not come into condemnation and that the unbelieving sinner shall not be able to stand in the judgment. All shall be manifest, but He that sitteth upon the throne of His glory shall divide them as a shepherd separateth the sheep from the goats. From that throne two processions shall move. One shall follow the Lamb to the New Jerusalem and the living fountains of water. And all jubilant with song the gates of the holy city will open for them. The Redeemed will sing, as the singers of David sang when the Ark of the Covenant was brought to Zion, and as the angels sang at the Ascension,[42]

"Lift up your heads, O ye gates, and be ye lifted up, ye
   everlasting doors and the King of glory shall come in!"
And the angelic sentries on the battlements of the City of God will reply,

"Who is this King of Glory?"
And that great host which no man can number, who have washed their robes and made them white in the blood of the Lamb will give answer,

"The Lord, strong and mighty, the Lord mighty in battle,
   the Lord of hosts, He is the King of glory."
And these shall go to be ever with the Lord, the contingent of grace in the armies of God.

---

42. Steward, Alexander, *Shoes for the Road*, 1940, pp. 46-52.

Those on the left hand take the other turn and the funeral procession of the second death winds its way slowly from the throne of God and of the Lamb. They pass through the gloomy portals over which is written, "They who enter here leave hope behind." The Jesus they once rejected has ever more rejected them. His "Depart from me, I never knew you" has banished them forever from the gates of glory. They go into outer darkness where there is weeping and gnashing of teeth, into endless sinning and endless punishment. Their cry is "Lost! Lost! forever lost!" They have lost all, for they have lost GOD.

The Generations in the Judgment. Believers and unbelievers, Jews and Gentiles, men who were entrusted with the oracles of God and men who only had the law written on their consciences, men who knew their Lord's will and men who knew it not, all shall stand before Him who is no respecter of persons, when God shall judge the secrets of men by Jesus Christ (Rom. ii.11-16; Lk. xii.48). Angels and men, sinners and saints, the quick and the dead, shall all be there. "Not one of all God's rational creatures shall be missing." [43] Moreover one generation shall appear with another; and the children shall report in the presence of the fathers the use they have made of their patrimony, physical and spiritual. When each one is giving account of his own stewardship to God, perhaps we shall be less caustic of those who witnessed valiantly for the faith in past generations — Thornwell, Dabney and Warfield. These men who labored and we who enter into their heritage and draw support from the foundations and convictions they established shall stand together before the judgment-seat of Christ. For,

> "In one vast conflux rolled,
> Wave following wave, are men of every age,
> Nation and tongue: all hear the warning blast,
> And led by wondrous impulse hither come."

The Puritans shall rise in the judgment to meet their detractors, the Reformers to confront their critics, pious Methodist to face

43. *Plumer, W. S.,* op. cit., p. 388.

grandchildren who fancy they have gone up from Methodism, the dour Covenanters to accuse those who have forgotten that the unborn children were pledged to the faith of the covenant. If King Saul bowed his face to the ground at the mention of the shade of Samuel, what shall Adolph Hitler do when he meets Martin Luther, or Rosenberg when he sees the Perceptor of Germany (Melanchthon), or the Governor of the Bahamas when Queen Victoria appears, Bertrand Russell when Jonathan Edwards rises, John Broadus Watson when John A. Broadus comes? How shall our generation which barely reproduces itself face the pioneer parents who supplied the children to build this nation? How shall this generation of champagne and cocktails look to the fathers who had the courage to prohibit the manufacture and sale of intoxicating liquor?

If we glance at only some of the specific references in Scripture we find that Sodom and Gomorrah, the generation of Abraham, the Queen of Sheba, a generation a thousand years later, Nineveh of the generation of Jonah are to stand in the judgment with the generation to which Jesus preached. Those who heard Noah will rise in the judgment to confront the men of Capernaum who heard Christ (I Peter iii.20;iv.6). Paul and his converts will be there to meet their persecutors (II Thess. i.4-10). The martyrs under the altar wait for their brethren to fulfill their course, perhaps in the Great Tribulation; then all who were persecuted for righteousness sake shall be avenged together (Rev. vi.9-11). Abraham and Isaac and Jacob shall enter into the Kingdom of God with men from the north and the east and the south and the west, while many of the children of the Kingdom are being cast out. Those who are persecuted for Christ's sake are to be greatly rewarded in heaven with the Old Testament prophets who suffered *causa Dei* (Matt. v.11-12). It is generally agreed that the Bible was not more than fifteen hundred years in writing. And yet it mentions generations from the days of Abraham, and the days of Noah, milleniums before Christ, to the Christians centuries that shall stand together in the judgment.

The earth and the sea shall give up their dead. And hell shall disgorge her minions. The devils shall not be absent, but shall stand condemned by the Lord who himself took the nature and status of a creature and therein met and conquered the Accuser of his brethren. The devil shall be cast into the lake of fire and brimstone where are also the beast and the false prophet; and they shall be tormented day and night forever and ever (Rev. xx.10). Indeed, the eternal fire has been prepared for the Devil and his angels (Matt. xxv.41) and needs not men to rush past the Gospel of grace and the Cross of atonement to feed its flames.

A Call to Repentance. Thus, even in the fearful judgment scene there are intimations of grace and the preaching of judgment is a call to repentance. Heaven is a kingdom prepared from the foundation of the world for those blessed of the Father, God would have all men to be saved, there is to be a great host that no man can number who have washed their robes and made them white in the blood of the Lamb, who are arrayed in white linen which is the righteous acts of the saints. Hell is prepared for the Devil and his angels. Jesus wept over the city which crucified Him. "As I live," saith the Lord God, "I have no pleasure in the death of the wicked. But that the wicked turn from his way and live: turn ye, turn ye from your wicked ways; for why will ye die, O House of Israel?" (Eze. xxxiii.11). While it is the day of grace, while the acceptable year of the Lord is with us may the judgment sober our lives. The fear of the Lord is still the beginning of wisdom. May we heed its message ere one say, "the summer is past, the harvest is ended, and we are not saved." Ere

> "The Lord, the Judge, before His throne
>   Bids the whole earth draw nigh;
> The nations near the rising sun;
>   And near the western sky.
>
> No more shall bold blasphemers say,
>   Judgment will ne'er begin;
> No more abuse His long delay
>   To insolence and sin.

Throned on a cloud our God shall come,
　Bright flames prepare His way;
Thunder and darkness, fire and storm,
　Lead on the dreadful day.

Heaven from above His call shall hear,
　Attending angels come;
And earth and hell shall know and fear
　His justice and their doom."[44]

III. The Vindication of Christ.

The judgment throne of Divine glory is specifically described as "the judgment seat of Christ" (II Cor. v.10). This great event will be the vindication of the Person, the Work and the Claims of the humiliated Saviour before an assembled universe. It is the teaching of the Gospels as well as the Epistles, of the Synoptics as well as John that the function of judgment is committed to Jesus Christ. This is so generally the rule in Scripture that the exception in Rom. xiv.10-12 is to be understood as explaining the rule. "God is here mentioned as Judge (see ii.16). He judges the world through Christ." [45]

The Sermon on the Mount closes with men pleading with Christ as *the Lord* Who has the final word concerning their destiny, and departure from Whom is Hell. The eschatological discourse in Matthew repeatedly emphasizes the same thought (xxiv.30, 31 ; 42, 45-51 ; xxv.11 ; 14-30 ; 31-46). When the Son of man comes in His glory His angels shall gather His elect. We, His servants, shall give account to our Lord at His coming of our diligence in the task He has assigned and for the talents He has intrusted to us. Except we be watching, our Lord will not take us in with Him to the marriage feast. The Son of man shall sit upon the throne of His glory and as King and Lord divide all the nations. From His word there is no appeal, only Heaven or Hell. According to John's Gospel, the Father hath given all judgment to the Son (v.22).

For Paul, the Resurrection of Jesus is God's assurance to all men that He will judge the world by the man whom He hath

---

44. Quoted Girardeau, J. L., *Sermons*, p. 25.
45. Sanday, *Romans*, p. 389.

raised up (Acts xvii.31). Thus, the Apostle says "He that judgeth me is the Lord;" and "God shall judge the secrets of men, according to my gospel, by Jesus Christ;" and "we shall all appear before the judgment-seat of Christ" (I Cor. iv.4; Rom. ii.16; II Cor. v.10). In Revelation, the Word of God who is King of Kings and Lord of Lords doth judge and make war (xix.11-16), even as in the earlier chapters He walks among the candlesticks judging the churches.

A. Christ's session upon the Judgment Throne is the proper reward of His humiliation. There is an especial propriety in this glorious coming to the Second Person of the Triune Jehovah. He came unto His own in lowly humility. His generation saw Him in the weakness of a babe, the poverty of a manger, the labor of a carpenter, the pain of a scourge, the shame of a criminal, the death of a Cross. And this portrayal has been broadcast to the generations since. Yea, prophets foresaw these sufferings generations earlier and angels looked into them (I Peter i.11, 13). His creatures have seen their Lord clad in the form of a servant, tempted in all points like as we are, offering up strong cryings and tears unto Him that is able to save him from death, taking our infirmities and bearing our diseases; they have seen His form more marred than any man and His visage than the sons of men; they have esteemed Him stricken of God and afflicted and have hid their faces from Him; they treated Him as a worm, and laughed Him to scorn as a reproach of men; they pierced His hands and His feet and cast lots for His vesture. They made Him a laughing stock and spit in His face. They heard His cry of foresakenness, His trouble with none to help, and His trust apparently put to shame. This may not be the end.

God shall yet make bare His mighty arm and vindicate His holy Child Jesus in the eyes of every creature. When He stood before the High Priest, Jesus said, "Hereafter shall ye see the Son of Man sitting on the right hand of Power and coming on the clouds of heaven." Because He humbled Himself and became obedient unto death, even the death of the Cross, God hath highly exalted Him and given Him a name that is above every Name. And as He sits upon the throne of His glory every knee shall bow at the name of Jesus, of things in heaven, and things on earth and things under the earth; and every tongue shall confess that Jesus, the Messiah, is Lord to the glory of God the Father (Phil. ii.9-11). Then men, demons and angels, assembled before the Great White Throne, shall bow in adoration and worship the Lord Jesus Christ. Having come in the form of a servant into this old world of sin and death; He shall come again in His native glory, a glory before which the fashion of this world shall be changed. At His shout the dead shall arise and death be vanquished; from His face the present earth and heaven shall flee away and there shall be a new heavens and a new earth in which dwelleth righteousness as the theatre for the manifestation of His Eternal Glory. "The Lord Christ shall appear in glory, display the wonders of His mediation and the perfection of his government, and will publicly be owned and crowned as Lord of all." [46] The hosts before His throne will take up the song:

> "Worthy is the Lamb that hath been slain
> to receive the power, and riches, and wisdom,
> and honor, and glory, and blessing."

> "Yea, Amen! let all adore Thee,
> High on Thine eternal throne:
> Saviour, take the power and glory,
> Claim the kingdom for Thine own:
> Alleluia! Thou shalt reign, and Thou alone."

B. Further, it is altogether fitting that the Father should give Christ authority to execute judgment because He was manifest in the flesh. The creature is to be judged by the heavenly One who took the lot and life of a creature. The very fashion of the Judge will hush the cavil of Satan that a free spirit cannot be an obedient subject. The simple life which the Judge lived as a carpenter will destroy the refuge of those who declare that

---

46. Plumer, W. S., *The Grace of Christ*, p. 388.

a proletariate lot justifies radicalism and revolt. And as He takes His seat in our own nature, God gives us the pledge that our constitution, circumstances, opportunities, weaknesses and temptations will be fairly and fully evaluated. "No foreigner to the human race will fill the judgment-seat before which the human race shall stand to receive irrevocable assignment to heaven and to hell." [47] A man who knows the measure of the case will be the judge.

In human nature Christ manifested the supreme act of faith in God. Forsaken by friends, subjected to torture, taunted with jeers, robbed of justice, crucified between thieves, His cry of forsakenness still maintained that God was His own God. God will justify this faith and show that justice is supreme when He seats upon the judgment throne of the universe the One who was taken away by the grossest miscarriage of justice which history records. There He will show that truth is not forever on the scaffold, nor wrong forever on the throne. Rather because

> Thou hast loved righteousness, and hated iniquity;
> Therefore, O God, thy God hath anointed Thee
> With the oil of gladness above Thy fellows (Hebrews i.9).

In the Gospel record of His human life, Christ has faced the moving generations. In Michal de Munkacsy's *Christ Before Pilate* our Saviour is pictured as He was arraigned before the Roman governor. Pilate sits on the judgment-seat in a niche of the praetorium. Clothed in the purple-bordered toga of a Roman senator, his strong Roman face is now the picture of indecision as worldly motives play for mastery. Almost in the center of the picture facing Pilate is the Prisoner, clothed in white with His hands bound behind Him. His face dominates everything. Serene, unshakable, with a glance that pierces men's souls, He is even here the One who is set for the rising and falling of many. Against His purity and sublimity the wickedness of a Pilate, a Caiaphas, a Pharisee and a soldier are evident.

---

47. Girardeau, J. L., *op. cit.*, p. 20.

As He was the touchstone there, so He has ever been the good paragon, the crystal Christ, who has measured and judged men as they have beheld the Man. Jesus Christ is God's magnet that passing over the human race draws to itself all that are not hopelessly bad. In His love, His character, His teaching, His deeds, His patience, His life and His death uplifted upon a tree, His Resurrection and Ascension He has drawn men of all climes and races and families unto Himself. He is the touchstone that God hath inserted into the stream of human life by which to measure every other life. He is God's idea of a man. And hence as every other man faces Him he evaluates himself.

Today we offer Christ to men. In His Name we beg them to be reconciled to God. Those who reject His mercy, disdain His dying love, scoff at His Resurrection, spurn the record of His saving revelation shall prostrate themselves before the throne of His glory and wait in breathless agony His Word. The judgment-seat of Christ lends new meaning to the Gospel declaration, "This is the work of God that ye believe on Him whom He hath sent." It gives poignancy to the Saviour's warning, "Except ye believe that I am He, ye shall die in your sins." It puts the weight of eternity into the question, "What then shall I do with Jesus who is called the Christ?" Nay more, it transmutes this into another question, "In that hour, what will Jesus, the Christ, do with me?" For,

> "Every eye shall now behold Him
> Robed in dreadful majesty;
> Those who set at naught and sold Him,
> Pierced and nailed Him to the tree,
> Deeply wailing. Shall the true Messiah see."

And in that day, many will sadly say,

> "Yonder sits my slighted Savior,
> With the marks of dying love;
> Oh, that I had sought His favor
> When I felt His Spirit move!
> Golden moments,
> When I felt His Spirit move!"

For those who have found in Jesus Christ their comfort and hope, there is life and blessedness in His session on the judgment throne. He became also man that He might be our Saviour. Christ took flesh and blood for our sakes rather than for His own. What He did in the body He did for us men and for our salvation. The life He lived He lived for us, keeping God's law perfectly. The death He died He died for us, as our representative and substitute enduring the weight of Divine wrath our sins deserved. He gives us His flesh and blood with all He did and endured therein. And when the Son of Man ascends the throne our hearts are lifted with hope even amidst the awesome glory of the Judgment. This is the human nature that was taken for us, that suffered and died in our stead, that He has given for us and to us. And grace is poured through His lips into our hearts as we hear Him say, "Lift up your heads for your redemption draweth nigh!" In the Middle Ages, Anselm taught dying men to put the death of Christ between them and the wrath of God. In the Scots' Confession John Knox draws consolation from the fact that the clean, pure, innocent Lamb of God was damned in the presence of an earthly tribunal that we might be absolved before the tribunal of God. In the Heidelberg Catechism Ursinus and Olevianus teach,

> "In all my sorrows and persecutions with uplifted head, I look for the judge, who has offered Himself for me to the judgment of God and removed me from all curse, to come again."

> "Lo! He comes with clouds descending,
> Once for favored sinners slain;
> Thousand, thousand saints attending
> Swell the triumph of His train;
> Alleluia! God appears on earth to reign."

"Even so come, Lord Jesus!"

C. "Our Saviour, as the final act of His redeeming work, shall shut the volume of grace and open that of eternal judgment." [48] When He finished the work committed to Him and

---

48. Girardeau, *op. cit.*, p. 20.

ascended to the Throne as the Lamb that had been slain, our Lord was declared worthy to loose the seals and open the counsels of God's peace to those whom He had purchased with His own blood. By His obedience and expiation Christ satisfied Divine justice and made it consonant with the rectitude of holiness to save those who believe in Him. He was given the task of administering the counsels of God's Providence and Grace in order to fill up the roll of His elect. The redemption He won will not be fully applied until He comes to reign in glory. Until then there will be men living on this earth struggling against the world, the flesh and the Devil, while those who have departed to be with Him will not be publicly vindicated and received in their completed personalities into the everlasting kingdom of our Lord and Saviour Jesus Christ. The Church will still be a struggling, spotted, imperfect body made up of such imperfect believers, such foolish leaders as we are.

Only then will she be the Church glorious, without spot or wrinkle or any such thing. Only as she shares in the radiancy of His Appearing will she be the Church Triumphant, the Bride arrayed in fine linen pure and white for her marriage to the Lamb. Then will the holy temple in the Lord which is built upon the foundation of the apostles and prophets, Jesus Christ Himself being the chief cornerstone, be completed, her top-stone brought forth with shouts of grace. Then will the scaffolding of earthly worship be removed, for the tabernacle of God shall be with men, and the Lord God Almighty and the Lamb shall be the sanctuary of the Holy City, the New Jerusalem. God, who has begun a good work in us will complete it in that day of Jesus Christ. Of Him are we in Christ Jesus who is made unto us wisdom from God, and righteousness, and sanctification and final, complete redemption (I Cor. i.30). In that day the wise man shall not glory in His wisdom, nor the strong man in his might, nor the rich in his wealth; but each shall glory in the Lord, as earth and heaven celebrate the vindication of his lovingkindness, justice and righteousness in the completed work of redemption (Jer. ix.23; I Cor. i.31).

> "Now redemption, long expected,
> See in solemn pomp appear;
> All His saints by man rejected,
> Now shall meet Him in the air:
>   Hallelujah!
> See the day of God appear."

When we shall see Him we shall be like Him, for we shall see Him as He is. And, according to the working of His mighty power, whereby He is able to subdue all things unto Himself, even these bodies of our humiliation shall be made like unto His glorious Body.

> "Oh Lamb of God who reignest,
>   Thou Bright and morning Star,
> Whose glory lightens that new earth
>   Which now we see from far;
> O worthy Judge Eternal,
>   When Thou dost bid us come,
> Then open wide the gates of pearl,
>   And call Thy servants home."

The judgment of God is the vindication of Christ. As we contemplate that glorious scene may we solemnly ask ourselves, Have I bound myself to Him with the cords of love, of faith and of hope? Does the Lord who knoweth all things know that even this treacherous heart of mine has a real affection for Him who loves me? And have I expressed that affiance of my heart in ways that recognize His Lordship — in ways of His ordering? With the heart man believeth unto salvation and with the lips confession is made unto salvation (Rom. x.10). As many as were baptized into Christ have put on Christ (Rom. vi.3; Gal. iii.27).

As baptism is a sign and a seal of our engrafting into Christ, so enrollment in the family of God on earth is an assurance that one's name is written on the Lamb's book of life, and membership in the Church visible attests one's incorporation in the body of Christ. Thus, the Apostle speaks of *a being baptized into Christ* (Rom. vi.3), and *of the Churches of God which in Judaea are in Christ Jesus* (I Thess. ii.14). The Church is the House and

Family of God, and Christ is the Saviour of His body the Church. One who is swimming the open ocean is exposed to the buffeting of the billows and the teeth of sharks, one who travels on an ocean liner rides the waves and meets the storms in that steamer. God grant that we may each be engrafted into Christ, travel this world, meet the Judgment and enter the world to come in Him, the Ship of Salvation!

CHAPTER VIII

THE THRONE OF HIS GLORY
MATT. XIX.28; XXV. 31

● *"King of Glory reign forever,
Thine an everlasting crown."*

MATT. xxv.1.31, 34

I. REGNUM INMOBILE. Hebrews xii.28.
    Christ, the First Fruits.
    The Three Tenses of the Kingdom.
    The City of God.
    Christ Sufficient and Indispensable.

II. REGNUM GLORIAE. Matt. xix.28.
    The Lord of Glory.
    The Glory of Holiness.
    The Glory of Happiness.
    The Glory of Beauty.

III. REGNUM CAELESTE. I Tim. iv.18.
    Sinful Earth a Contrast to Heaven.
    The Hope of a Heavenly Earth.
    This Hope, the Renewal not the Annihilation of the Earth.

IV. REGNUM AETERNUM. I Peter i.11.
    The Eternal Kingdom, in distinction from:
    Chiliasm, an intermediate Kingdom.

The Judgment. The Kingdom of Heaven and the King-
  dom of God.
No Place for an Intermediate Kingdom.
The Throne of David.
A Glorified Church in a Fallen World.
The Apocalypse.
The Blessed Hope.

The Reign of Christ is a Kingdom that cannot be shaken
(Hebr. xii.28). This Reign becomes the Kingdom of Glory
when the King comes to sit upon the throne of His glory (Matt.
xxv.31) and to bring those whom He has saved into His heavenly
Kingdom (II Tim. iv.18). These enter into the eternal Kingdom
of our Lord and Saviour Jesus Christ (II Peter i.11), they
inherit the Kingdom which is eternal life (Matt. xxv. 34, 46).
For, "Christ has redeemed the world and won an eternal Kingdom through His death." [1]

I. REGNUM INMOBILE. Hebrews xii.28.

Christ, the First Fruits. The exaltation of Christ is the earnest
of the Kingdom of Glory. He is the first fruits of the Reign of
Glory as He is the first fruits of the Resurrection. God promised
David that he should never lack an heir to sit upon his throne.
Gabriel promised Mary that God would give unto her holy Child
the Throne of His father David. That promise has been and is
being kept in the enthronement of Christ at God's right hand
(Acts ii.30). Our King has been raised in glory (I Cor. xv.43;
Phil. iii.21) and enthroned at God's right hand in heaven, angels
and authorities and powers being made subject unto HIM (I
Peter iii.22; Eph. i.20-22). Thus He has been given an everlasting dominion and a reign that shall not be destroyed (Dan.
vii.14). When the nations rage and the kings set themselves
against the Lord and against His Christ in order to break their
bonds asunder, He that sitteth in the heavens will laugh. Jehovah
has set His King upon His holy hill of Zion in order to give

---

1. Alleman, H. C., *The New Testament*, p. 140.

Him the nations for His inheritance. Therefore, He shall break His enemies with a rod of iron (Psalm ii). The Maker of heaven and earth hears the prayers of His people and fills them with the power of the Holy Spirit to do mighty things through the Name of His Holy Child, Jesus, so that the threats of their enemies are dashed aside and the reign of grace is advanced (Acts iv.23-33).

Hebrews, the book which dwells so richly upon the Messianic teaching of the one hundred and tenth psalm that it may be called an exposition thereof, is the epistle that declares most explicitly: Christ's Kingdom cannot be shaken. The finality of Christ's one sacrifice carries the assurance that He shall reign till His enemies are made the footstool of His feet (Ps. cx.2; Hebr. x.12-13; I Cor. xv.25). Since the heavenly High Priest ever liveth to make intercession, there is an unchanging Throne of Grace (Ps. xc.4; Hebr. v.6, 10; vi.20; vii.17, 21; iv.14-16). Christ's enthronement (Ps. cx.1; Hebr. i, 3, 13; viii.1; x.12; xii.2) and His unending Priesthood give His people a Kingdom that cannot be shaken (xii.28). The Kingdom exists as long as the King is reigning on His Throne. He, who is above all rule and authority and dominion both in this age and in that which is to come, shall reign until the last enemy is crushed under His feet. Many things are being shaken in this world of ours, but the Kingdom can no more be moved than Christ can be torn from His Throne at God's right hand.

What God has done for the King, He has done in principle for the Kingdom. The good work which He hath begun He will continue unto the day of Jesus Christ. If we suffer with Him now, we shall reign with Him then. The Captain of our salvation tasted death for every man and has been crowned with glory and honor as our Forerunner. He shall come to be glorified in His saints (II Thess. i.10; Eph. i.18). Ere He departed Jesus bequeathed unto His diciples His Kingdom, even as the Father had bequeathed it unto Him, that in His Kingdom they might eat and drink and sit upon judgment thrones (Lk. xxii.29-30). Those whom He has redeemed and made a Kingdom shall reign upon the earth (Rev. v.9-10). After Daniel sees the Son of Man receiving the indestructible Kingdom, he is troubled with other visions. However, the interpreter assures him that, after four kings have arisen out of the earth, "the saints of the Most High shall receive the Kingdom and possess the Kingdom for ever and ever" (vii.13-18).

The Three Tenses of the Kingdom. From different point of view past, present and future tenses are all predicable of the Kingdom. "God's Kingdom has come. God's Kingdom is coming at the present time. God's Kingdom will come." [2] The Kingdom came when the King was enthroned in His Kingship and poured forth the Holy Spirit upon His disciples . The Kingdom is coming as righteousness, peace and joy in the Holy Ghost (Rom. xiv.17). The Kingdom will come in power and glory when the Son of Man comes in the glory of His Father with His holy angels. The present existence of the Kingdom of Grace is a pledge, a promise, an earnest, a first fruits of the coming Kingdom of Glory. And conversely, the coming Kingdom of Glory is a rebuke to our present earthly confusion and an undying inspiration to strive after the heavenly perfection. The vision of the Holy City that will come down out of heaven judges our wicked civilization, our war-torn world, our guilty society, our empirical church, our rebellious wills, and at the same time it beckons us onward to better things. The revelation of the heavenly Kingdom provokes unending dissatisfaction with the present muddle and an unmoveable steadfastness in the work of the Lord. For, Christ on the Throne and the glorious consummation testify that our labor is not in vain in the Lord (I Cor. xv.58). In the philosophical terminology, Althaus has called this judgment upon our present condition axiological eschatology, and the impetus to better things teleological eschatology. The goal of the ages calls us to the task of the hour.

The Bible is the only book which can meet the current need of man. It portrays man as man is revealing himself in these

---

2. Wendland, H. D., *op. cit.* p. 145. cf. Westminster Larger Catechism, 191; Shorter, 102; Heidelberg, 123; Calvin's, 270.

sad days of the twentieth century with the mask off and the
glamor gone. "Man being a fallen creature cannot grow in
goodness," nor does he apply Christian solutions to the problems
of an unchristian society.[3] And yet this volume, shot through
with theocentric realism, is the most hopeful book ever written.
Sin in its utter heinousness is only a parenthesis between the
Garden of God's fellowship and the New Jerusalem. God made
man to be clothed with glory, honor and dominion. "Everything
that was once thought and done by God, though it be unappre-
ciated, effaced, nullified by men, nevertheless as God's thoughts
and deeds will not be ultimately nullified but again made visible,
again established." [4]

Moreover, the written Word reflects the living Word. After
the Voice from heaven had turned His eyes to the Servant of the
Lord whose lot is suffering, after John had acclaimed Him as
the Lamb of God that beareth the sins of the world, after He
had confessed Himself the Bridegroom that was to be snatched
suddenly from the Bride, our Lord taught His disciples:

"Blessed are the meek: for they shall inherit the earth."
"Blessed are the peace-makers: for they shall be called
        sons of God."

"Thy will be done on earth as it is done in heaven."
In His life and in His teaching He drew the lines of the heavenly
life in the midst of our crooked lives and so established among
us the impelling vision of compassion, peace and good will among
men. Since His meat was to do the will of God, our hearts can
never find peace doing the will of the world, the flesh and the
Devil.

When the throne of Caesar was filled by the maniac Caligula
or the tyrant Nero, Luke penned the angel chorus. However
arbitrary the will and brutal the rule of modern totalitarians, the
paean of praise to God in the highest and of peace on earth
good will to men shall arise from the host of the redeemed. And

3. Davies, D. R., *The Two Humanities*, p. 121.
4. Schmidt, K. L., *Die Polis in Kirche und Welt*, 1939, p. 38.

this song that the catacombs could not crush never allows hope to fail. Christ hath conquered and Christ is our hope. More than any other He faced sin in its heinousness, met Satan in his seductiveness and tasted death in its hellishness. Yet Christ overcame the world, the flesh, and the Devil, sin, death and the law. Therefore, He is the hope of the world, the assurance of the world's ultimate redemption, the guarantee of the New Jerusalem.

The City of God. When the ancient Roman world was going to pieces under the attacks of the Goths, Vandals and Huns, Augustine turned from man's achievements to the consideration *De Civitate Dei*. No doubt many of his contemporaries thought he was a theorist, far removed from the actual problems of the day. But the City of God became the inspiration and the guiding star for the New Europe that through the slow travail of the Middle Ages emerged into the modern world.

Today, "Modern history is drawing to its close; we are approaching an epoch analogous to the end of the ancient world" (Berdyaev). "The dream of Humanism has turned into the nightmare of Nazism" (Davies). "Man is a failure as a political animal" (B. Shaw). Karl Marx's prophecy that when the proletariat obtained power she would surrender it has proved untrue. Man has not been able to make the world safe for democracy. Peace has not issued from the League's Palace of Peace on Lake Leman. And man's dream of an ideal Republic, an island of Utopia, a New Order, or a New Prosperity is tarnished.

With the crumbling of our dreams and the crashing of our civilization shall we then allow the people to perish for lack of a vision? Is the golden age only a mirage without either history or hope? Shall we look for nothing but increasing skill in war, for attrition and starvation until man has destroyed himself on this planet, and for the grimace of the Devil leering over the ruins of this earth? Nay, "the sons of God have much in hand and more in hope." The Gospel of the Kingdom of glory has come to men for such a time as this. The revelation of the New

Jerusalem calls men from the human mirages to the Divine
reality, from empires that are collapsing and economies that are
tottering to the Kingdom that cannot be shaken, from the baseless
fabric of a dream to the City that hath foundations whose maker
and builder is God. "Whether new darkness or new dawn, the
new humanity, God's kingdom in the world, will go marching
on." [5] The banners of God are going forward until the Coming
of Christ transforms the Kingdom of Grace into the Kingdom of
Glory in the new heavens and the new earth. As the rising sun
hangs the morning glories upon the trellis of the skies, so in
heavens torn to shreds by bomb and shrapnel, the Victory of
Christ plants the hope of glory to brighten the hearts and lighten
the eyes of the sin-cursed, fear-smitten, death-driven sons of
men. The Gospel of Christ hangs again the halo of hope over
the black-out of human night. As we pray, *Thy Kingdom come,
Thy will be done on earth as it is done in Heaven,* the vision of
the heavenly Kingdom becomes the inspiration of our present
lives.

Christ Sufficient and Indispensable. Since the primary meaning of Kingdom is Kingship, the Kingdom is as indestructible
as Christ's Reign at the right hand of God. Even though His
vineyard should be so ravaged that it would be difficult to find
faith on the earth, yet would the King reign until every enemy
were destroyed. Since by the Resurrection He has been made a
life-giving Spirit, He is ever able to raise up subjects for the
Kingdom by His sovereign grace. Therefore, Christ is alone
sufficient and alone indispensable to the continuity of His Kingdom. And no earthly individual, group, congregation, denomination or nation is indispensable.

If any people ever had occasion to think that God could not
do without them it was the Jewish theocracy. On Palm Sunday
the daughter of Zion beheld her King coming unto her and
heard the multitudes crying,

5. Davies, D. R., *The Two Humanities,* p. 256.

"Blessed is the King that cometh in the Name of the Lord."
"Blessed is the Kingdom that cometh, the Kingdom of our
    father David."

The Jewish leaders may well have reasoned: "We are the Israel-
ites. Ours is the adoption, the glory, the covenants, the giving
of the law, the worship of God, the promises, the patriarchs.
Of our race is the Messiah. God has no hands but our hands to
do His work. The Kingdom cannot do without us. Therefore,
we are free to make any compromise or concession we see fit to
the demands of Judaism, of the Temple and of circumcision and
still maintain our leadership in the Kingdom. It is unthinkable
that any other people can carry forward the Kingdom that has
rested upon Israel from the days of Abraham and of David."

The King, however, told these leaders a story with a different
moral. In the parable of the vineyard the husbandmen beat one
servant, handled another shamefully, cast a third out of the
vineyard and finally killed the son and heir. Therefore, when
the Lord of the vineyard came, he destroyed those husbandmen
and gave the vineyard to others. "The Kingdom of God shall
be taken from you and shall be given to a nation bringing forth
the fruits thereof." The stone which the builders rejected
became the head of the corner. The Jewish nation, the city of
Jerusalem, the Temple and its worship, the centers around which
Hebrew race, blood and soil clustered were shaken and fell. The
Kingdom was taken from the Jew and given to the Gentile. The
saying, "We are Abraham's children," no longer carried with it
any guarantee of salvation. Judaism was shaken out of her
privileged position, but the Kingdom of God could not be shaken.
Jerusalem and the Temple were moved; the Church that was
founded upon the eternal throne of Christ went from strength
to strength in the Lord. Across this New Testament record is
written the lesson: "Whoever pursues a political aim to the cost
of the *Politeuma* in the heavens (Phil. iii.20) can have no part
in the Kingdom of God." [6]

---

6. Vischer, W., *Calvinistic Congress*, 1938, p. 254.

Will the Gentile continue to repeat the error of the ancient Jew? In his solemn *Admonition to My Beloved Germans* Martin Luther wrote: "What's gone is gone. The Jews had Christ, but they rejected Him, and they are now scattered abroad. Greece had the pure Gospel, but now she has the Turk. Rome and the Latin nations had the truth, but now they have the Pope. Germany has now her great opportunity, but unfaithfulness will drive it away." France rejected the Reformation and received the Terror. German universities exchanged the truth of the Gospel for the rationalism of the Enlightenment and all their boasted freedom of thought has been engulfed by National Socialism.

America is a privileged nation, founded by those who came to these shores to worship God according to their understanding of His Word. However, this does not mean that we are indispensable to the ongoing of the Kingdom and can play fast and loose with French infidelity, German destructive criticism, Continental Sabbath desecration, Modernistic compromises with ethnic religions. An American policy of appeasement will be answered in the same way every other such policy has been answered in the past: "The Kingdom of God shall be taken away from you." Only to a faithful people does God say, "Open ye the gates, that the righteous nation which keepeth faith may enter in." He that hath the key of David openeth and none shall shut, and shutteth and none openeth (Rev. iii.7).

Mordecai did not tell Esther that in view of her exceptional privilege God had no hands but her hands, no voice but her voice by which to save Israel. This is the answer which Mordecai bade them return unto Esther: "Think not with thyself that thou shalt escape in the King's house, more than all the Jews. For if thou altogether holdest thy peace at this time, then will relief and deliverance arise to the Jews from another place, but thou and thy father's house will perish: and who knoweth whether thou art come to the Kingdom for such a time as this?"

"God does not need us." [7] The God who made the world and all things in it, being the Lord of heaven and of earth, is not served by men's hands as though He needed anything, seeing He giveth to all life and breath and all things (Acts xvii.24-25). When we bring polluted offerings, Jehovah of hosts replies, "I will accept no offering at your hands. For from the rising of the sun even unto the going down of the same my name shall be great among the Gentiles; and in every place incense shall be offered unto my name and a pure offering (Mal. i.7-11)." The Lord God has given unto His Son the Throne of David and He shall reign over the true Israel of God forever (Lk. i.32-33; Isa. ix.6-7). Of the Son He saith, "Thy throne, O God, is for ever and ever; and the sceptre of righteousness is the sceptre of Thy Kingdom." (Heb. i.8). The Kingdom given the Son of Man shall not be destroyed (Dan. vii.14), but those who fail to lift aloft the torch that has been given them shall be shaken out of their privileged position in the Kingdom.

The true disciples of Moses were those who went forth unto Him who suffered without the gate bearing the reproach of Christ (Hebr. xi.26; xiii.13). Those who suffer with Christ shall also be glorified with Him (Rom. viii.17; I Peter iv.13-14; v.10). When the Son of Man comes to sit upon the Throne of His Glory He shall also welcome those who ministered unto His brethren. *"The least of these my brethren* are specifically those who witness for Him before a despising and uncomprehending world and who suffer for that witness." [8] Those whose faith has shown itself in their ministering to His witnesses, however unpopular that witnessing may have made them, shall inherit the Kingdom prepared for them from the foundation of the world (Matt. xxv.34). God's Kingdom is rooted in His sovereign purpose, promised in His holy Word, anchored in Christ the King of glory; it cannot be shaken. God hath said it, it shall stand!

7. Barth, K., *The Epistle to the Romans*, pp. 35-36.
8. Lamont, D., *The Evangelical Quarterly*, October, 1935.

II. Regnum Gloriae. Matt. xix..8.

The Lord of Glory. Glory is the most distinctively charac-
terizing attribute of the God of the Old Testament. Jehovah is
the God of glory, the King of glory, whom the heaven of heavens
cannot contain, and who yet manifests His glory in His Shekinah
Presence in the Holy of Holies. He is the glory in the midst of
His people (Zech. ii.5). Israel is exhorted, "Arise, shine for
the glory of Jehovah is risen upon thee and the LORD will be
unto thee an everlasting light and thy God, thy glory" (Isa. lx.
1, 19).

In the New Testament Jesus Christ is "the outshining of the
glory of God" (Heb. i.3), "the Glory" (Jas. ii.1), "the Lord of
Glory" (I Cor. ii.8). He came trailing such unquenched clouds
of Divine glory that the disciples recognized His glory, glory as
of the only begotten of the Father (Jn. i.14). His triumphal
Parousia shall be the epiphany of the glory of our great God and
Saviour (Tit. ii.13). Jesus Himself speaks of the Son of Man's
coming on the clouds with power and great glory (Mt. xxiv.30)
to sit upon the throne of His glory (Mt. xxv.31), and of the
regeneration in which His disciples shall also sit on thrones judging Israel (Mt. xix.28). Our Lord prayed that His disciples
might see His glory (Jn. xvii.5, 22, 24). Those who partake
of Christ's sufferings rejoice in the blessed hope of the revelation
of His glory (I Pet. iv.13). The light of the knowledge of the
glory of God shined into Paul's heart from the face of Jesus
Christ, so that he knew his Saviour to be the Lord of glory
even when He was crucified (II Cor. iv.6; I Cor. ii.8). In his
Patmos vision John sees the Lamb in the midst of the Throne
receiving the worship of the four living ones and the four and
twenty elders, while myriads of angels sing, "Worthy is the
Lamb that hath been slain to receive the power, and riches,
and wisdom, and honor, and glory, and blessing" (Rev. v.12).
According to the New Testament the Word became flesh, Jesus
Christ is the Shekinah Glory, God tabernacling among us, God
manifest in the flesh. Thereafter, He ascended to the state of
heavenly glory which was His before the foundation of the world

and in this glory is receiving the worship of those who have washed their robes and made them white in the blood of the Lamb (Rev. vii.9-14).

"In the days of His flesh" this Divine glory was veiled by the form of a servant and the likeness of men, and it has not yet been publicly manifested to the world which crucified Him. Therefore, there shall be a manifestation of His glory, such a manifestation as, perhaps, this present form of the world with its law of sin and death is incapable of receiving. There shall be new heavens and a new earth as a fit theatre for the revelation of His eternal glory. All the might and magnificence of the God who created the innumerable starry hosts, the galaxies of heaven, the spiral nebulae, all the wisdom of the Spirit of God who ordered the light waves, the atomic structure, the electrical forces and the course of history, all the splendour of the Triune Jehovah before whom the heaven of heavens are unclean and the seraphim veil their faces, crying, HOLY, HOLY, HOLY, shall be brought into play to create a new world for the display of the glory of our King. And the glory of the King carries with it the glory of His Kingdom. According to His gracious word, we also shall see His glory; we shall share His glory; we shall reign with Him in the throne of His glory.

The Glory of His Grace. The glory of God's righteous justice is manifest in rewarding the faithful and punishing the wicked angels. But even the angels desire to look into the sufferings of Christ and the glories that shall follow them (I Pet. i.11-12), for the grace of God hath appeared in Him and that grace shall be fully brought to the redeemed at the revelation of Jesus Christ (Tit. ii.11; I Pet. i.13). We have been redeemed unto the praise of His glory, that is, especially unto the praise of the glory of His grace which He freely bestowed on us in the Beloved (Eph. i.12, 14, 6). We are each one monuments of God's mercy, testimonies of His love to the unlovely, brands plucked from the burning by the redemption that is in Christ Jesus, children of wrath made alive together with Christ.

In the ages to come God will continue to shower His mercies upon us showing the exceeding kindness of the heart of Him who has made Himself our Father in Christ Jesus (Eph. ii.7). And every new act of mercy will testify the greatness of His love, the wonder of His grace. In these limitless aeons we shall learn the breadth and length and height and depth of the love of Christ which passeth knowledge (Eph. iii.18). God shall cloth His people with the garments of salvation and the robe of righteousness as the bridegroom adorneth himself with a garland and as the bride adorneth herself with her jewels (Cf. Isa. lxi.10). And with each new understanding of the plan of salvation, each new appropriation of the greatness of His heart, there shall go forth a paean of praise to Him who loveth us. There is a story of an old Scottish Divine to whom God spoke in a dream saying that he wanted this minister to know just how much God loved him. And ever after that experience there was a fragrance and a sweetness about that life such as one seldom sees. When we see Him as He is, when day by day He unfolds to us the wonders of His love, our lives shall also take on the fragrance and the beauty of His grace. By looking to Him we shall reflect His likeness.

The closing book of the Bible clearly indicates that He shall appear then, as He does now in Heaven in the character that marks Him as the Redeemer. In the first twenty-six books of the New Testament the Saviour is occasionally designated the Lamb; in the closing book which pictures Him in heaven and in the New Jerusalem He is given that designation some thirty times. And the Lamb is a term descriptive, not of His gentleness, but of His death.[9] Thus the Apocalypse reveals the death of Christ as the center and heart of the throne of the universe today,[10] the event that shares with creation itself the worship and praise of heaven (Rev. v, vii). And the Kingdom of Glory

9. Alleman, H. C., *op. cit.*, p. 140. Cf. Schmidt, K. L., *Die Polis in Kirche und Welt*, p. 39, "Das Lamm, das in der Johannes-Apokalypse, das geschlachete Lamm ist."

10. Lewis, Edwin, *A New Heaven and a New Earth*.

is ushered in by the marriage of the Lamb (Rev. xxi.2.9; xix.7).
The holy city, New Jerusalem, which cometh down out of heaven
having the glory of God, is none other than the Lamb's wife, the
glorious Church without spot, or wrinkle or any such thing (Rev.
xxi; Eph. v.27). There is no temple in this holy city: for the
Lord God the Almighty, and the Lamb, are the temple thereof
(Rev. xxi.22). The river of the water of life that brings healing
for the nations flows clear as crystal from the throne of God and
of the Lamb (Rev. xxii.1-2). Redemption is the theme of heaven.
Redemption will be the theme of the New Jerusalem. The blessings of that city flow to us from the green hill without the city
wall of Jerusalem where the dear Lord was crucified who died
to save us all. Accordingly grace is the never failing keynote of
our praise. As we look to the pit whence we were hewn, and
then to His image which His grace shall have pressed upon us,
and to the Lamb standing as it had been slain we shall praise
the glory of His grace. All eternity will not be too long to
thank the God of all grace Who called us unto eternal glory in
Christ and to praise the Lamb Who loveth us and Who loosed us
from our sins in His own blood.

> "The bride eyes not her garment,
> But her dear bridegroom's face;
> I will not gaze at glory,
> But on my King of grace;
> Not at the crown He lifteth,
> But on His pierced hand:
> The Lamb is all the glory
> Of Emmanuel's Land."

The Glory of Holiness. For sinners all other glories flow out
of the glory of God's grace. We can never cease to praise Him
that He looked upon us in our sins and raised us up with Christ
and made us sit with Him in the heavenlies until the revelation
of His grace conforms us to His image. Yet the glories of the
Kingdom that begin in grace issue in every spiritual virtue and
every physical beauty. The glory of the only begotten of the
Father was grace and truth (Jn. i.14). His life manifested the
glory of perfect obedience to the Father, of love unspeakable, of

humility, of righteousness, of compassion, of zeal for the Father's glory; and we shall be like Him. Yea, we shall be raised Spiritual bodies; and the fruits of the Spirit are the virtues of Christ. The New Jerusalem shall be marked by such spiritual glories as truth, righteousness, peace, harmony, love, joy, gentleness, longsuffering, patience, faithfulness, kindness, goodness, meekness, temperance. It shall be resplendent in the peaceable fruits of rightousness. "According to His promise we look for a new heaven and a new earth wherein dwelleth righteousness" (II Pet. iii.13). Kant used to say, "The starry heavens above me, and the moral law in me . . . are the two things which fill the soul with ever new and increasing admiration and reverence." [11] But what Kant's practical reason operating with the categorical imperative and the autonomous will of man have been unable to do, the grace of God in Christ will consummate. In the new world the glory of moral righteousness will shine from the redeemed children of men as the stars adorn heavens on a cloudless night. Truth shall spring out of the earth as righteousness looks down from heaven (cf. Ps. lxxx.11). The Father's house will be glorious in the beauty of its order, and the blessedness of His bounty to His family. The Church shall be glorious and without blemish in purity, truth, peace, unity, concord, holiness. The City of God, resplendent in the glory of God, shall gather into her bosom the nations of earth and heal their wounds with the leaves from the tree of life.

The Glory of Happiness. His throne shall bathe this holy city Jerusalem with the glory of joy and blessedness. Happiness is ultimately dependent upon holiness. The pleasures of sin are fleeting, at His right hand there are joys forevermore. God chastiseth us today that we may be partakers of His holiness and the chastisement that seemeth to be not joyous, but grievous yieldeth the peaceful fruits of righteousness (Heb. xii.10-11). For the joy that was set before Him Christ endured the cross, despising the same; and our chastisements are signs that we

---

11. Cited Kirkpatrick, A. F., *The Psalms*, p. 101.

also are sons beloved of the Lord, who is thereby preparing us
for these eternal joys (xii.1-6). "Our light affliction, which is for
the moment, worketh for us more and more exceedingly an
eternal weight of glory" (II Cor. iv.17). Yea, even in the trials
of our faith Peter urges our great rejoicing in view of the exceeding joys of this celestial inheritance, incorruptible, undefiled and
unfading (I Pet. i.4-6). God Himself shall dwell with His people
and be their God and wipe all tears from their eyes and death
shall be no more; neither shall there be mourning, nor crying, nor
pain any more: the first things are passed away and all things
are made new. "For Jehovah will be thine everlasting light and
the days of thy mourning shall be ended" (Isa. lx.20). Before
the throne of the Lamb there shall be no more curse. And all
the beatitudes of God shall be filled and overfilled in the city of
God, as God maketh those who take refuge under the shadow
of His wings to drink of the river of His pleasures (Ps. xxxvi.
7, 8). God shall bless us with His presence, and the Saviour's joy
shall be in us that our joy may be full.

"For behold, I create new heavens and a new earth: and
the former things shall not be remembered, nor come into
mind. But be ye glad and rejoice forever in that which I
create; for, behold, I create Jerusalem a rejoicing, and her
people a joy. And I will rejoice in Jerusalem, and joy in
my people; and there shall be heard in her no more the
voice of weeping and the voice of crying." (Isaiah lxv.17-
19).

> "For the darkness shall turn to dawning,
> And the dawning to noonday bright,
> And Christ's great Kingdom shall come on earth,
> The Kingdom of Love and Light."

The Glory of Beauty. These glories of the Kingdom are not
confined to spiritual relationships and moral integrity such as
grace, holiness and blessedness. Glory means manifested beauty,
light, splendor. "Rapt Isaiah" in the Old and the Seer of Patmos
in the New Testament have not exhausted human language in
their closing chapters without showing that there shall be a

physical glory as the place for this spiritual loveliness. Men chose beautiful Lake Lemon and the background of Switzerland's snow-capped peaks for the Palace of Peace. Shall God's Kingdom of Glory have a less resplendent setting? A visitor to Patmos says that, as one looks at this island nestling in the blue waters of the Mediterranean and rising against the brighter blue of an evening sky, he sees high in the mountains a beautiful white city. And when light clouds pass between, it seems that this city is just settling down out of heaven. So John saw the New Jerusalem coming down out of heaven, adorned as a bride for her husband, reflecting the splendor of the glory of God, her light like unto a stone most precious. How can one describe the City of God? The city was pure gold, like unto pure glass. The foundations of her walls were adorned with all manner of precious stones. Her twelve gates were twelve pearls; her street was pure gold like unto transparent glass. There is no night there; neither is there need for sun or moon; the glory of God lightens it and the Lamb is the lamp thereof. The LORD will be an everlasting light and thy God thy Glory. Her gates are open continually to bring in the glory and the honor of the nations. Her wall shall be called Salvation and her gates Praise. Her glory shall surpass that of Lebanon and Herman. She shall be a crown of beauty in the hand of Jehovah and a royal diadem in the hand of her God and His glory shall be seen upon her.

Thus the imagery drawn from our lives and observations is exhausted to set forth the glorious beauty of the New Jerusalem. Among all people the wedding is the occasion for the display of plenty and beauty. The City of God is garlanded as a bridegroom and adorned with jewels as a bride made ready for her husband, for "as the bridegroom rejoiceth over the bride so shall thy God rejoice over thee." Among nations we think of the Arch of Triumph and the Victor marching home with kings and princes swelling his triumphal procession. Even so "they shall bring the glory and the honor of the nations" into the Holy City. Nations shall come to thy light and kings to the brightness of thy rising." Men will bring unto thee "the wealth of the nations and their kings led captive." When Jehovah makes Jerusalem a praise in the earth, the glory of God which lightens her shall eclipse the splendor of the skies, so that the city will have "no need of the sun neither of the moon to shine upon it." And "at evening time it shall be light" (Zech. xiv.7).

We have no way of distinguishing which parts of this rich terminology are figurative and which parts literal. But the figures God employs are true figures; the reality is not less glorious than the figure indicates. Perhaps the glories are beyond the power of tongue to tell or pen to write, and the prophets have used the highest lights of our temporal language, the top flights of finite imagery to indicate eternal glories. The glories so indicated are set forth in a physical environment that is worthy of the Father's bountiful hand, and of the beauty of His holiness. "The world of nature is full of beauty." As we see and enjoy this beauty we learn that God, the Creator, is not only truth and love, but also beauty. "God creates not only living hearts, but also form and figure," color and contrast. "He establishes not only inwardness, but also corporeality, visible beauty. He will be glorified not only in His spiritual cosmos, in the living building of the Church which worship Him, but also in the visible cosmos of nature." Beauty is to be understood not only as a means to the true and the good, with which it is properly related, but beauty is a thought of God in its own right and consequently a special attribute of the reality of God.[12] This truth is perhaps clearer if we remember that nature is more a scientific than a Biblical term,[13] and that the Scriptural concept *creation* is related immediately to God. While the category of physical nature excludes the spiritual, the category of creature includes both the physical and the spiritual, and makes it easier to think of the one as well as the other reflecting the glories of the Creator. The foretastes of God's appreciation of the beautiful which we see in the tints of autumn, the fresh green of the spring, the dazzling

---

12. Althaus, P., *DLD*.4.330.
13. Sasse, H., *Th.W.*,I.677.

diamonds of the skies, the rosy tints of the dawn, the glowing
colors of the evening, and the radiant smiles of children's faces
point to the beauty of the Infinite Artist. "The renovation glory
of the Resurrection is not to be confined to the Lord Jesus Christ
and the saints. It is to extend even to the material universe." [14]
The holy city shall show forth the glory of God in her beauty
as well as in her order, in her physical as well as in her moral
and spiritual adornment. "Reborn Paradise shall in its visible
form shine forth eternally and resplendently to the glory of
God." [15] The King has a new heaven and a new earth of unutter-
able beauty and glory prepared for the blessed of His Father,
in which every created form shall shine in a beauty that reflects
God's glory and every redeemed child shall show forth the praise
of Him who called us out of darkness into His marvelous light.

III. Regnum Caeleste. I Tim. iv.18.

The last testimony from the Apostle Paul is his assurance that
God will save him unto His heavenly Kingdom (II Tim. iv.18).
And whatever else may be true of the New Jersalem that was
revealed unto John, it is both heavenly and divine in its origin.[16]

A. *Sinful Earth a Contrast to Heaven.* Sometimes HEAVEN
designates the "dwelling-place" of God, His Throne transcendent
even above *heaven* as the state of the angels and the blessed.
Compared with God the heaven of heavens is unclean and the
seraphim with veiled faces cry, HOLY, HOLY, HOLY.

Heaven in the second sense is the society of those who live
blessed, eternal lives of perfect obedience, the innumerable hosts
of angels, the spirits of just men made perfect. He that doeth
the will of God abideth forever, and His will is done in heaven.
Basil the Great, one of the Eastern doctors, thought of the Holy
Spirit as perfecting and establishing in holiness these inhabitants
of heaven. "The angels are perfected through the communion

14. Cameron, J. K., *op. cit.*, p. 167.
15. Kuyper, A., *The Revelation of St. John*, p. 343.
16. Pieters, A., *op. cit.*, p. 349.

of the Spirit, who is the source of the law, order and distinctness
of the heavenly army." Empowered by the Spirit, they cry,
"Glory to God in the Highest," and "Holy, holy, holy, Lord God
of hosts." "In creation the presence of the Holy Spirit confers
on them the grace that flows from Him for the completion and
perfection of their essence." The Spirit enables them to behold
the Father, to obey perfectly, to worship acceptably.[17] This work
of the Spirit is not apart from, but in Christ in whom and unto
whom were the things of heaven created and through whom they
are reconciled and summed up (Col. i.17, 20; Eph. 1.10). This
abode of those who are confirmed in holiness is transcendent
above our world of sin and death.[18]

This distinction between sometimes becomes an opposition of
earth to heaven, so that Scripture speaks of them as two worlds,
earth below and heaven above. Believers are strangers and pil-
grims in the earth (Hebr. xi.13) who ought to be dead to things
on earth and have their minds on things above (Col. iii.2, 5).
However, this opposition ultimately goes back to the fact of sin.
Since earth is a fallen creation it is in a different relationship to
God than heaven is. Since the world lieth under the law of sin
and death the fashion of it passeth away (I Cor. vii.31) together
with the lust thereof (I Jn. ii.17). We are not to lay up treasures on earth, where moth and rust consume and thieves steal,
but in heaven where they are neither consumed nor stolen (Matt.
vi.19-20).

The sharpness of this contrast, however, never destroys the
unity of Divine creation according to which heaven and earth
together constitute the world. Heaven and earth are in indissoluable connection at the same time that they are in sharp distinction (Mt. vi.10; xxiii.9; Lk. ii.14). Heaven and earth, the
present cosmos, will pass away; and God will make a new heavens

17. Basil, *De Spiritu Sancto.*
18. Althaus, P., *D.I.D.*v.a.345.
19. Sasse, H., in Kittel's *Theologisches Worterbuch,* I:677-679.

and a new earth as the future world of the coming age (Mk. xiii. 31; Mt. v.18; Lk. xvi.17; II Peter iii.7, 10; Rev. xxi.1f; Isa. lxv.17; lxvi.22).[19] God's unchangeable eternity stands in contrast to the impermanent form of the heavens and the earth (Hebr. i.10-12).

B. *The Hope of a Heavenly Earth.* Since this opposition of earth to heaven comes from sin and the fall it will be done away in redemption. In the turbulence and suffering of their day, the Old Testament prophets looked for the coming of a new heavens and a new earth that would obliterate even the memory of their bitter experiences (Isa. lxv.17). To a world shattered by the Assyrian, the rod of God's anger, the Prophet promised, "They shall not hurt nor destroy in all my holy mountain" (Isa. xi.9). "They shall build houses, and inhabit them; and they shall plant vineyards and eat the fruit of them. They shall not build and another inhabit; and they shall not plant and another eat . . . They shall not labor in vain nor bring forth for calamity" (Isa. lxv.21-22). "But they shall sit every man under his vine and his fig-tree; and none shall make them afraid: for the mouth of Jehovah of hosts hath spoken it (Mic. iv.4)." In that day the Lord will make a covenant of peace with the beasts (Hos. ii.18; Eze. xxxiv.25). "And the wolf shall dwell with the lamb, and the leopard shall lie down with the kind; and the calf and the young lion together; and a little child shall lead them (Isa. xi.6)." "In that day there shall be upon the bells of the horses, Holy unto Jehovah" (Zech. xiv.20). Creation which was subjected unto vanity for man's sin shall be delivered from its groaning (Rom. viii.19-22).

The foundation of this hope is the Messiah, the branch out of the stock of Jesse who shall be filled with the Spirit of wisdom and understanding, of counsel and might, of knowledge and the fear of the Lord (Isa. xi.1f; xlii.1f; xlviii.16; lxi.1f). The great characteristic of His reign is RIGHTEOUSNESS. "With righteousness shall He judge the poor and decide with equity for the meek of the earth . . . Righteousness shall be the girdle of his waist, and faithfulness the girdle of his loins" (Isa. xi.4-5). "A sceptre of righteousness is the sceptre of thy kingdom. Thou hast loved righteousness and hated iniquity" (Hebr. i.8-9; Psa. xlv. 6-7). The knowledge of the LORD who exalteth this righteous King shall cover the earth as the waters cover the sea (Isa. xi.9), for the law shall go out of Zion and the word of the LORD from Jerusalem (Isa. ii.3; Mic. iv.2). The blessedness of this reign is the banishment of war and fear. "He will judge among the nations and decide concerning many peoples and they shall beat their swords into plowshares and their spears into pruning hooks; nation shall not lift up sword against nation, neither shall they learn war any more" (Isa. ii.4; Mic. iv.3; Hos. ii.18; Psa. xlvi.9).

As the Old Testament promised a Messiah filled with the Spirit, so the New begins with the Christ-child conceived by the Holy Ghost and anointed at His baptism with the Spirit. In the power of the Spirit Jesus overcomes the Tempter (Mk. i.12), enters upon His public ministry (Lk. iv.4), casts out demons (Mt. xii.28) and rejoices in heart (Lk. x.21). The Father gave not the Spirit by measure unto Him and He did always the things that pleased His Father. He delighted to do the will of God on earth as it is done in heaven, obeying Him even unto the death of the Cross. Now enthroned as the life-giving Spirit He seals His people with the earnest of the Spirit, as a foretaste of that heavenly Kingdom when we shall have Spiritual bodies and the sins of the old man will be put aside forever. The fragrance of His life in the Spirit here, and the gifts of the Spirit He now bestows point to the Kingdom in which the works of the flesh will be done away, and the fruits of the Spirit will abound. For there shall in no wise enter into the City of God anything unclean or that maketh an abomination or a lie (Rev. xxi.27).

As Christ is the center of the heavenly Kingdom, so also is He that goal revealed in time. He went about doing good and words of grace were poured forth from His lips. The heavenliness of His walk and words drew the lineaments of the new life in the midst of the disordered lines of our false and fallen lives. His own life is the promise that the meek shall inherit the earth, that we shall be perfect even as our Father in heaven is perfect (Mat. v.5, 48). In the heavenly Kingdom that appears in Him, the lightest motion of ill-will is a breach of the order of love. In the City of Heavenly Love there will be no misunderstandings, no unsympahetic attitudes, no bickerings, jealousies or strife. "There'll be no distinctions there." In the City that lieth four-square there will be no lust. They that are accounted worthy of the resurrection neither marry nor are given in marriage, but are as the angels of heaven. When our delight is in the fear of the Lord, there will be no need for oaths. When the greatness of His love constrains every motion of our heart, there will be such a wealth of love that dissolves both the need for and the consideration of maintaining one's rights. When by the grace of the Lord Jesus Christ the Fatherhood of whom every family in heaven and on earth is named has gathered His children into the many mansions, enmity will be forever gone.[20]

The Son of Man was not from earth, but came down out of heaven (Jn. iii.13; vi.33, 38, 42, 51, 62). Thus, "In Christ the heavenly man was on earth,"[21] and the coming aeon broke into this world of sin and death. The "unearthly Son of Man" forgave sins on earth and sealed that forgiveness with miracles which show that suffering and sighing have no place in the heavenly Kingdom (Mk. ii.1-12). The prayers of His disciples on earth are heard by the Father in heaven (Mt. xviii.19). What His Church binds on earth is bound in heaven (Mt. xvi.19; xviii. 18), and the redeemed of earth stand with the Lamb on Mount Zion (Rev. xiv.3). The same God is Lord of heaven and earth (Mt. xi.25; Lk. x.21; Acts xvii.24), and as Lord of the earth

20. Thurneysen, E., *Die Bergpredigt*, pp. 22, 26-27.
21. Althaus, P., *D.L.D.*, v.a.345.

(Rev. xi.4) has decreed the ultimate victory to His Christ. "As in Him the *there* became *here*, but in the hiddenness of the form of a servant, so will His Parousia finally make the *there* to be *here*." The contradiction between heaven and earth will cease, sin will be banished, Satan will be vanquished, death will be destroyed, and the Kingdom of Heaven will fill the renewed earth. "Jehovah shall be King over all the earth" (Zech. xiv.9).

C. *This Hope, the Renewal not the Annihilation of the Earth.* In its echatological passages Scripture pictures the visible heavens passing away with the earth and being replaced by new heavens and a new earth. It is tautology to speak of a Kingdom limited to heaven as heavenly. Rather, "the Seer sees the holy city coming down out of heaven from God; the earth has now become the place of the presence of God, of His salvation, of His life. The transcendence of having *heaven* over against *earth* is at an end." [22]

The Biblical conception is distinct from that Hellenic spiritualism which, denying that our existence is essentially a corporeal life in a world of things, finds its hope in a purely spiritual existence without body or world. The mediaeval mystic had no place in his eschatology for a world created by God. For him, God is the highest and the only good whom he will love to the exclusion of all creatures, and for whom the true joy in God is the immediate joy in Him alone. On the other hand Luther rejoices in God the Creator, praises Him for the beauty of His creation, and imitates God by rejoicing in the works of God's hands. God is all in all, but blessedness includes in it joy in the world God has created. Accordingly, Luther taught not the annihilation, but the transformation of the world. Later Lutheran orthodoxy reversed him declaring, "Man needs the world no more, either for a dwelling-place, for food, for clothes, or for a mirror of

---

22. Althaus, *DID*, v.a.346.
23. *Ibid*, pp.327, 339, 341-342.

the knowledge of God." "The new heaven is in the future the 'earth' of the soul." [23] This change was in part due to an over-emphasis on the intermediate state when the souls of believers are apart from their bodies and the life of this visible world. The Kingdom of Glory was pictured as a continuation of this spiritual state. In opposing the premillenarian theory, Snowden holds that humanity will never be perfected on this earth and that heaven will be ushered in as the eternal state.[24]

In considering this matter one should keep in mind the three moments of the Divine activity, creation, redemption and consummation. On the morning of creation when the sons of God shouted for joy, God saw the earth and pronounced it very good. Then He saw it in its sin and cursed the very ground for man's sake so that creation itself has since groaned and travailed in pain awaiting its deliverance from this curse. In the consummation of Christ's redemption He saw it as the new heavens and the new earth wherein dwelleth righteousness and admired its beauty, and crowned His Son for His glorious success in "the restitution of all things." [25]

Creation presupposes a consummation that includes earth. "God is a successful being, and it is incredible that He should be a failure in anything." [26] What He purposes that He brings to pass. At the beginning the Spirit brooded upon the deep and God declared all His creative work very good. All that God has thought and done will neither be ultimately obliterated, nullified nor destroyed by the creature. Nothwithstanding the parenthesis of sin, the earth will fulfill her destiny. The living God is a jealous God. The Redeemer made no compromise with Satan in the Temptation. God will not concede to Satan the ultimate Lordship over even this marred and fallen earth. In the end

---

24. Snowden, J. H., *The Coming of the Lord*. 2nd Ed., pp. 277, 278.
25. Webb, R. A., *op. cit.*, p. 95.
26. Webb, R. A., *op. cit.* p. 88.

Anti-christ may not boast, "The earth remains true to me, my brother." [27] This planet on which God's honor has been challenged by sin and death will see His glories set in dazzling light. Sin and death shall be done away, but God's purpose shall stand. There shall be a "restoration of the world," a *palingenesis* not an annihilation of the earth He has created. For this world is the destined theatre of glory.[28] "The Scripture in all manner of ways continually also emphasizes this corporeal, external and formal nature of the eternity that is to come." [29]

A purely spiritual eschatology is contrary to the fundamental conceptions of the creation of man. God made man not only to be His child, but also to be the ruler of a visible creation. "Our existence is essentially a being in the world of things." God reveals Himself in the mirrors of His creation and calls us to tasks in the world. It is because we are bound, body and soul, to the world that sacrifice is sacrifice and death is death. Because we do love the world, God calls us to love Him above all things. All that we have to do with on earth places us in the great decision for or against the Kingdom of God.[30] The handiwork of God manifests the richness and fullness and greatness of His inexhaustible thought. It is inconceivable that when He ushers those who have been faithful over a few things into rulership over many things that His own hand should be shortened and the manifestations of His glory limited to the spiritual.

Since God so loved the world that He gave His only begotten Son to be the Saviour of the world, the whole creation looketh for its deliverance from corruption at the revelation of the sons of God (Rom. viii.19-22). In the work of Redemption *the Word became flesh* and descended *to the lower parts of the earth*. Here on the earth where sin attacked the Throne of the Almighty,

27. Rogaz, *Der Kampf um das Reich Gottes*, p. 47, cited Althaus, DID, 4:303.
28. Calvin on Romans viii.21; *Institutes*, III.xxv.11.
29. Kuyper, A., *op. cit.*, 339, 341.
30. Althaus, P., *DID*.4328-331.

Christ glorified Him in His atoning death. Is it too much to look for the consummation of that reconciliation in the regeneration of the same earth?

By His Incarnation, Christ became subject to all our human needs and entered into everything human, the sinful and defective alone excluded. "Jesus Christ has repudiated nothing in the creation." [31] "It is emphatically told that after His crucifixion no bones of Christ were broken, but that intact He was carried to His grave; that He rose in bodily form and thus entered upon the glorification which He on Tabor had momentarily enjoyed in advance . . . that the Mediator shall come down to this earth in a visible observable form, and, as the exponent of the human form that shall be observable with the eye, shall execute judgment." [32] "God has, in the Resurection of the Lord, spoken a 'Yea' to the whole of nature." It was the bodily Resurrection of Christ which led the Church to affirm "the resurrection of the flesh." The resurrection of the body and the new earth belong together. In redeeming fallen man God does not translate him into an angel or a purely spiritual being. "Rather the plan, the object and effort of the work of Redemption has been to restore what was lost, and even so to restore it that it never could be lost again." [33]

The real seat of sin is the soul, and from that center it has contaminated the body. God has visited the punishment for transgression upon the body of man and has cursed the earth for his sake. Thus, the creation itself has been subjected to vanity. "Its sickness is our sickness; the not-yet under which it groans rests on the not-yet under which our life stands. But just on that account our hope is at the same time its hope. To the solidarity in the riddle and in the need corresponds the solidarity in the

---

31. Vischer, W., *Calvinistic Congress*, 1938, p. 225.
32. Kuyper, A., *op. cit.* p. 342.
33. Webb, R. A., *op. cit.* pp.90-91; Peck, T. A., *Miscellanies*, II.200-201.

promise. With the cessation of our dissension and war, ceases also the world's form of death. Our resurrection, our redemption to 'Glory' will also make it free, solve its riddle, bring it from brokenness to wholeness. Therefore, the earnest expectation of the creature waiteth for the revelation of sons of God." "We hope for the redemption of this world, this nature and this corporeality." [34]

Both the Old and the New Testament speaks of a new heavens and a new earth. The word new designates something already existing now appearing in a new aspect. The new heavens and the new earth are created in the sense of recreation. They are made new and emerge out of the ruins of the old by the power of God, on the day of the resurrection. This is not creation *ex nihilo,* but transformation. "Of the fathers generally, as of Justin Martyr in particular, Semisch states, that they regarded the future destruction of the world by fire, 'far more frequently as a transformation than as an annihilation'." [35] If we follow the most ancient manuscripts, Peter tells us not that the earth and its works are burned up, but that they are *discovered,* thus predicting the transformation rather than the destruction of the present physical world (II Peter iii.10).[36] The new heavens and the new earth constitute a new world, a cosmos with a new aspect, a new character, a heavenly Kingdom.

> "Blessed be the LORD God, the God of Israel,
> Who only doeth wondrous things.
> And blessed be his glorious name for ever:
> And let the whole earth be filled with his glory;
> Amen, and Amen. Psalm lxxii.18-19.

IV. REGNUM AETERNUM. I Peter i.11.

Second Peter exhorts the Christians to diligence in making their calling and election sure that entrance into the *Eternal Kingdom* of our Lord and Saviour Jesus Christ may be richly sup-

---
34. Althaus, P., *DID.*4.335, 306.
35. Semisch, *Life and Times of Justin,* cited Fairbairn, *Typology,* I:317.
36. Richardson, D. W., *The Revelation of Jesus Christ,* pp. 179, 180, 183.

plied unto them. Our Lord taught His disciples to make to themselves friends by means of the mammon of unrighteousness that when it fails they may receive the sons of light into the *eternal tabernacles* (Lk. xvi.9). In the regeneration the Son of Man shall sit upon the Throne of His Glory and those who have left loved ones for His sake shall inherit *Eternal Life* (Matt. xix.28-29). When the Son of Man comes in His Glory with the angelic hosts swelling His train, the King shall sit upon the Throne of His Glory and usher those on His right hand into *the Kingdom prepared for them from the foundation of the world,* and they shall go away into *Eternal Life* (Matt. xxv.31, 34, 46). In the midst of afflictions, bonds and sufferings the Apostles bid their converts look for the salvation which is in Christ Jesus with *Eternal Glory* (II Cor. iv.17; I Peter v.10; II Tim. ii.10). At the blowing of the seventh trumpet, the Almighty takes His great power to destroy them that destroy the earth and to visit angry nations; and lo, "the kingdom of the world is become the kingdom of the Lord and of His Christ: and *He shall reign for ever and ever.*" (Rev. xi.15-18).

Thus, in the Christian faith we strive for an eternal Kingdom, we suffer for a Glory that shall not be marred by sin, death, persecution or rebellion, we believe: "He shall come again, with glory, to judge both the quick and the dead; whose Kingdom shall have no end." And we understand that the glorious Coming or Parousia of our Lord is the beginning of this unending Kingdom.

> "Reascend, immortal Saviour,
> Leave Thy footstool, take Thy Throne;
> Thence return, and reign forever;
> Be the Kingdom all Thine own!"

Chiliasm. Writing near the middle of the second century, Justin Martyr admitted that "many who belong to the pure and

pious faith and are true Christians" understood that the Coming
of Christ would bring in the Eternal Kingdom. On the other
hand Justin himself followed Papias in expecting a Millenium
Kingdom.[37] This doctrine of an *intermediate kingdom* either
before or after our Lord's return is designated Chiliasm, from
the Greek word meaning a thousand. "The essence of Chiliasm
is the expectation of a coming preliminary fulfillment of the
Kingdom of God on earth through the immediate interposition
of the exalted Christ." [38] Strict Chiliasm or Premillenarianism
dates the beginning of the intermediate kingdom with the visible
return of Christ, the resurrection and glorification of the believers and the establishment of the glorified Church on earth. Then,
"the Kingdom of God will really be an external force in the
world," with Jerusalem as its capital, Israel at the head of
humanity, and the civil and ceremonial law of the Pentateuch
"unfolding its spiritual depths" in the worship and the constitution of the millenium Kingdom.[39] The great revival led Jonathan
Edwards, John Wesley, and Samuel Hopkins to a mild Chiliasm
or Postmillenarianism.[38] In this, the intermediate kingdom is "a
hope of a better time" which awaits a victorious efflorescence of
the Church from a spiritual return of Christ, or a new advance of
Christianity marked by the conversion of the Jews, great missionary progress with Christendom becoming the ruling power and
her principles permeating every province and ordinance of life.[39]

As those who magnify the intermediate state of the soul
between death and the resurrection use texts written of the final
or resurrection state to describe the intermediate state, so some
Chiliasts of each school "plunder" *the Kingdom of Glory* to deck
out their intermediate kingdom with promises written to describe
the *Regnum Gloriae.* J. H. Snowden, a prominent Postmillen-
arian, explicitly uses Revelation xxi.5 and implicitly uses II Peter
iii.13, Isaiah lxv.17 and Revelation xxi.1 to describe the new

37. Justin Martyr, *Dialogue with Trypho,* lxxx.
38. Niebuhr, H. R., *The Kingdom of God in America,* pp. 142, 144, 146.
39. Althaus, P., *DID.*v.a. 294-295. Citing for strict Chiliasm: Hofmann, Frank, Auber-
len, Sperman; for mild Chiliasm: Spener, Bengel, Delitsch, Martensen, Ragaz.

heavens and the new earth he prophecied as a result of the first
World War.[40] In a widely circulated Premillenarian volume
written by W.E.B. the following passages, descriptive of the
eternal Kingdom, are explicitly quoted and applied to the millenial
reign: Revelation xxi.9-19; iii.12; xxi.14; xxi.19; xxi.21, 22, 23;
xxi.11; xxi.24-26; xxi.27.[41] This erroneous practice has called
forth a sharp critique from Klieforth, thus: "This alleged Millenium is nothing else than a chimerical hybrid between the form
of the Kingdom of God in the present as the Church and its
future form as *Regnum Gloriae* by which both are plundered
and robbed of their characteristic peculiarities in order to deck
itself out." "Since their Christian hope satisfies itself in the
Millenium Kingdom, they are silent concerning the *Regnum
Gloriae,* because they have retained no content for it." [42] While
this criticism may not be applicable to every representative of
either school of Chiliasm it serves as a warning.

A principle for understanding prophecy is that history furnished both the occasion and the mould of prophecy. The agency
of the serpent in the Temptation furnished the occasion and the
mould of the Protevangelium, without thereby teaching that
Jesus must crush one or many snakes with His heel. The thought
of the return from captivity furnished the mould of Isaiah xl.3-4
without thereby asserting that John the Baptist must be a road
contractor or that seismic disturbances must accompany his
preaching as he prepared the way for the Messiah. As the Apostles could only speak of the future world in concepts of this world,
so the prophets spoke of the salvation and worship of the New
Covenant in concepts which they derived from the situation of
God's people in the Old Covenant. And the New Testament
does interpret a part of these prophecies as fulfilled in the Kingdom of Grace and a part of them await their fulfillment in the
Kingdom of Glory.

---

40. Snowden, J. H., *The Coming of the Lord*, 1919, pp. 275, 276.
41. W.E.B., *Jesus is Coming*, pp. 192-193.
42. Cited by Althaus, P., *DID.*v.a.304-305.

In view of its unity Scripture is to be collated with Scripture
and the simpler and clearer passages used to interpret the more
difficult ones (Westminster Confession I.ix). Since the Revelation of John is the last and not the first book in the Bible and
since it is difficult to distinguish between picture and fact in
the Chiliasm of the Apocalypse, it is more fitting to begin with
the simpler passages of the Gospels than to draw up a detailed
chart from a questionable reading of this difficult "hieroglyph,"[43]
and then to force the plainer prophecies of the Gospels and
Epistles out of their *prima facie* meaning to conform to this
chart. Let the simple passages of the Word be first interpreted
in their own context, for the context determined the meaning
and the context discloses the meaning. And then let the more
intricate and figurative passages be interpreted to fit into the
plain lines drawn by our Lord and His Apostles in their literal
passages.

The Judgment. Those who start with the Gospels find our
Lord repeatedly representing one generation standing with
another *in the judgment, the* Queen of Sheba with His generation (Lk. xi.29-32), Sodom and Gomorrah standing with Caper-
num, Tyre and Sidon with Bethsaida *in the day of judgment*
(Matt. xi.22, 24; x.15; Lk. x.12-15), men of every generation
giving account of their idle words *in the day of judgment* (Matt.
xii.36). Men in whose presence Jesus ate and drank will see
Christians coming from the four corners of the earth to recline
with the Patriarchs in the Kingdom of God while they themselves are being cast out (Lk. xiii.25-29). In entire accord with
this usual method of speaking Jesus gives the great judgment
scene in Matthew xxv.31-46. The Son of Man is to come in
His glory and all the angels with Him. Then shall He sit upon
the throne of His glory and before Him shall be gathered all
the nations and He shall separate them. As a result of that

---

43. Faulkner, J. A., *op. cit.* p. 105; Luthardt, C. E., *op. cit.*, p. 431.

separation some shall go away into eternal punishment and others into eternal life. This scene has all the marks of the final judgment that the Great White Throne has in Revelation xx. 11-15. All the nations naturally and literally means all that have ever lived, all the nations that have inhabited Palestine, and Egypt, and the valley of the Tigris-Euphrates, and Asia Minor, and Mexico. It includes the Amalekites, the Mongols, the Pharoahs, the Byzantines, etc. Thus the climax of our Lord's teaching on the judgment takes up all He had previously said about one generation standing with another *in the judgment.*

However, the Chiliast splits up the judgment into a series of different judgments, one at the beginning of the Millenium upon the nations then living, another a thousand years later upon the dead. In order to carry through this scheme most of them interpret Matthew xxv.32 as a judgment upon only the living nations. There is nothing in this verse, in the scene (31-46), or in the Gospel teachings of Jesus to support the insertion of this qualifying adjective. It runs counter to every representation of the judgment in the Gospels.

The Judgment Scene intimated in the close of the Sermon on the Mount concerns *every tree,* it is addressed to *every one* among which some shall enter the Kingdom of heaven, and others shall be banished from the King (Mt. vii.16-27; cf. Lk. vi.46-49). Similarly, in the discourse in John on the Son's authority to give life and to execute judgment, Jesus repeatedly describes the resurrection as *the hour* in which all that are in the tombs shall hear His voice and come forth, some to the resurrection of life, others to the resurrection of judgment (v.25-29). In accord with this view, the Apostle Paul wrote the Thessalonian Christians, who were suffering for the sake of the glorious Kingdom of God, that their persecutors — wicked men of the year 50 A.D. — would suffer eternal destruction at the revelation of Jesus Christ from heaven with His angels, when the Lord shall be glorified in His saints (II Thess. i.4-10). If

one looks still more widely, there is no intimation in Daniel xii.2
that the resurrection of some to everlasting life is not simultaneous
with the resurrection of others to shame and everlasting contempt. According to the plain reading of Daniel the awakening
from the dust of the earth takes place at one time, and John
v.25-29 indicates that this was Jesus reading thereof. It is in
accord with Jesus' repeated references to *the judgment, the day
of judgment, the last day, that day* and His constant weighing
of one generation with another as well as with the explicit
affirmations in the text to understand Matthew xxv.31-46 of the
final judgment upon all generations, the final division, the entrance
into a life on the one hand and into a punishment on the other that
is eternal. Thus, no place is left for another crisis and terminus
after a millenium. "Jesus knows nothing of the intermediate
kingdom." [44]

The Kingdom of Heaven and the Kingdom of God. Many
Chiliasts distinguish between the Kingdom of Heaven and the
Kingdom of God and then use this distinction to introduce an
additional or intermediate kingdom. The phrase, the Kingdom
of Heaven. is found exclusively in Matthew, followed by the
Gospel according to the Hebrews. In John iii.5 the phrase does
not occur in the best manuscripts. Even in Matthew the term
gives place from three to five times to the Kingdom of God
(Matt. xii.28; xxi.31, 43; perhaps vi.33; xix.24). Since in the
reading of several of the manuscripts and in the parallel passages
in the other synoptic gospels the Kingdom of God is interchanged
with the Kingdom of Heaven, "it must be concluded that they
are used promiscuously and have the same significance." [45] In the
speech usage of later Judaism the word Heaven is often substituted for the word God. Accordingly, Jesus seems to have used
the Aramaic idiom "Heaven" for which Matthew often gives
a literal rendering, "the Kingdom of Heaven." In other passages
the first gospel and in parallel passages the second and third

44. Althaus, P., *DID*.4 287.
45. Schmidt, K. L., *Th.W-b.z.NT.*, I.582.

gospels offer a freer translation, "the Kingdom of God." The Kingdom of Heaven is the Kingdom of God, or the Kingdom of the Father (Matt. xiii.43; xxvi.29; vi.10; xxv.34; Lk. xii.32). It is His Reign whose holiness and glory so weigh upon our minds that we hesitate to speak of it save by the majestic circumlocution, HEAVEN. The Kingship of Heaven is a Lordship perfectly realized in Heaven, brought into this world by Heaven's own intervention that supernaturally overthrows Satan's dominion. God's Reign is the actual exercise of the Divine supremacy in the interest of the Divine Glory (Mk. xii.34; Matt. vi.33). For Thine is the Kingdom and the Power and the Glory.

No Place for an Intermediate Kingdom. Jesus' doctrine is the more significant just because He was an eschatologist and placed His disciples before a keen tension of expectation concerning the End. The expectation of an intermediate Kingdom of various lengths is taught in Jewish apocalypses, such as Enoch, Baruch and Esra. In allowing no place for such a limited Kingdom in His presentation of the last things, Jesus, so it seems to us, remained *consciously* behind His contemporaries. That he did not teach such a temporally limited intermediate Kingdom, but presupposed an eternal Kingdom, leaves the implication that He rejected the intermediate and accepted instead an eternal kingdom.

The same picture is presented in Second Peter, the epistle in which the term, *Regnum Aeternum* occurs (i.11). The third chapter of this epistle is devoted to the question of Christ's Parousia. In answer to deep concern about this matter, in view of the fact that all things continue as they were from the beginning of the creation, the writer gives this assurance: "The day of the Lord will come as a thief; in the which the heavens shall pass away with a great noise and the elements shall be dissolved with fervent heat, and the earth and the works that are therein shall be burned up (or discovered)." Again Christians are exhorted to look for and desire "the Parousia of the day of God, by reason of which the heavens being on fire shall be dissolved, and the elements shall melt with fervent heat; but according to His promise we look for a new heaven and a new earth, wherein dwelleth righteousness" (iii.4, 10, 12-13). The natural reading of this Epistle is that believers are to make their calling and election sure in order that an entrance into the eternal Kingdom of our Lord and Saviour Jesus Christ may be richly supplied unto them at the Parousia of the Lord which synchronizes with the change of the old heavens and earth and the introduction of the new ones.[46]

In Isaiah, the LORD says, "Behold, I create new heavens and a new earth," and "The new heavens and the new earth, which I will make shall remain before me." (lx.17; lxi.22). While the Chiliasts apply these passages to their intermediate kingdom, the language more naturally and more literally befits the eternal Kingdom in a future cosmic system that will be perpetual and immutable, imperishable and everlasting.

The Throne of David. God's promises to David are only adequately met by a reign of his seed without major interruptions. God promised David: "I will set up thy seed after thee . . . I will establish the throne of his kingdom forever. I will be his father, and he shall be my son: if he commit iniquity, I will chasten him with the rod of men . . . but my lovingkindness shall not depart from him, as I took it from Saul . . . Thy throne shall be established forever" (II Sam. vii.12-16). When chastisements do come and there is a temporary interruption of the reign or of the glory of the house of David, the psalmist pleads before the Lord: Thou hast said, "My lovingkindness will I not utterly take from him, nor alter the thing that is gone out of my lips. Once have I sworn by my holiness; I will not lie to David. His seed shall endure for ever, and His throne as the sun before me." (Psa. lxxxix.33-36, 29, 37; cf. Psa. lxxii.17, 5, 7). When the house of David trembled before a mighty confederacy, Jehovah gave them the sign of the Virgin born Immanuel (Isa. vii.13-14).

---

46. Cf. Bromall, W., *The Issacharian*, Winter, 1940, p. 3.

In the midst of the darkness the Prophet lifted the great light of the promised Messiah:

> "For unto us a child is born, unto us a son is given: and his name shall be called Wonderful, Counsellor, Mighty God, Everlasting Father, Prince of Peace. Of the increase of his government and of peace there shall be no end, upon the throne of David, and upon his kingdom to establish it with justice and with righteousness from henceforth even for ever" (ix.6-7).

In fulfillment of this promise Gabriel promises to a virgin of the house of David a Holy Child named Jesus, the Son of the Most High, to whom the Lord God will give the throne of His father David so that He will reign over the house of Jacob forever (Lk. i.32-33). As Luke's first book opens with this promise so his second book opens with Peter's declaration that the promise is fulfilled in the Resurrection and Ascension of Jesus Christ to God's right hand. Thereby God has kept His promise to David, seating Jesus Christ, David's Son and Lord, upon the throne of David (Acts ii.30).

During the Old Testament theocracy the messianic promise was the life of David's throne. For the Messiah's sake God did not break off His lovingkindness, but after chastening the Davidites for their sins restored them to the throne. Now in the Messiah the promise has its eternal fulfillment. God has elevated Christ to His own right hand to reign with Him in His throne (Rev. iii.21). For nineteen hundred years the Lamb has reigned in the midst of a throne invisible to the world. In the new heavens and the new earth His Throne shall be manifest in its glory and its heavenly blessedness to all eternity. However, if one deny that Christ has been invisibly reigning on this throne of David for the last nineteen hundred years what becomes of God's promise to David? Nineteen hundred years is a greater interruption than any caused by the chastisements visited on the Old Testament heirs of David. Are the chiliasts ready to say that God has so chastised His Holy Child Jesus? When He was wounded, it was for our sins. After He had borne our sins in His own body on the Tree, God exalted Him to His own right hand above every dominion both in this age and in that which is to come (Eph. i.20, 21) and enthroned Him in a Kingdom that shall not be destroyed (Dan. vii.14). Nor can we conceive of any future sin on the part of this Davidic King for which God will chastise Him even temporarily and take the dominion from Him for the little period called for in the chiliastic rebellion of Satan at the end of their millenium.

A Glorified Church in a Fallen World. The effort to present a half-way step in which the Church will be living a supernatural, risen life, the believers having new glorified bodies, at the same time as the world is living in the fallen state of sin and death and force involves a fundamental contradiction. The resurrection of believers and the glorification of the Church cannot be isolated from the rest of nature. The creation also waits the revealing of the sons of God (Rom. viii.19). Our risen Head and King is not living visibly among us today. Will millions of risen glorified believers live amidst a humanity still subject to the laws of sin and death? Will a glorified Church live in this old earth amidst the ruins left by war, disease, famine and death? Althaus describes such a conception "as nothing else than mythology." [47] At least the combination is so difficult to formulate that it has led to all kinds of detailed differences among Chiliasts. Quite generally they teach that the reign of the risen saints is on this earth.[48] Some are positing a secret rapture that will take the saints out of the earth at least during the tribulation. One widely read Premillenarian teaches that Jesus Christ will reign upon this earth as King for a thousand years, while the redeemed, having new bodies will reign in the heavens with Him.[49] How may one reign in heaven with Christ when He is seated on

---

47. Althaus, *DID*.v.a.305.

48. W.E.B., *Jesus is Coming*, pp. 53, 75, 189, 190, etr. G. H. Gilmer, *The Thousand Years*, in *The Evangel*, V.11.1.

49. McIntire, C., *The Beacon*, V.26.3,6.

David's throne in old Jerusalem? Shall new bodies reign in heaven rather than on earth (cf. Rev. v.10)? And if new bodies reign a thousand years in heaven, will they have a new earth thereafter, or is the promise of a new earth in which dwelleth righteousness to be spiritualized away?

The Apocalypse. My outline and exegesis of *Revelation* do not yield the Parousia of Christ before the millenium passage. The Apocalypse has a prologue at the beginning, an epilogue at the end and the main body of the book covered by seven series in each of which there are seven symbols. There are seven churches (i.9-iii.22), seven seals (iv.1-viii.1), seven trumpets (viii.2-xi.18), seven signs (xi.19-xiv.20), seven bowls (xv.1-xvi.21), seven sayings (xvii.1-xix.10) and seven visions (xix.11-xxii.5). The whole book, in its prologue, its epilogue and in each of its series of visions seems to be stretched from the first coming or the time of the writer to the second coming. Thus there is a large amount of parallelism or recapitulation. But it is not a perfect or a mere parallelism, there is movement. The emphasis in the prologue and the earlier series of visions is on the first coming and the situation of the writer with just a suggestion of the second coming, *Behold He cometh with the clouds* and *He that overcometh, I will give to sit down with me in my throne, as I also overcame and sat down with my Father in his throne.* The latter series still begin with the situation the writer faces but are richer and fuller in their account of the second coming and the glories that shall follow. Even in the epilogue where the emphasis is on the second coming, Jesus is the Alpha as well as the Omega, the root and the offspring of David.

The seven visions which constitute the last series are: the Word of God (xix.11-16), the Victory over the Beast (17-21), the Binding of the Dragon (xx.1-3), the Millenium (4-6), the Victory over the Dragon (7-10) the Judgment Throne (11-15), and the New Jerusalem in the New Heavens and the New Earth (xxi.1-xxii.5). The first two of these, the Word of God and the Victory over the Beast, fit the situation which existed when John wrote. In the pericope xix.11-16 there is a revelation of Jesus

Christ in heaven followed by the armies of heaven. But there is no more reference in that vision to His coming to earth than there is in the earlier vision of Him in i.9-20, or in v.6-14, or in Acts vii.56, or ix.3f. In xix.13 His Name is the Word of God and in xix.15 out of His mouth proceedeth a sharp two-edged sword, but in i.16 out of His mouth proceedeth a sharp two-edged sword as also in ii.12 and 16. The sceptre of Christ is the sword of the Spirit, the Word of God (Hebr. iv.12; Isa. xlix.2). In other words the seventh series of visions is introduced in somewhat the same fashion as was the first series and the second series, that is, by a vision of the heavenly risen Christ. The second vision in the seventh series, the war and victory of the Christ (xix.17-21), is His spiritual conquest of the pagan persecuting Roman Empire which He accomplishes through His martyrs by spiritual weapons. "The exalted Saviour is still a warrior King and from the Throne to which He has been exalted in Heaven, He goes forth conquering and to conquer through the ministries of His Church on earth." [50] In neither of these two visions is Christ said to come down out of heaven as the holy city does in xxi.2. The interpretation of the millenium vision offered in earlier chapters of this book do not support Chiliasm.

The second coming of Christ and the transition to the new order are in the last two rather than the first two of the seven visions. The coming of the Son of Man in His glory to sit upon the Throne of His Glory and to judge all the nations is not in Rev. xix.11-16, but in Rev. xx.11-15. Here the Judgment immediately ensues with the Parousia as it does in Matthew twenty-five and Second Thessalonians one; here it is followed by the new heavens and the new earth (Rev. xxi.1) as it is in Second Peter, three. "It is here clear that the Judgment is the great transition to the new order; because there, not only is heaven and

---

50. Stewart, A., *op. cit.*, p. 53.

earth to flee away to create space for a new order, but sin and
wickedness are destroyed." [51]

Christ and His Kingdom of Glory will come in a sudden, a
visible and a catastrophic manner. That change will be more
thorough-going and complete than Chiliasm imagines, and more
visible than Revelation xix.11-16 states. This interpretation of
Scripture does not rob the believer of the millenium hope in
the popular understanding of that word as an era of righteousness and love and peace on earth, but it puts it in its right place
and makes it far more wonderful and glorious than a thousand-
year reign ending in a fresh outbreak of Satan's power. In the
Holy City Satan will never show his face. [52]

> "It was the New Jerusalem
> That would never pass away."

The conflict pictured in Revelation culminates in the visible Second Coming of Christ, the Great White Throne of Judgment and
the Kingdom of Glory in the new heavens and the new earth.
The Coming of our Lord inaugurates the Golden Age, which is
the popular connotation of the word Millenium. However, in
the heavenly Kingdom which the Parousia will bring, sin, sorrow, suffering and death are forever done away and righteousness, peace and love shall forever prevail.

The Blessed Hope. Thus the blessed hope of the Appearing
of the Glory of our great God and Saviour Jesus Christ is not
tied to Chiliasm in either of its forms. "There is a great difference between Chiliasm and faith in the imminency of the
return of Christ. That was the faith of the Apostolic Church.
Apostolic believers lived in the faith of that return, but it was
always a faith in which the personal equation prevailed. It was

---

51. Lohmeyer, F., *Die Offenbarung des Johannes*, 1926, p. 162.
52. Cf. Caldwell, E.C., *The Millenium*, pp. 25-27.

a matter between the believer and His Saviour; it was the living nerve of the endless devotion of the apostolic believer and of his indestructible hope; its spirit is felt in all the apostolic literature." [53]

Our Lord kept His disciples in expectation of His Parousia without any mention of an intermediate kingdom. Paul speaks of the return of Christ in almost every chapter of each of his epistles to the Thessalonians, but there is no reference in either of these epistles to any intermediate Kingdom. The Thessalonians waited for God's Son from heaven, Jesus who delivereth us from the wrath to come, expecting the eternal destruction of their persecutors when Christ would come to be glorified in His saints, not a thousand years later (I Thess. i.9-10; II Thess. i.9). According to Hebrews Christ hath appeared *at the end of the ages* to put away sin by the sacrifice of Himself, once for all. And as it is appointed unto men, once for all, to die and after this judgment; so also Christ having been offered, once for all, to bear the sins of man shall appear a second time apart from sin unto the salvation of those who wait for Him ix.26-28). Here the parallelism places the appearing of Christ a second time for the salvation of His people at the judgment of the dead, as the final event closing this last dispensation of grace and opening the door of the Kingdom of Glory.[54]

The conservative Reformation rejected the Chiliasm of the Anabaptists.[55] "The Reformers are as unchiliastic in their thoughts of the last things as Jesus was, and yet at the same time they are as full of tension with reference to the End as He was." [56] The Westminster Confession gives no countenance to either form of Chiliasm, but closes with an appeal to all men to watch and to be every ready to say, Come Lord Jesus, come quickly. The Larger Catechism interprets the second petition of the Lord's

---

53. Dosker, H. E., *Chiliasm*, in *The Christian Observer*.
54. Smyth, T., *Works*, IX.398.
55. *Conf. Aug.* 17; *Conf. Helv.* 11; *Institutes* III.xxv.5.
56. Althaus, *DID*.v.a.290-291.

Prayer as including the prayer that Christ would "hasten the time of His second coming, and our reigning with Him for ever." "Be ye also ready; for in an hour that ye think not the Son of Man cometh" (Matt. xxiv.44). "What I say unto you I say unto all, Watch." (Lk. xii.35). "He that testifieth these things saith, Yea I come quickly." (Rev. xxii.20).

Christ — The Hope of Glory

(Continued from front flap)

earth, then our redemption for body, soul and spirit would be incomplete, for the very nature of the hope within demands its fulfillment and awaits His return.

Having given us a foretaste of the kingdom which is to come by the gift of the Holy Spirit, He cannot but manifest it in full glory on this earth. "The miracles of the Bible," Dr. Robinson asserts, "are not isolated phenomena, but the first rays of eschatological dawn breaking into this age from the age which is to come." We need also to see that the miracle of the Resurrection (His, and because of Him, ours) is a mighty movement of life going out from God to recreate the Cosmos and lead to its final consummation.

The collapse of evolution and the apocalyptic explanation of history, drove men to eschatology in the twentieth century. The first period of the century looked on it as *ancient history*, the second as *super-history*, and the latest as *end history*.

The judgment of Christians and unbelievers in its relation to all phases of eschatology is fully discussed. The conclusions concerning Chiliasm, the doctrine of the Millennial Reign, are worthy of the sincere consideration of every true believer.

The reader is left with a sense of the imminency of the Coming of the Lord, and our vital personal place in the completed plan of redemption, objective as well as subjective. He will be conscious of an urgent desire to enter into all the marvels of the Kingdom by the grace of God and the power of the indwelling Spirit, into the eternal scheme of our mighty God. and our Savior, Jesus Christ.